CHATSWORTH

THE

HOUSEKEEPER'S TALE

Christine Robinson

CHRISTINE ROBINSON

ILLUSTRATIONS BY JANET BITTON

First published in Great Britain in 2014 by

Bannister Publications Ltd
118 Saltergate
Chesterfield
Derbyshire S40 1NG

ISBN 978-1-909813-06-9

A catalogue record for this book is available from the British Library

Typeset in Palatino Linotype by Escritor Design, Chesterfield, Derbyshire
Printed and bound in Great Britain by SRP Ltd, Exeter, Devon

Contents

Foreword

by

The 12th Duke of Devonshire

Christine Robinson and her family have been deeply involved in Chatsworth for several generations as has that of her husband, Clive.

They have lived in the midst of this unusual Estate for most of their lives and this book is thus a fascinating and authoritative account of what goes on and who does what. Unusually, Christine, despite the years she has worked at Chatsworth, is still enthusiastic about the changes that have happened over the years, and especially in the last eight years since my wife and I have been living here. Many people perceive the changes as a criticism of what went before, but Christine realizes that this is not the case, just a matter of the same objective being pursued by a different route.

This is a beautifully written book, full of stories and facts new to me, and therefore highly likely to be new to almost every reader. For these alone it is worth reading.

Christmas at Chatsworth was started, at the suggestion of my father as a result of the closure of the countryside owing to the Foot and Mouth disaster of 2001. Christine Robinson has been totally involved since that first, highly successful but somewhat chaotic, decorated Chatsworth. The six weeks that Chatsworth morphs into a winter fairyland, based on a different theme every year, is now easily our busiest time of year. In 2013 there were over 134,000 visitors in that short time. Christine remains one of three key people in the planning and delivery of this amazing success. Her experience and imagination combine together brilliantly. Although it is probably her most exhausting part of the year I am sure that she is very proud of what she and her colleagues achieve, year in, year out. She certainly should be.

And she must be very proud of this book, a project at last fulfilled and a brilliant account of her happy and successful life and career … so far.

Stoker Devonshire, June 2014

Acknowledgments

It has taken over ten years to finally complete this book, which would not have been accomplished without the encouragement of family and friends. I am especially indebted to Janet Bitton for her enchanting line drawings, and to the Duke, for his very kind foreword and for allowing me to use photographs belonging to the Devonshire Collection and reproduced by permission of Chatsworth Settlement Trustees and Chatsworth House Trust.

Friends, family and colleagues have also given permission to use their photographs, and have reminded me of stories about the Chatsworth characters of days gone by. Many of those are now long gone, but I hope the part they played in Chatsworth's story may briefly come to life again through these pages.

I would also like to offer enormous thanks to my editor, Tom Blyth, who has guided me with endless patience through the tortuous process of finally achieving the long-held ambition of publishing these memoirs.

Photographs on cover and back end paper by Matthew Bullen
Photograph on front end paper by Phil Robinson

Introduction

At the annual Chatsworth staff party on 14th March 2003, I was presented with a gold watch to mark 25 years' service to the Cavendish family, and Nick Woods, at the time deputy land agent, introduced the presentation of the long service awards with the words,

"This evening, ladies and gentlemen, we are gathered for the presentation of the long service awards, and to mark 180 years of service to Chatsworth…"

One hundred and eighty years! I felt near to collapse at the thought of it. As Nick continued, he went on to add that there were in fact six recipients of awards; two for 40 years' service, and four for 25 years' service, 180 years in all. It was a lovely occasion, as four of the six were from the House staff: Sean Doxey, House clerk of works (25 years), Tony Hubbuck, electrician (40 years), Henry Coleman, butler (40 years) and myself, housekeeper (25 years). The other two to receive awards were Sean Feeney, river bailiff, and Andy Fletcher from the farms, both for 25 years.

The Dowager Duchess used to say that people came to work at Chatsworth for either half a day or a lifetime, and I certainly could not imagine working anywhere else. On the reverse of the watch are my initials: CER, 25 years, and the Cavendish snake, and I have worn the watch every day ever since. Now my number of years' service is nearly 40, and I realise that my entire working life has been devoted to the service of one family and one house – Chatsworth. It doesn't seem that long, and yet it seems like forever – a lifetime of infinite variety, yet comfortable regularity; fresh challenges and constant changes.

Sean and I are the only two still working from that presentation in 2003, myself as head housekeeper, and Sean as head of special projects. We are both still amazed every day at the power the House has over us, and how, even after all these years, there is still more to discover about it.

In March 2013, fire prevention work was on-going during the closed season to introduce compartmentalisation within the doors and door panels, and on taking out the panel in the doorway between the North Entrance Hall and the Sylvester Lobby, a hidden recess was discovered between the doorway and the Entrance Hall fireplace. The edge of the fireplace could be seen within the recess, the work probably dating back to the alterations of the 6th Duke of Devonshire in the 1820s, and possibly even longer ago, and within the recess, the workmen found a handmade step ladder, with wedged joints attaching the rungs, thick with the dust of nearly 200 years. The rungs of the ladder are worn with the tread of countless feet, all playing their part, as we still do today, in caring for this great house.

1

⌘

A Sense of Place

On my way to work from Edensor this morning, windows wound down, I turned off the road at Sandy's Turn in Chatsworth Park and had to slow down to allow some young fallow deer bucks to cross the road. It was a glorious summer's morning, bright sunshine slanting through the trees, and I could hear the soft thud of their feet on the sun-baked parkland. What a wonderful hold-up on one's way to work! No traffic jams and road works, no irate horn-tooting drivers, no sweaty fellow travellers on the underground or a commuter train; no sitting thigh to thigh, day after day, with the same people, never smiling or making eye contact. Just the tranquillity of beautiful sun-dappled parkland, a sparkling river, a flock of sheep and a herd of deer.

It reminded me of the day in 2004 when the road through the Park was closed for the funeral of the 11th Duke of Devonshire. When the deer came down to the roadside that day it was so much quieter than usual. It was almost as though they had come to pay their respects to His Grace, along with the hundreds of people lining the route to Edensor Church from Chatsworth as the funeral procession wound its way across the river from the House.

In the years since that day so much has changed at Chatsworth, yet in essence it is the same - devoted staff and the Cavendish family, both serving a beautiful house set in magnificent parkland. The Cavendish family are custodians of it all, but in their way, so are the families who have worked here over many generations. Although, inevitably, there is not the same long-standing service by the same families as there once was, those who come to work here quickly become captivated by the place and, whilst they may come initially as a stepping stone to something else, once Chatsworth has woven its spell, then they cannot tear themselves away.

For my own part, I feel a sense of place and of belonging. For generations my family, and that of my husband Clive, have worked on the Chatsworth Estate, walked the land, raised our children, played our part.

Resistance to change is part of the human condition, and it has been interesting to observe how changes at Chatsworth have been approached by different members of staff, by residents of the local villages, and also by visitors to Chatsworth House and Gardens. For the staff, the death of the 11th Duke had a huge impact, as he had been in position for 54 years. No member of staff had ever worked under any other Duke, although we did, of course, know the 12th Duke and Duchess as regular visitors to Chatsworth. Long before acceding to the title, they had, as the Marquis and Marchioness of Hartington, played their part in the running of the Estate, particularly on the Yorkshire Estate at Bolton Abbey.

I think we all wondered what it would be like working for the 'new' Duke and Duchess, and I wouldn't be surprised if their unease was fairly similar! Here was a couple with a well-established home life 80 miles away, who were now required to take up the reins at Chatsworth in a quite high profile way and at a time of life when most people would be thinking of slowing down. I think they were concerned to try to make everyone feel at ease during the transition, and were acutely aware of how difficult things were for all of us, and especially for the Dowager Duchess.

There was talk initially of Her Grace moving away; some said she had a house prepared ready for her at Swinbrook in Gloucestershire where she grew up, whilst others said she was moving to a cottage on the Bolton Abbey Estate. I don't know the truth of the matter, but I always understood that the 12th Duke and Duchess persuaded her not to make any hasty decisions. It was a time of great stress and she might later come to regret a hasty decision; and so she stayed on at Chatsworth. In the days before the funeral, hundreds of cards were received by Her Grace and we filled all the steps and floor in the Chapel and the shelves in the Library with them. It was such a moving time with very many well-wishers.

18 months later, the Old Vicarage in Edensor became vacant and Her Grace decided that she would like to move into it. It is a wonderful house and garden and with the help of her secretary for many years, Helen Marchant, she has done so much to make it comfortable. She had a stylish summerhouse built, which is affectionately called 'The Ticket Office'. The floor of this summerhouse is made up of all the minerals to be found under Cavendish land: copper from the Ecton copper mine, lead from Magpie Mine near Sheldon, fossilised limestone from the Duke's Once-a-Week mine, Duke's Red marble from Ashford-in-the-Water. The Old Vicarage has been a wonderful place for Her Grace to entertain her friends in a private setting. Over the years her visitors have ranged from The Prince of Wales to Alan Titchmarsh, Tom Stoppard, Alan Bennett, and two of her oldest friends, now sadly dead, the late Sir Nicholas Henderson and Paddy Leigh Fermor.

Paddy would visit often when the 11th Duke and Duchess were living at Chatsworth and he invented the titles for the false book spines on the door leading up to the gallery in the Library: titles such as *Sideways through Derbyshire* by Crabbe, *Gloucester in all Weathers* by Dr Foster, and *Consenting Adults* by Abel N. Willing. Henry Coleman, devoted butler to the 11th Duke and Duchess for many years, moved with Her Grace to the Old Vicarage and told me about a visit Paddy once made there. He told Henry at dinner that earlier that day he had taken a bath, carefully lowering himself into it, whilst cursing the infirmities of old age as he did so. It was as he stood up to get out of the bath that he glanced down at his feet, which were still underneath the water. 'My God!' he had exclaimed. 'My ticker's dodgy, my rheumatism's a nightmare, and now something terrible has happened to my feet!' It was at that point that he realised that he had forgotten to take off his socks!

My earliest acquaintance with Chatsworth goes back to my junior school holidays when I used to travel up from the West Midlands to stay with my grandmother in Darley Dale. We would catch the bus from her flat on Lime Tree Avenue to Rowsley and then walk the mile to Beeley, where we would visit two of my grandmother's sisters in the Club Yard. It was a large family, four boys and seven girls, all born in Beeley village at Moor Farm. My grandmother Annie Muriel, was the youngest, born on 24th July 1892.

Annie Muriel's great-grandfather was Samuel Grafton, who farmed Moor Farm at Beeley and married Hannah Downs from Edensor. They had a large family of girls including Annie's grandmother, Sarah, who was born in 1815 and baptised in Edensor Church. Sam worked his daughters on the farm as hard as if they had been sons and my grandmother thought they must have been rather frightened of him. She had a story that was passed down through the family that one night he called for some hot water for a sick horse, but there was no hot water to be had, so the girls all pee'd in a bucket and one of them took it out to him, as they were too afraid to say there was no hot water. He put his finger in the bucket and exclaimed, 'Call that 'ot! It's abaht as warm as piss!'

In the 1830s, once the morning milking was finished, the sisters would drive carts loaded with stone from their family quarry near the Burnt Wood, above Beeley, to Chatsworth to build the 6th Duke's North Wing. Another load of stone was then hauled in the afternoon before evening milking. A family legend tells that when Sam Grafton's wife Hannah fell pregnant again, there was a fervent hope that the child would be the longed-for son to continue the family business. It was a dark and stormy night when Hannah eventually went into labour. Things did not progress well, so in the lashing rain Sam left his wife in the care of their daughters whilst he set off on horseback along the old road via Pig Lane in Beeley to fetch the physician from Baslow. The old road emerged opposite the coal gate above the Blue Doors entrance to Chatsworth Park, and there the Devil was waiting for him in the shadows. The creature stepped out in front of Sam's horse as he stooped from the saddle to open the gate. The horse startled and reared in fear, and the stranger took the bridle to steady it.

'Now Sam Grafton, and where might you be bound?' he asked.

'Ter fetch t'doctor for me missus,' Sam replied. 'Ah canna wait abaht talking ter thee, her's in labour, and ah canna lose me son.'

'How can you be sure it is a son?' queried the Devil.

'It 'as ter be. Ah need a son. Me daughters are grand lasses, but they'll be off to 'ave families of their own – it must be a son!'

'I can help you there, but it will cost you,' said the Devil. 'What would you give me for a son to be born?'

'A son! Ah'd give anything for a son, but ah've nowt ter give thee,' said Sam. 'Now let me past, whoever you are, Hannah's waitin' for me.'

'Anything? You'd give anything for a son?' said the Devil. Sam stopped and turned in the saddle to look at the stranger. 'You have got one thing you could give me,' continued the Devil.

'And what's that?'

'Your soul. Sell me your soul, and you will have a son!'

A son was duly born, and they named him after his father, but the young Samuel never made anything of himself, turned to drink, and ended his days without a farthing to his name. When his father, old Sam, died on 17th December 1866 he was buried in Beeley churchyard, and to this day no grass will grow on his grave…

As the young Samuel had been no help to his father Sam, his sisters continued to work with their father on the farm and with the haulage business. One daughter Sarah (my great-great-grandmother), married Joseph Burdekin from Alport on 7th March 1837 in Beeley Church when she was 22 and he was 24. She made a kneeler to use during the marriage service that is still used by brides in Beeley Church to this day. It may well be that Joseph Burdekin had been working on the farm already as a hired hand, because after their marriage, Sarah's father Sam went into partnership with Joseph. He eventually took over the tenancy of Moor Farm after his father-in-law's death in 1866. They continued the haulage business with horse and dray and were part of the team which fetched coal from Rowsley, once the Midland Railway opened there in 1849.

A recent Master Plan (renovation works to Chatsworth House begun in 2006), discovery in March 2013 was a piece of old packing case underneath the floorboards of the North Sketch Gallery, which was probably put in there in the 1820s at the time of the 6th Duke's alterations as insulation and sound proofing. It was about to be thrown away when someone noticed on the reverse of the old packing case the words, 'Cromford Canal, to Chatsworth'. What did the packing case originally contain? Who knows, it might have been brought to Chatsworth from the canal at Cromford by Joseph Burdekin.

The Burdekins continued to fetch coal from Rowsley to Chatsworth throughout the remainder of the 19th century, providing the coal to feed the eight stoves that heated Joseph Paxton's Great Conservatory in the gardens. It was completed in 1841, and was also known as the Great

Stove. Joseph Paxton had arrived at Chatsworth on 9th May 1826, having been spotted by the 6th Duke working in the Royal Horticultural Society gardens next to Chiswick House in London. The Society rented the gardens from the Duke, and it was there that Paxton started work at the age of 14. The Duke was so impressed with Paxton's capabilities that when he heard that the young man was thinking of emigrating to America, he offered him a position at Chatsworth as head gardener. He was only 23 when he arrived to take up the post.

Fortunately for posterity, Paxton kept a journal and this is what he wrote about his first day at Chatsworth:

I left London by the comet coach for Chesterfield and arrived at Chatsworth at half past four o'clock on the morning of the 9th May 1826. As no other person was to be seen at that early hour, I got over the greenhouse gate by the old covered way, explored the pleasure grounds, and looked round the outside of the house. I then went down to the kitchen gardens, scaled the outside wall and saw the whole place, set the men to work there at six o'clock and then returned to Chatsworth and got Thomas Weldon to play me the waterworks and afterwards went to breakfast with the housekeeper, poor dear Mrs Gregory and her niece. The latter fell in love with me and I with her, and thus completed my first morning's work at Chatsworth, and all before nine o'clock.

They were married less than a year later, on 20th February 1827, and enjoyed a long and happy marriage. A love letter received by Sarah from Paxton sometime during 1826 indicates how much they were in love. In it Paxton tells her that she is his '…lovely endearing angel, the adorable object of my heart. To say I love and adore thee my dear is but trifling – you are the very idol of soul… rest assured while I draw breath it will be my study to make myself more dear… I am and shall ever be yours till Death.'

For some time, Paxton had been dreaming of building a greenhouse magnificent enough to house the plant collection he and the 6th Duke intended to gather. Whilst one of Chatsworth's most promising young gardeners, John Gibson, was overseas collecting specimens, Paxton was busy with his plans for a spectacular showcase in which to display them. The scale of his project surpassed anything already in existence. The glasshouse was 227 feet long, 123 feet wide and 67 feet high, covered an acre of ground, and took four years to build, from 1836 until 1840.

Gibson had sailed out to Calcutta with a friend of the Duke's, Lord Auckland, Governor General of India. The intention was for Gibson to take choice plants from the Chatsworth collection, such as dahlias that would thrive in the Indian climate, as a gift to the botanical gardens in Calcutta. In due course he would return to Chatsworth with orchids and other exhibits for the Duke's Great Stove. In addition to the collection of orchids, Gibson was tasked by Paxton and the 6th Duke to bring back *Amherstia nobilis*, which had been discovered in 1826 by the curator of the botanical gardens in Calcutta, Nathaniel Wallich, near the Burmese town of Martaban on the Salven River. His description of the beauty of *Amherstia*, dubbed 'The Pride of Burma' ensured that it was the one plant every collector desired above everything else, and so it was no surprise that Paxton and the Duke wanted one. The journey to Calcutta took six-and-a-half months, and on the way Gibson collected plants for Chatsworth at every port of call: oranges, lemons, myrtle and fuchsia from Madeira, ericas and proteas from the Cape of Good Hope. He finally reached Calcutta on 8th March 1836.

Gibson dispatched countless specimens for the Great Stove, and a year later, left Calcutta on 3rd March, 1837, bringing with him over a thousand tender exotic plants, over one hundred species of orchid, and also, *Amherstia nobilis*. Paxton and the Duke met Gibson and his precious cargo in London. Paxton then commissioned a narrow boat to take the plants from London to Cromford, where they were loaded onto sprung wagons (possibly one of Joseph Burdekin's), for the twelve mile journey to Chatsworth. Sadly Paxton could not encourage *Amherstia* to flower and the race to produce the first blooms was won in March 1849 by another avid collector, Mrs Lawrence of Ealing Park. Paxton never managed to persuade *Amherstia nobilis* to flower, but when Kate Colquhoun, author of Paxton's biography, gave the 12th Duke a plant in thanks for her research for the book at Chatsworth, the head gardener at the time, Ian Webster, succeeded where Paxton had failed and *Amherstia nobilis* bloomed at Chatsworth in 2010.

At any one time from the 1840s to the outbreak of the First World War in 1914, there were three of Burdekins' haulage carts to be seen heading northwards from Beeley with coal to feed Paxton's stoves and the brew house furnace, and three heading southwards from Chatsworth with ice to go by train from Rowsley to supply hotels in Derby.

In those days nearly every country house had its own ice pond. Chatsworth has two, one in the Garden at the end of the Canal Pond, and the other in the Park itself. The Canal Pond was a less efficient ice pond than the one in the Park, as it was too wide and too deep to have the ideal thickness of ice. Also, because the pond was open to the elements all year round, the ice from it was invariably soiled and not acceptable for use in the Kitchen.

The ice pond in the Park was constructed in 1693 for the 1st Duke and is a crescent shaped pond 150 yards long and averaging ten yards in width, cut into a sloping bank. It has its own controlled water feed and outlet, and at the northern end of the pond there is a circular beehive-shaped underground chamber. At the first sign of a keen frost, the water was allowed to flood through the pond until the surface was clear of leaves and twigs. A gamekeeper was tasked with keeping watch over it throughout the day, and to drive away birds and animals that might foul the water. Men's boots and tools were also kept scrupulously clean throughout the operation, and care also had to be taken not to stir up the water when breaking the ice that formed over the shallow water.

Ice was never gathered if it had a covering of snow, as the snow melted and prevented the complete solidification of the ice. When the pond was frozen over to a depth of an inch or so, the ice was cut with a spade all around the pond about a yard from the edge and the main area was then broken up into large sheets which were dragged along to the ice house using a long pole with a spiked horse-shoe shaped attachment on the end of it. The ice was then broken into smaller pieces with a wooden mallet and pushed down a wooden chute into the underground chamber. Any melt water drained through the slatted base of the chute into a waste drain, so that only ice was allowed to enter the chamber. As the ice piled up inside, a man with clean boots went down a ladder into the chamber to break the slabs into smaller pieces and to pack it down tightly within the space, and this process was repeated until all the available ice was stored. The top of the chamber was then sealed up and the passage leading into the building was tightly packed with straw to make it airtight. The ice then solidified, and further supplies were added as and when the pond froze.

What is fascinating is that the ice house at Chatsworth was built in the late 17th century, yet ice was not used generally as a means of preserving food until the 1840s, when a shipment of frozen ice was imported into Britain by an American entrepreneur. When this first shipment arrived, the customs officers were so puzzled as to how to classify it that all 300 tons of ice had melted away before it could be moved from the docks.

Robert Aughtie, a gardener at Chatsworth in the 1840s, kept a journal in which he describes the collecting of ice at the ice pond. His entry for 23rd December 1848 reads: 'The ice house was filled today by George's men', and again on 6th January 1849, 'William Bland got a ducking while getting ice at the pond in the park.'

Dennis Fisher, the husband of my father's cousin, remembered gathering ice from the Chatsworth ice pond in the first half of the 20th century. He described the process in a note for the Chatsworth archives:

Usually about six men were occupied with this work and were allowed a day to clear the pond. The youngest member of the gang was the 'fetcher', tasked with keeping the fire going and fetching the morning and afternoon ration of ale from the House. The men were paid a bonus for this job and it was traditional, though unofficial, for them to make up a kitty and send the 'fetcher' to a pub in Baslow for a gallon of rum. They normally finished the job by mid-afternoon and would then sit around the brazier drinking rum and ale until knocking-off time!

The ration of ale he mentions is a reference to the fact that beer was the everyday drink for most people, not just those serving in a large country house, because it was a way of purifying water supplies that were otherwise unfit to drink. The first brew was the strongest, but when the malt was brewed a second time, it was less potent and it was this 'small beer' which was drunk at meal times. It also formed part of the servants' wages, and in order to keep pace with the demand, most country houses had their own brew house.

The Chatsworth brew house was located behind the Stables where the brewing copper held 400 gallons and was one of the largest in any country house in the country. Brewing at Chatsworth in the 19th century was a two-man operation involving an open, coal-fired furnace and a good deal of heavy physical work, lifting, hand-pumping, and scalding and scrubbing vessels. Long hours were spent watching the boil and fermentation, and could mean that the men would need to stay up for one night and two days for each brew, with only short breaks for food, drink, and odd snatches of sleep. Additional help would have been employed for grinding the malt, and a cooper would have maintained the casks in the beer cellar below the House itself.

There were originally twelve of these casks, which were known as 'The Twelve Apostles'. The barrel heads were decorated with the coat of arms of the 1st Duke of Devonshire, intricately carved in 1714 by Samuel Watson, who also did much of the elaborate carving in the House itself. Three of these barrels remain in place in the Beer Cellar for visitors to see during some of the 'Behind-the-Scenes' tours at the House. The pipe running from the Chatsworth brew house down to the cellar was three inches wide and over 1,000 feet long. At some point in the 20th century, a tap into this pipe was discovered in the 1st Duke's greenhouse, which suggests that the gardeners' ingenuity provided them with their own private supply! Our younger son, Michael, works as a brewer at Peak Ales, the microbrewery currently operating on the Chatsworth Estate, and amongst their several brews, Peak Ales produce a special brew called 'Gardeners' Tap'. It is sold exclusively on the Chatsworth Estate and is very popular with Chatsworth visitors.

Sarah and Joe Burdekin had nine children, and after she was widowed in 1861 her 17-year-old son, Tom, took over the haulage business and the running of Moor Farm in Beeley. It must have been a big responsibility as he had five younger brothers and sisters, the youngest being four-year-old George. When George grew up, he took over Sheeplea Farm at Spitewinter on Beeley Moor with his wife Maria, and eventually Sarah went to live there with them. Sarah would drive with her horse, Kit, in the trap to Shentall's in Brampton, Chesterfield, with cheese and eggs for sale.

These family bonds remained strong as the years went by, and as Sarah grew older, my grandmother and her brothers and sisters took it in turns, two at a time, to stay with her at Sheeplea Farm, sleeping on a truckle bed at the foot of her huge four-poster bed in case she needed anything in the night. My Nan remembered the giggling that ensued when they heard the old lady break wind in her sleep!

Vast birthday parties were held for Sarah at Sheeplea, with up to 100 relatives from Stanton, Darley Dale, Rowsley and Beeley, and those without their own transport were fetched and returned home in the landau carriage. On their way back to Sheeplea from delivering everyone safely home, the landau could go on the main road past the Spitewinter pub, or take a short cut. Nan told me that the men on the landau would shout, 'Which way shall we go, Bill?'

'I'll let the horses have their head!' was Bill's reply from the reins, and of course they always went by the pub.

Sarah Burdekin died in 1910, aged 95, and is buried in Ashover Churchyard. George had a gravestone with the simple inscription, 'Mother', placed for her.

Young Tom Burdekin continued at Moor Farm with the haulage business as well as the farm. In addition to hauling coal to Chatsworth, he once went up to Thornton-le-Dale in Yorkshire to fetch a load of timber, returning with not only the wood but also Mary Wilton as his bride. They had eleven children, my grandmother being the youngest. All eleven children survived, and all four sons became tenant farmers or worked on the Chatsworth Estate. They all held the village of Beeley in very great affection, with family funerals being great occasions for a family reunion.

Millie was the fifth child, born in 1880, and aged 20 was engaged to be married. One summer's day, she and her fiancé went on an outing, when he was tragically drowned in a boating accident. Not long afterwards Millie discovered that she was pregnant, and in a panic, ran away to Manchester. Her mother, Mary Burdekin, followed her and managed to discover where she was living and brought her back to Beeley. Mary Burdekin was herself illegitimate and did not want her grandchild to have to grow up with the same stigma, nor for her daughter Millie to have to cope with bringing up a child on her own. So once the baby was born, Mary brought him up as her twelfth child, and she was widowed shortly afterwards. My grandmother said that her mother took the baby with her to one of the Sheeplea gatherings for her mother-in-law, old Sarah Burdekin. Mary's sister-in-law Sarah said,

'Why Mary, we'er hast tha got thee childt?'

'Why he's mine!' replied Mary.

'Well who's 'is fayther?' queried her sister-in-law.

'Your Jim!' laughed Mary. Jim was Sarah's husband, a big, friendly, jovial man, who gave a great guffaw. The whole company laughed and that was the end of the matter, and the child, named Eric, was henceforth referred to by the family as the youngest son. In time Millie went on to enjoy a long and happy marriage with her husband Harry.

After my great-grandfather, Tom Burdekin's death in 1902, aged 58, his widow Mary left Moor Farm and took on the tenancy of the Post Office and Tea Room in Beeley. When Chatsworth was busy with the annual round of winter House parties she earned a little extra money for her family by working in the kitchens at the big House.

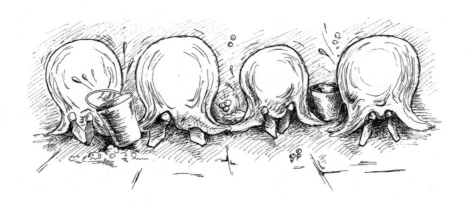

2

❧

The Country House

At the time my great-grandmother was working at these late
Victorian and Edwardian House parties, Chatsworth was only
occupied by the Cavendish family for part of the year as their other
houses also had to be visited. From January until after Easter the
Devonshires went to Lismore Castle in Country Waterford for the
salmon fishing and then travelled to London to stay at Devonshire
House from April until mid-July. From mid-July until mid-August, it
was time for the seaside at Compton Place in Eastbourne and then, from
mid-August until mid-September, they went up to Bolton Abbey in
beautiful Wharfedale in the Yorkshire Dales for the grouse-shooting.
Mid-September until mid-October was spent at Hardwick Hall and then
it was back to Chatsworth from mid-October to January for the
pheasant-shooting and to celebrate Christmas and New Year. In her
book, *The House*, Deborah Duchess reminisces that she once asked
Duchess Evelyn, the 9th Duke's wife, 'So when did you go to Chiswick?'

'Chiswick? Oh we sometimes used Chiswick for breakfast!' her
grandmother-in-law replied.

My grandmother sometimes went with her mother when she was
called to help out in the Chatsworth Kitchen at these busy times, and
she could remember as a girl of about eleven helping her mother in the
kitchen over Christmas. The recipe for Christmas pudding that I use
today is the one she gave me. It is in my recipe book as 'Chatsworth
Christmas Pudding' and is the best Christmas pudding I have ever
tasted. At the time great-grandmother was helping in the Christmas
Kitchen at Chatsworth, my grandmother found herself with other, less
welcome tasks. These included scrubbing the long almost subterranean

service passageway that runs the length of the North Wing at Chatsworth, which is the only below-stairs means of accessing one part of the House from the other. Nan knelt alongside three housemaids at one end of the passageway as, on hands and knees, they scrubbed their way to the other end. She told me that the housekeeper said to her, 'Annie, have you ever worked so hard in all your life?'

Whilst she was working in the House with her mother over this particular Christmas, probably 1903, they slept on the Kitchen-maids' Landing, which is now home to the textile department, and is reached via the 'Cally', or California Passage. Nan said they used to talk about going 'up the California' to bed, but no one knows why it was called the California. The Victorian kitchen they worked in was built in the 6th Duke's North Wing and would have been the height of modernity in its day with all the latest fixtures and fittings; there was even a tank for keeping live fish until they were needed.

The Kitchen faced north to avoid the heat of direct sunlight and has a very high ceiling to take away the hot air, steam and smells. The fittings included steam cupboards and a hot steam table, the steam being produced by coke, whilst wood was used to fuel the huge ranges. The Kitchen was only used for cooking and would not have contained a sink, as all the washing up and vegetable preparation would have been done in a separate scullery. This meant that every dish and pot had to be carried into the next room to be washed, dried and put away. These details were probably unknown to the owners of these great houses. In a book written in 1851 by the wife of Charles Dickens, under the pen name of Maria Clutterbuck, a lunch menu for six people was proposed, which would have generated over 450 pieces of washing up!

The working day began early for the kitchen staff. The nightwatchman on his final round would wake the scullery maid at 5.30am and her first job was to clean the kitchen range with brushes, blacking and ashes. It needed to be burning well by the time the cook and kitchen maids arrived at about 6.30am to prepare breakfast, first for the staff and then for the family, who took breakfast at 9am.

Generally at this time, mechanical jacks were used for turning roasting meat. Some were powered by a hand crank, some by a small dog called a spit-hound, running on a treadmill rather like a hamster wheel. Other contraptions used the heat from the fire to turn the spit.

The one at Chatsworth used water power from water piped under-ground from a pond in the gardens called the Jack Pond, where more recently Angela Conner's water sculpture, 'Revelation', was situated. The water passed from the Jack Pond through a lead pipe to turn a waterwheel in the Kitchen at the side of one of the three vast fireplaces. As the waterwheel turned, so the spit above the fire turned with it.

Whilst the Kitchen was used for cooking, and the Scullery for vegetable preparation and washing up, any cakes or sweet pastries were prepared in the Confectionery, otherwise known as the Still Room. They were then baked in a separate room adjoining the Still Room, called the Bake House, which was my office for a long time. The name 'still room' dates back to medieval times when any great house or castle had its own distillery, where medicines such as throat lozenges were prepared, herbs and flowers processed for use in food or cosmetics, rat poison, soap, and furniture polish would be made, hair restorer concocted, and rose water distilled. As physicians and apothecaries became more common and the products they made became more readily available, the Still Room was used less as a chemist's laboratory and more as an addition to the Kitchen, used when making jams and jellies, icing elaborate cakes for the dining table above stairs, and producing ice creams and sorbets away from the heat of the Kitchen. The concoction of these sweet confections led to its change of name to that of Confec-tionery. In my first winter working at Chatsworth we made Seville orange marmalade in the Confectionery for sale in the Orangery Shop, and in subsequent years, the Farm Shop.

The winter parties at Chatsworth included Christmas and the New Year, and provided the opportunity to offer lavish House parties at which King Edward VII, when he was Prince of Wales, and later, after he became King, was a regular guest, with Queen Alexandra. He had set the pattern for these country house parties at Sandringham and the 8th Duke of Devonshire (who inherited the title in 1891), and his lively wife Louisa soon established a routine of similar entertainments at Chatsworth.

Louisa Von Alten was the widow of the 6th Duke of Manchester and became a duchess for the second time in 1892, at the age of 59, when she married the Duke of Devonshire. She has always been known by the family at Chatsworth as 'The Double Duchess'. Louisa Von Alten was a great beauty in her youth, and when she first arrived in England as the young bride of Lord William Mandeville (who would succeed to the dukedom of Manchester in 1855), Lord and Lady Ravensworth held a party in her honour at Ravensworth Castle, where my grandmother became a housemaid. Here, Duchess Louisa made such an impression on one of the guests, William Charlton, that the event is recalled in the memoirs of his wife written 40 years later, and she wasn't even at the party herself, as she was in Paris!

The winter shoots hosted by the 8th Duke and Duchess of Devonshire also incorporated spectacular evening parties for events such as Twelfth Night. One regular guest at these evening parties was the local physician, Dr Wrench (1833-1912), who had learned his trade as a very young man in the Crimean War. He became the physician to the Duke of Devonshire, who engaged the doctor's services not only for his own personal care, but also to look after his staff and the inhabitants of the surrounding villages. He lived in Park House in Baslow and my husband Clive's great-grandfather, William Strutt, was his coachman. He was so highly thought of by Dr Wrench's family that he was buried alongside his master in Baslow churchyard. A wonderful journal was kept by Dr Wrench, now in the care of Nottingham University and waiting for someone to have the time to edit and publish it. In the journal, Dr Wrench describes some of the parties he was invited to at Chatsworth.

Dr Wrench attended a dinner at the House in 1895, when the Prince of Wales was the principal guest. In his journal, Dr Wrench described there being 35 people in the party and that one of the guests was a millionaire Parsee called Remben Sassoon, who had brought a persimmon for the Prince of Wales. As no one had seen a persimmon before, the Prince cut it up and shared it round the table with everyone else.

On 7th January 1898, Dr Wrench, his wife Annie and daughter Nancy were present at the theatricals at 10pm, followed by supper at 1am for 160 guests, half in the Dining Room at circular tables, where the Prince sat, and half in the Statue Gallery where the Princess sat. Dr Wrench remembered that the guests were waited on by 60 footmen, moving so quietly that they could enjoy the band playing in the gallery. They were so busy enjoying the scene, however, that they had not done justice to all the wonderful food when the Prince rose from the table, and the guests all had to do same, leaving the fruit on their plates and their champagne glasses full of wine. Dr Wrench goes on to say that during that House party there was excellent shooting, the fountains were floodlit, beautiful women were in their diamonds, servants were in livery and that there was lots of 'gaiety at dinner, plays, and Johnson's string band for entertainment'.

In January 1899, Dr Wrench was invited to take his own party to a ball at Chatsworth, lit by electric lamps. They took supper in the Orangery at two dozen round tables under the tree ferns and camellias with lights amongst the foliage. The tables were laden with gold and silver plate, and 'the Blue Hungarian Band played dance music and National music'. Coffee was served at 2am in the Painted Hall while they waited for their carriages, and the Duke provided a special train for guests from Derby which left Rowsley at 3am. It must have been a very colourful scene, with ladies in their jewels and beautiful dresses. The Duke wore the ribbon and Order of the Garter, the men wore their medals and orders, mayors wore their chains, and Dr Wrench wrote that the Master Cutler had a badge on his chest as big as a warming pan. There is a 'suggested list' in the Chatsworth archive for the Chatsworth Ball of 12th January 1899 which extends to ten pages, and there were 410 local acceptances, which must have also meant 250 horses, whilst a special train brought a number of guests from London. The Daily Graphic of Saturday 14th January describes the Duchess of Devonshire: 'Her dress was of cloth of silver with point d'Alencon lace and red roses, with a tiara and collar of diamonds. The Duchess of Marlborough was in white tulle embroidered with pink roses, with a coronet of diamonds and a collar of pearls.'

The Prince of Wales visited Chatsworth again the following year, and Dr Wrench dined at the House every night of the visit, when they ate what he says were reputed to be 'the best dinners in England'. At one of the dinners, Dr Wrench says that the Double Duchess's grand-daughters, the Acheson sisters, asked their grandmother if she had ever eaten blackberry and apple pie – she hadn't and there followed an animated discussion about bicycles and flying machines. These three sisters played a lot of golf on the Chatsworth course, striking in their modern plus-four trousers, and my grandmother's brother, my great-uncle Joe, and other boys were fetched out of Edensor School when their services were required as caddies on the golf course, much to the annoyance of the school master. The Acheson sisters were really striking women, as can be seen in the painting by John Singer Sargent at Chatsworth.

On the 4th January 1904 the royal party arrived by train at Rowsley station at 5pm. When they were half a mile from Chatsworth the party was met by 300 torchbearers, who ran beside the coach all the way through the Old Park to the House. The gardeners filled the Gardens with illuminations and the public were admitted in their thousands. As the blinds in the House windows were raised, they were able to see the King taking tea in the Drawing Room and he went to the window and waved to the crowd in response to their calls.

Dr Wrench records the dinners and diners on each of the five nights of the royal visit. Most evenings there were 43 at dinner, dining from gold plates. He only mentions two items, cold boiled beef, with a savoury of bloater soft roes at the end. One night members of his family were also invited to the theatricals, and on another night the public paid to see the play and all the money was given to a local charity. It may well have been one of these performances that my grandmother and her family attended as she could remember as a child going along to see them. During his visit Dr Wrench had to see the King several times as he had a sore throat, and when the King left, he presented Dr Wrench with a memento of a scarf pin in gold and enamel, set with 30 diamonds and within a crown enclosing 'VII'. On the same visit Queen Alexandra also visited the Poorhouse in Bakewell and left £50 'for the old people'.

On the 24th November 1904, Dr Wrench was again at Rowsley station, this time to meet the King and Queen of Portugal and the Duke provided a dozen carriages for the party. It was snowing hard and the River Derwent had frozen over for the first time in eight years. There were great dinners, as was expected by royal guests. Dinner usually consisted of fish, entrée, game, sweets, ices and desserts. One of the meals was recorded by Dr Wrench as:

Potage a la Bolton
Crème d'Orge a l'Allemande
Cabillard grille aux Huitres
Mignons de Volaille a l'escargots

Crepenette de Becassines
Dindes aux marrons
Filet de boeuf a la Jardiniere
Cailles rotie
Haricots verts a la crème
Tortes aux pommes
Crème de fromage

In January 1905 Dr Wrench again met King Edward VII and Queen Alexandra at Rowsley and again dined at Chatsworth on every evening of their visit. He observed that, 'He enjoyed the company more than the food because it was interesting talking to Sir Francis Young who had just returned from Tibet'. He also says that three golf professionals had been hired and they played golf nearly every day. On one day, eight motor cars went up to Devonshire Hospital at Buxton where the King presented a glass operating table.

January 1906 was the first time that the King and Queen were met with motor cars. My great-uncle Joe was chauffeur to the Duke by then, and he may well have been driving one of the cars whilst his mother and sister Annie were helping out in the Kitchen. There was much hilarity at dinner and Dr Wrench noted that:

If laughter aids digestion, then dyspepsia should never be known at Chatsworth! The Twelfth Night Party was much enjoyed by the Queen. Soon after dinner we proceeded to the Statue Gallery, the band played the National Anthem, and we promenaded round a twenty-foot Christmas tree covered with crackers and penny toys. The fun commenced when several gentlemen attempted to bob for apples. This afforded great hilarity, for the Queen stood by and gave the unprepared a ducking by a tap on their heads when they were fishing for the apple. I avoided the baptism by water and was crowned by the Queen with a paper crown from a cracker. She beckoned me to her, I bowed, and she fixed the crown with three good pats on my bald pate. We all crossed hands and danced round the tree, singing Auld Lang Syne, John Peel, and other choruses. Then Lord Acheson, Miss Wilson, Lord E. Vane Tempest and Princess Henry of Pless danced the cake dance against each other to the accompaniment of penny whistles. I noticed Princess Victoria blowing two at once. Of course, we had the cutting of the great

cake, eight feet in circumference, and made of sponge cake, with the
search in our portions for trinkets. After the cake, we returned to the
dining room, the table was converted to a glissade, and venturesome
ladies and gentlemen seated on the cloth were dragged by willing hands
as fast as possible the whole length of the table. The ladies were caught,
and the gentlemen made their own landings!

The days of the house parties would revolve around outdoor pursuits followed by evenings of dining, cards and theatrical entertainments in the wonderful Victorian Theatre at the end of Chatsworth's long North Wing. This Theatre was first designed as a Ballroom by Sir Jeffrey Wyatvillle in 1833. The ceiling is decorated with late 17th century panels painted by Louis Cheron (1660-1725) and Sir James Thornhill (1676-1734), and include views of Thor's Cave and Peveril Castle, which are the earliest known depictions of Derbyshire landscapes. They were originally painted for the 1st Duke of Devonshire's Long Gallery and were removed from there when that room was converted to the Library by the 6th Duke. He also commissioned the Crace brothers to decorate the spaces in between the panels on the ceiling of this new Ballroom.

The gallery in the Ballroom was originally a music gallery for the orchestra. There are two boxes beneath it, which were for playing cards if guests preferred to sit out the dancing; one of these boxes was used by Queen Victoria when she attended a ball at Chatsworth in 1843. Guests would have eaten their starter and main course in the Great Dining Room and then strolled through the Sculpture Gallery and Orangery and then on up to the Ballroom for dancing and dessert. The men would have taken their port and cigars on the roof.

In 1896 Duchess Louisa transformed the 6th Duke's Ballroom at the top of the Belvedere tower into a Theatre, with the help of William Helmsley, a leading London designer and supplier of theatrical scenery and appliances. It was fitted out with a stage, proscenium arch, front drop curtain (featuring a painting of Elizabethan Chatsworth), and a number of scenery sets, including a woodland scene, a cottage interior, a baronial hall and a grand French drawing room. Prior to the discovery of the scenery at Chatsworth, only one other piece of Helmsley's scenery was known to have survived, the act drop at the Gaiety Theatre and Opera House in Douglas on the Isle of Man, which dates back to 1900. In addition to the scenery, other items of historic theatre interest were discovered at Chatsworth in the small room beneath the stage including electric lights, seating plans, tickets, small early electric follow-spots and footlight pillars, no examples of which are known to exist anywhere else but at Chatsworth. The Theatre was used so regularly by the 8th Duke and Duchess when King Edward VII came to stay that the press dubbed it 'The Theatre Royal'. The Theatre is now one of only three private theatres surviving in country houses. The other two are at Capesthorne Manor in Cheshire and Craig-y-nos in Powys, but Chatsworth's is reputed to be the finest.

The mornings during these country house parties would have included shooting for the gentlemen, while the ladies could do as they pleased after breakfast, letter-writing, riding, reading or gossiping, before joining the gentlemen for luncheon out with the shoot. There, an elaborate meal would be laid out in a specially erected marquee with tablecloths, silver, porcelain and crystal glassware. In the afternoons, the ladies would change for tea, which would be followed by games or a retreat to the Library, before another change of clothes for dinner. Ladies were not expected to wear the same dress more than once, so a four day visit would have required 12 to 16 complete ensembles. Dinner would be served at 8.30pm with guests entering the Great Dining Room in strict order of rank. Although the ladies wore the finest of beautiful jewellery, they would have worn little or no makeup, so as to demonstrate the fine quality of their complexions. After dinner there would have been conversation, music, and cards, when baccarat or whist would have been played.

The number of staff working at Chatsworth to provide the kind of service that was required for such lavish entertainment was immense. The Gardens alone required 80 men to tend the 105 acres of main garden and six acres of kitchen garden at Barbrook, where the Chatsworth caravan site is now situated. Here they would have been cultivating fruit, vegetables, and flowers for the table. There were also 30 glasshouses to look after, including Paxton's Great Conservatory, the Conservative Wallcase for growing peaches, apricots and figs, the Victoria Regia Lily House, three orchid houses, four pineapple houses, three ranges of vineries (each 250 feet long), a mushroom house, cucumber and melon houses, several further peach houses, strawberry and cherry houses and the Orangery. Nowadays only just over half an acre is under glass.

Cooks and housekeepers were always given the courtesy title 'Mrs' whether married or single, and footmen were hired for their looks as much as their ability, with the tallest footmen commanding the highest wages. Lady Maud Baillie (daughter of the 9th Duke), described the State livery as being 'pale yellow cloth with silver lace strappings and pale blue cuffs, knee breeches, white silk stockings and buckled shoes'. This livery was worn until 1938 if there were more than six for dinner, and until 1924 footmen still powdered their hair if there was a party.

Because house parties were generally from mid-October to January, the hot-houses must have been invaluable in the provision of fruit and vegetables for the meals, and flowers for the table decorations. Unfortunately, there are no records at Chatsworth of these table displays but it is certain that they would have been very elaborate in order to impress the guests, and a returning visitor would not have expected to see the same design used a second time. I gave a talk to a group in Cheshire a number of years ago, where an elderly lady told me that her grandfather had worked in the gardens at Chatsworth and once described a table setting for a grand dinner, when Paxton's Rockery was reproduced in miniature on the dining table, complete with the water feature of the Wellington Rock. She confirmed that there was always a member of the gardening team who was the 'decorator', with the responsibility of creating the beautiful arrangements for drawing rooms, library, bedrooms, dining room and so on, and that is still the case today.

Flower displays within the family part of the House are arranged by members of the gardens team rather than flower arrangers brought in especially for the purpose, and when flower festivals are staged at Chatsworth, the gardening team works very closely with the flower arrangers to show the House off to best advantage. For private dinners, the Duchess consults closely with the gardeners to decide which flowers are to be used on the table and always incorporates what is seasonally available in the Gardens, whether it be flat silver dishes of blood red camellias, or tall vases of spiky lupins, flutes of peonies and hostas, or a simple vase of roses. Depending on the occasion, table decorations may not always be of flowers. When Her Grace was Duchess at Chatsworth, she once requested a pen of live piglets on the dining table.

His Grace refused to sit down at the table until they were removed, so they were taken away after the first course, when he agreed to join the rest of the guests. On another occasion, a pen of live chickens were placed on the table.

In 1907, when 80 gardeners were busily employed in the Gardens alone, there were 262 in total on the Chatsworth staff list, including seven housemaids and three laundry maids. Interestingly, the laundry maids received more than twice the wage of the housemaids (£35 per year, compared with £17 for the housemaids), but they were much lower in the 'below stairs' social hierarchy and never mixed with the rest of the staff, apart from very briefly at Christmas. At that time the house-keeper's salary was £100 plus a 10 per cent bonus from the money received from House party visits. In 1907 there were 773 staff employed in total on all the Devonshire estates; in 2013 there were 567 staff employed at Chatsworth alone.

As was the tradition, girls leaving home went away into service, unless they went into service locally as laundry maids. In 1908 at the age of 16 my grandmother went into service as parlour maid at Ravensworth Castle, near Lamesley, just outside Gateshead. The permanent staff for a grand house were seldom sourced locally, but from a distance away so that there would be less gossip in the locality about what went on above stairs. Local staff were only brought in to help out at particularly busy times, or to work in the laundry. Annie therefore, went to join her sister, Nellie, six years her senior, who was already in service at Ravensworth. When Nan died she left me the wonderful brown domed trunk that was bought for her when she left home. It has her initials AMB stencilled on the side and is filled with all kinds of poignant mementoes. When she went away to Ravensworth, her brother George took her and her trunk from Beeley Post Office to the station at Rowsley in the pony and trap, charging her sixpence for the ride. George always had a reputation for being a bit tight-fisted, and when he later took on the tenancy of a farm of his own at Crossroads Farm, Belper, he never fed his pigs on Sundays as he said it did them good to have a day of rest.

There was a young gardener working at Ravensworth called John Edward Matthewson Tindale (always known as 'Jack'), who was born there on 4th March 1892. His father, Edward Tindale, was head gardener to the Estate and his mother was formerly Margaret Cameron, a Gaelic speaking Scot from Abernethy, Inverness. She refused to have playing cards in the house, declaring that they were 'the Devil's pictures', but enjoyed making rather potent dandelion and other wines, which packed quite a punch by all accounts.

Ravensworth was a small estate, and it wasn't long before the pretty red-haired housemaid, Annie, caught the eye of the young gardener, Jack. He volunteered for the Northumberland Fusiliers in the Great War, and on a short leave they were married on 15th February 1917 in St. Philip's Church, Chorlton, in Manchester where my grandmother was living with her sister Millie, and working in munitions. On 21st March 1918, my grandfather was wounded and taken prisoner, spending the last months of the war in a prisoner of war camp at Soltau, near Hannover, from where he and other prisoners were sent to work on a nearby farm.

In the old domed trunk, Nan left an embroidered handkerchief box for me, containing all the cards and letters she received from him while he was a prisoner of war. He was allowed to send two cards and three letters home per month, but the return mail was so inefficient that he did not receive a reply from her until 20th July, by which time he had sent seven cards and six letters home. In many of the cards and letters he urged the folks at home to 'remember the silver lining', and he never lost his sense of humour, enquiring about his Annie's holidays and adding, '…am spending mine once more on the Continent'. He was always thinking of the Gardens at Ravensworth too: 'Father will be busy, I hope the melons finished well. I know the chrysanths will still have that unquenchable thirst.'

After the War, he returned to Ravensworth Gardens, where the young couple had an estate cottage in a wood. Here, the underground coal mine workings were so close to the surface that Annie and Jack could hear the miners' conversations in the ground beneath them. My father, Eric Cameron Tindale was born here on 5th November 1924. In 1926, old Edward Tindale died, aged 70, and I have a lovely letter of condolence to his widow from the Newcastle Lord Mayor's Chamber.

Ravensworth's days were numbered; with the mine workings so close to the surface, the whole building became unstable and my grandfather and his young family moved to a succession of municipal gardens in Newport, then Cambridge and Leeds. Finally, they moved to Queen's Park, Chesterfield, where he took up the appointment of parks superintendent in 1939 and remained there until his retirement in 1956. My grandparents always remembered Ravensworth with great affection, and I made a pilgrimage there in 2009 with my mother and elder son, Philip, to see what was left of it. The castle is a ruin now, but the atmosphere was amazing, and I found the head gardener's cottage intact, hardly changed at all from the photograph I found in Nan's old trunk and the picture my grandfather had painted of 'the old home'.

3

❧

Early Days

After several house moves up and down the country, my grandparents eventually returned to Derbyshire. Visits to stay with them at Darley Dale, and later in Beeley, when my grandmother moved back there after my grandfather's death in 1964, always involved a visit to Chatsworth. We would walk past Beeley Church, where so many ancestors, both Burdekins and Graftons (and now also my grandparents), are buried, and into Beeley meadow. Then the mile-long stroll through to the one-arch bridge and Bridge Farm. The farm was last tenanted as a working farm to Sam Burdekin, one of my grandmother's brothers, and subsequently to his son Albert. Next we would pass through the kissing gate into Chatsworth Park, and then past the ruined mill, originally built for the 4th Duke of Devonshire by James Paine in 1756-7.

We have recently discovered that my husband Clive's ancestor, John Strutt, took the tenancy of the 1st Duke's mill in 1700. It lay on the east side of the river below Chatsworth and was demolished during the 4th Duke's landscaping of the Park with Capability Brown. John Strutt's grandson, William Ward Strutt, was the first miller in the new mill built in 1756 and the Strutt family continued to work the mill until 1859. Francis George Ward Strutt was the last Strutt to mill there and the tenancy was then taken over by the Hodkins, descendants of the Burdekin family by marriage (Nan's brother George married Lillie Hodkin). They milled there until it was closed in 1952. Thus it was that only our two families have ever milled in the Park in the last 400 years.

The walk then continued from Paine's ruined mill past the bottom weir and along the riverbank to the Duck Pen Wood and the top weir, with the first tantalising views of Chatsworth.

I would like to say that I was stunned by my first view of Chatsworth on this walk through the Park, but in truth I can't distance myself enough from how I think of it now. Fitting perfectly into the landscape and in total harmony with its natural surroundings, Chatsworth looks as though it has always been there. With its warm and mellow honey-coloured stone, and golden window frames glowing, burnished in the afternoon sunshine, Chatsworth extends the warmest of welcomes to all who visit.

In 1967, when I was twelve, and staying with my grandmother, I wrote a letter home to my parents. I still have the letter, and it is plain that my first visit had been an enjoyable one. It reads as follows:

On Wednesday we got on the Baslow bus and got off at Edensor and walked over to Chatsworth. We had a good look round – the paintings were wonderful and we saw a real Rembrandt worth half a million pounds. On most of the ceilings there were beautiful paintings, and round the door frames there were lovely carvings. In the Sculpture Gallery there was a lovely cake of Chatsworth covered in icing including the gates, which must have taken a lot of work. There was a lovely marble table with three little babies curled up asleep on it all beautifully carved in marble.

A holiday in Derbyshire always included a visit to my grandmother's brother, Joe, who had been chauffeur to the 9th Duke, and was now retired to a pensioner's flat in the Cavendish Flats at Edensor. His daughter, Joyce Fisher, and her husband Dennis also lived in Edensor, and when they were away on holiday we would come as a family to house-sit for them in their beautiful house, Norman Villa. It's the sort of house you always dream of living in, and now my own dream has come true, as we moved into this house ourselves in 2006.

A fascinating piece of our family history was discovered only recently, when we started to investigate the Strutt family and discovered that Norman Villa was actually built for Clive's great-great-great-grandfather, William Strutt, in 1840 at a cost of £1,200. William's father and brother were the millers and as a younger son, William did not go into the mill with them, but became the park keeper to the 6th Duke.

When his wife Sarah died aged 41 in 1834, William engaged a house-keeper, Mrs Martha Outram, to help him raise his young family, Henry (aged 13), Charlotte (four) and Maria (two), and a new house was built for him in Edensor Village as part of the 6th Duke's alterations. The house has a back staircase leading from the kitchen and small sitting room up to an enclosed bedroom, which would have been perfect for a live-in housekeeper. On his death in 1852 William was buried in Edensor Churchyard and the inscription on his tomb reads, 'Park Keeper to the Duke of Devonshire for forty years'.

Henry Strutt's oldest son, William, became the coachman to Dr Wrench in Baslow, and his son Francis was employed by the Rutland garage in Bakewell to run the stables and garage at the hotel. The youngest of his four children is my mother-in-law, Janet.

My parents moved to Chesterfield in 1973 when I was in my second term at Newcastle-upon-Tyne University, where I was studying History, Norwegian, and Religious Studies, so the following summer, I was looking for a holiday job. At that time there was a large Trebor sweet factory near the railway station in Chesterfield and I got a job working on the factory floor. The work alternated between filling 'lucky bags' with different sweets, and picking the misshapen sweets off the white conveyor belt as they bounced along in front of me, before going down a chute to a lower floor to be packaged. The sweets in production always seemed to be cherryade or menthol-eucalyptus, so I either had dancing red sweets in front of me, dazzling my eyes all day, or fumes from the menthol eucalyptus making them water! At the end of the day, the sugar on the factory floor that had stuck to the soles of my shoes collected dust from the path in Tapton Park as I walked home at the end of my shift, and after three weeks of that I decided to try my hand at something else.

Dad suggested contacting Chatsworth, as it seemed reasonable to suppose that they would take on extra staff at busy times of year. Although Dad's cousin's husband, Dennis Fisher, was comptroller at Chatsworth at that time, I did not want to ask him for a job but preferred to try to get one on my own merit, so I rang the Chatsworth switchboard and they put me through to the housekeeper, Mrs Dean. I asked her if there might be anything for me, and so one Saturday afternoon in 1974, I walked again from Beeley through the meadow and the Park to visit

Mrs Dean for an interview. It went well and as I walked back to Beeley, I felt lucky to have been offered a job. In addition to running the part of the House that was open to visitors, Mrs Dean was also responsible for the Orangery Shop, ice cream sales in the Gardens, guide book sales in the North Entrance Hall, and ticket sales in the Scots Apartments, a suite of rooms within the House which weren't always open to view, and for which there was a small extra charge.

I learned later that Mrs Dean's father had worked as a woodsman for the Royal Household and that she was born in Windsor Great Park. She went into domestic service, achieving the position of second housemaid with the Duke and Duchess of Windsor, having previously spent the war years driving a motor bike in the Army. Before she came to Chatsworth, she was working at a private hotel called the Ramjam Inn on the A1 near Grantham, when a friend saw an advertisement in *The Lady* magazine for the position of housekeeper at Chatsworth. Mrs Dean applied, came for an interview with Her Grace, and started work at the House on 1st August 1968.

On her arrival at Chatsworth she found that the housekeepers she was to be working under were the Hungarian sisters, Ilona and Elisabeth Solymossy. It seems that for most of the housekeeping team working under them, a day without tears was an unusual one. The Solymossy sisters arrived in England as refugees in 1938, one a chemist, and the other a teacher. They were engaged by Kathleen Kennedy, sister of JFK and widow of William Hartington, who would have become the 11th Duke had he not been killed in action in Belgium in 1944. Kathleen employed the Solymossy sisters as cook and housemaid at her house in Smith Square, London, and they stayed on there as caretakers after her death in a tragic flying accident on 13th May 1948 when she was aged only 28. Afterwards, the 10th Duke and Duchess invited the sisters to Chatsworth to engage a team to clean and prepare the House for opening to visitors. They moved in on 23rd August 1948, together with nine other Hungarians, and amazingly, the House was ready for opening at Easter 1949. In spite of petrol-rationing, 75,000 people came to visit at half-a-crown each for entry to the House and Gardens, or a shilling just to see the Gardens.

In 1955, Hugo Read, the Agent at Chatsworth at that time, suggested to the 11th Duke and Duchess (who had succeeded to the title in 1950), that they move from their home at Edensor House in Edensor village into the House at Chatsworth. The Solymossy sisters, who had been looking after the House full-time since their arrival in 1948, were now called upon to prepare the private living quarters for the Duke and Duchess and their young children. The family moved into the House in November 1959, and the Solymossys stayed until Mrs Dean came to join them in 1968. Mrs Dean had a very strong character, and I can imagine a clash of wills when she joined the team. She told me that she went to see Her Grace about it and declared, 'It's me or them! I was told I was going to be housekeeper, and I won't be told what to do by those dictators!'

The Solymossy sisters retired and Miss Dennis was engaged to run the private side of the House while Mrs Dean took over the public areas and the Orangery Shop. Mrs Dean moved into the flat on the Cavendish Passage (now a suite of offices) and the two Solymossy sisters moved from there into a delightful little cottage in Baslow. That is now a quaint holiday home, Park Cottage, with its own private gate into Chatsworth Park. From all I have heard, the two Solymossy sisters were formidable. There was no wonder the House was ready for opening in such a short time – it would not have dared to be otherwise.

Miss Elisabeth Solymossy died in 1975, so I never met her, but I met Miss Ilona many times and always found it difficult to have a conversation with her, as she was so very easy to upset. She always tried to be the first across the threshold on the day the House opened every year, and whilst I found this irritating, it was a sign of her absolute devotion to Chatsworth. I'm sure her determination to be the first visitor every year was just to make sure the House was being looked after properly. In fact, it was her keen sense of how things ought to be that alerted us to the fact that there was something wrong in the Great Chamber. On this occasion, Miss Ilona said that she could feel a strange vibration under her feet as she walked across the room, and on exploration it proved to be caused by a crack in the beam beneath the floor.

I remember one occasion many years ago, after a Christmas party at the House, when we were putting our coats on in the North Entrance Hall. Clive held the door open for Miss Ilona and wished her a happy Christmas.

'Oh I don't tsink it vill be zat!' she replied, in her thick Hungarian accent. 'I shall be at home alone and tsinking about my family behind ze iron curtain.'

When she died in 1991 she had left instructions that her elderly dog be put to sleep and buried with her in the churchyard at Edensor. It was a raw wintry day just before Christmas, and as is traditional on the Estate, the men from the House were the pall bearers. It was very slippery with slushy snow around the edge of the grave, and when poor Trevor McDowell's foot slipped, we all thought he was going to fall in and join her.

Mrs Dean was a very different prospect; she stood no nonsense and ran a very tight ship, but I really did love her and we got on very well indeed. She had a cracking sense of humour and such a love of speed that a trip out in the car with her was always a white knuckle ride – it must have been a hangover from her days on a motorbike during the war. I never go through the Sculpture Gallery without humming the song, 'Red sails in the sunset, Way out on the sea, Oh, carry my loved one, Home safely to me'. It's what I remember Mrs Dean singing or whistling the most; she was always whistling or singing something, and I remember her years as housekeeper as being a time of a very happy team.

Her flat at the end of the Cavendish Passage was on the first floor of the North Wing. It ran parallel to the main North Drive of the House and comprised three interconnecting rooms: a bedroom, a sitting room and another bedroom, with a tiny kitchenette in the corridor and a small bathroom. This flat has since been converted to offices for the chief operating officer, the head of operations, and the events manager, and the bathroom is now a small lobby with a staircase leading up to the marketing offices. When John Oliver was comptroller, the servants' rooms in the attics were converted to these marketing offices and he had a hole knocked through so that a new staircase could be put in. This was fashioned from a piece of the old cast iron spiral staircase from Paxton's Great Conservatory in the Gardens that had survived at the old kitchen gardens behind the cricket ground at Barbrook. It has made a stylish staircase up to the new offices, though the ascent is more comfortable than the descent for anyone suffering from vertigo.

The switchboard at Chatsworth has always been manned 24 hours a day and when Mrs Dean was housekeeper, it was situated directly beneath her flat. One night she woke up, wondering what could have disturbed her and as she lay trying to go back to sleep, she thought she could hear a cry from outside: 'Help! Help!' She opened the window to make sure she hadn't been mistaken, and then rang the switchboard, who were convinced that she must have been hearing things.

'Just you open your window, Mr Oldale, and you'll hear that I'm not mistaken! Someone out there sounds in trouble!'

No doubt grumbling, Alan Oldale went and listened at the window, and realised that someone was indeed in trouble, and that the sound was coming from the direction of the river. He contacted the night watchman, who set off for the riverbank with his torch and found one of the lads from Home Farm at Barbrook standing on the roof of his car in the middle of the river. It was a good job it was a summer's night and that the river level was low or he would most probably have been swept away. He had been on his way back to Home Farm from a rather heavy night out and missed the bridge entirely.

The switchboard operators at this time worked shifts to give each other relief, and one of the operators working a different shift from Mr Oldale was notorious for listening in to the conversations – I suppose it relieved the monotony of the evening. Whenever you were on the phone if Tom was on duty, you could hear the switchboard clock ticking in the background. One evening, someone on the phone suddenly asked, 'What time is it Tom?' and the ticking suddenly stopped as he put the phone down.

John Oliver (comptroller 1996-2006), remembers an incident during the great gale of February 1962 when hundreds of trees came down on the Estate (over 1,000 in Stand Wood alone), and many buildings were damaged, including Paine's Mill at the south end of the Park where two large beech trees destroyed the roof of the mill. At the time, John was a 15-year-old apprentice joiner at Chatsworth. As he walked down the Stables hill to work he saw the panes popping out of the windows of the Theatre tower, four or five at a time, as the glazing bars broke under the strain of the wind. Just after 8am he had an emergency call to go to the Solymossy's flat on the Cavendish Passage, where Miss Ilona was trapped inside her bedroom. She had gone to bed with the top sash of her window open and the pressure of the wind on her inward opening door prevented her from opening it. John managed to force open the door and then tried to close the window but he had to admit defeat, as when he touched it, panes of glass started to blow in on him.

My journey to work involved catching a Hulley's bus from Chesterfield to Baslow and then walking through the north end of the Park to arrive at the House in time for work at 8am. I vividly recall the excitement of my first day at work, when I took the opportunity to cross the rope in the State Music Room to examine the violin door at close quarters. The violin and bow hanging on the door is actually a *trompe l'oeil* painting executed by Jan van der Vaardt in the late 17th century. It is thought to have been brought to Chatsworth after it was rescued from the fire that destroyed Devonshire House in Piccadilly in 1733. It deceives many of our visitors who can't believe that what they are looking at is actually a painting.

After a day spent dusting, vacuuming, selling tickets or ice-cream, or working in the Orangery Shop, I would walk back to Baslow to catch the bus home. I did this for three summers and I can't ever remember it raining. Sometimes I was able to borrow my mother's old Ford Anglia and drove to work. I remember driving home on one occasion in the summer of 1976, a particularly hot one with a long drought, and seeing a huge pall of smoke hanging over the hillside. Beeley Moor had caught fire and as the peat beneath it blazed away, the firemen fought to bring it under control. The family were away at Bolton Abbey, but His Grace came back to help and I remember thinking how absurd it seemed that he had to stay at the Cavendish Hotel in Baslow because there was no one to look after him at Chatsworth. Part of the problem might also have been that the whole kitchen was packed up and travelled with the family up to Bolton Abbey, saucepans and all.

In those days there was nowhere at Chatsworth for people to get a cup of tea, although there was always a bowl with the notice, 'Water for Dogs', by the North Gate. There was just one shop in the Orangery, a small ice cream hut in the Gardens (now Flora's Temple Teas), and a small tent erected each summer in the car park on Lodge Hill where Gladys Hopkins (wife of head gardener Dennis Hopkins) would sell tomatoes and other surplus produce from the Gardens. Mrs Dean enjoyed running the Orangery Shop and did all the buying for it, together with Her Grace. She ran the shop until 1978 when it grew too big to be run alongside housekeeping, and a separate manager, Gill Mason, was engaged to organise it the following season.

Her Grace always took a keen interest in the running of the shop, and I can remember her telephoning regularly from Bolton Abbey during August wanting to know how many of the Chatsworth trays had been sold. I enjoyed the camaraderie of working in the Orangery Shop, which in those days sold a variety of souvenirs: Chatsworth matches, dusters, bon-bons and paperweights, soap, lace, tin trays, Blue John eggs and the like. It also sold hand-knitted garments made from the Jacob's wool produced by the sheep on the Estate and knitted up by local women (myself included), who were urged into production by Her Grace's maid, Maud Barnes.

Her Grace's regular visits to the shop usually involved her working behind the counter to lend a hand when we were busy. We had many busy days in there, with no electronic till, just a wooden cash tray that had been made by the joiners to fit inside the shop counter, which was also made in the Joiners' Workshop in the House. On one of these busy days when I had not been working at Chatsworth long, Her Grace was helping out behind the counter. We couldn't help getting in each other's way, and I said, 'Sorry, sir' instead of 'Sorry, Your Grace'. Something had subconsciously told me I needed to give a title, and flustered, I just picked the wrong one. She thought it highly amusing and we both just laughed and got on with the job. Their Graces' younger daughter, Lady Sophie, also enjoyed helping out sometimes in the shop when she was at home. I also vividly recall one Saturday morning, just before the House opened, when Mrs Dean and I heard the most curious scraping sound advancing through the Sculpture Gallery and getting louder and louder. Finally, the noise arrived in the Orangery, and proved to be Lord and Lady Hartington's young daughters, Lady Celina and Lady Jasmine, in their mother's coats and shoes, trailing along to the shop. I told the Duchess this recently, and she remembered how much both the girls enjoyed wearing her shoes when they were little.

A colleague, Sue Lumb, recalled an occasion when she was in the Orangery Shop with Her Grace and her whippet, Nobby. There were quite a few visitors in the shop, and one of them, spying the notice on the door which read, 'No dogs or ice-creams inside the shop', decided to evict Nobby from the premises. Nobby planted his paws firmly on the ground – he was not going anywhere. The earnest visitor tried to drag the unwilling animal across the floor towards the door, but paused and turned his head as Her Grace said, 'Oh look, Sue. Nobby doesn't want to go outside!' I think visitors might not expect a grand house like Chatsworth to be a living home, with dogs and children and all the other things that are part of family life. Another occasion involving a dog was when Her Grace had a black labrador called Pronto. When she went through the House one day, the dog caused some consternation for a group of visiting Italians who suddenly put on a spurt when they heard the Duchess shouting, 'Pronto! Pronto!'

At this time Her Grace had a blue Mini Clubman, and on many a summer's evening you could see it abandoned somewhere off-road in the Park, door left open and Her Grace nowhere in sight. After a minute or two scanning the landscape, a distant figure could be spotted, moving purposefully along with her 'thistle-spudder' taking out the thistles. It is a thankless task, but one she could never resist, and she always carried a spudder in the car in case she noticed a clump of thistles that needed to be dealt with.

Her son, the 12th Duke, once bought her a notice for her bedroom door, saying 'Manager'. Nothing could have been more appropriate, for she did truly manage Chatsworth all the time she lived there. John Oliver used to say that the 11th Duke and Duchess's tenure at Chatsworth was 'An iron fist in a velvet glove', in as much as Her Grace was always the apparent organiser and decision-maker, but it was His Grace who was actually very much in charge and made the ultimate decisions. I have often seen that in action myself at meetings when once His Grace had spoken, that was that, and Her Grace gave up trying to pursue what she had wanted. He had made up his mind, and she knew that nothing would budge him.

Her energy was boundless, and right up until her leaving Chatsworth to live in Edensor in December 2005, when she would have been 85, she still had the most amazing stamina. I was on the Chapel Passage one day when I heard running feet, as she came flying round the corner from the Grotto, with the butler, Henry, in hot pursuit.

'Is Henry still keeping up with me?' she cried as she ran past.

'Yes, Your Grace, he's not far behind!' I replied.

'Good! Come along Henry, let's go!' and off she went, with Henry trotting along behind her.

When I first started working at Chatsworth as a holiday job, Her Grace had a Border collie called Collie, and as a keen dog-lover, I made a great fuss of him the first time I met him. I found out afterwards that he was rather sharp and had a tendency to nip people, but I think this was because they were wary of him. I never had a problem and he was always pleased to see me, a result, I think, of our relaxed first meeting. His tongue always seemed a little too long for his mouth and protruded slightly, and for a number of years there was a postcard on sale in the Orangery shop with a photograph of him taken in the greenhouse, with his pink tongue-tip peeping out.

Collie had a particular dislike for men, and a very keen aptitude for rounding up anything that moved, and these combined traits proved a problem on numerous occasions for some of the male employees. In 1982, Her Grace's book, *The House, a Portrait of Chatsworth*, was published, and signed copies were sold in the Orangery Shop. It was a regular duty for one of the shop store men to deliver copies of the book to Her Grace's office for her to sign, where Collie was always on the lookout. He would herd the nervous man into a corner, and every time he tried to get away, the dog would growl and he was pinned in a corner until someone came along to call Collie to order.

The housekeeper of the private rooms at this time was Miss Dennis, who came originally from Norfolk and spoke very rapidly in her Norfolk accent, which was sometimes difficult to follow. She always wore her grey hair scraped back into a tight bun, a white overall, sandals, and her stockings were invariably wrinkled. Miss Dennis was in the Sabine Dressing Room one day and opened the door onto the West Sketch Gallery, only to find Collie sitting in the corridor outside. He knew she was terrified of him and teased her dreadfully, always cornering her in a room with only one means of exit. On this occasion, as soon as she closed the Sabine door he strolled away, knowing that it would be some time before she dared to open it again. She telephoned the switchboard, saying that Collie had her trapped in the Sabine, but of course by the time someone got up there Collie had long gone.

Her Grace worked Collie with the sheep, and they made a good team, with Collie getting in a little extra practice rounding-up the hens by the

Game Larder when Her Grace wasn't about. Her Grace's other dog at this time was a lovely black labrador called Chip, who was always very affectionate.

The dogs were often a good early warning system as they would appear ahead of Her Grace so we knew she couldn't be far behind. She often used to whistle as well, which was always useful. In an old staff newsletter, Bill Grindey, who worked in the Gardens before the Second World War, recalled Duchess Evelyn, wife of the 9th Duke, walking round the garden with her little dog, Chatty. In Bill's words, 'As she caught up with the first group of gardeners they would shuffle their feet, making the dog bark. This was a signal to the gardeners that the Duchess was on her way, so all crafty cigarettes were put out and they were all working their socks off when the Duchess reached them.'

During the war, Bill learned to drive and on his return to Chatsworth he went to work as a driver in the Building Yard. He also remembered a time sheet being put in regarding the cleaning of a pensioner's back yard, which read, 'Two hours cleaning Mrs so-and-so's back side'! Sadly, Bill died in 1981.

Mrs Marjorie Link was the first person I worked with on the housekeeping team and she told me a lot about how things used to be on the Estate 'in the old days'. She took great pride in the cleaning of her area on the North Wing, and she would stand back from the beautiful table in the Great Dining Room with a critical eye, and her arms folded; then a sniff, and then the comment, 'A blind man on a galloping horse would be pleased to see that!' Sometimes she would wistfully reminisce about the staff parties held in the Sculpture Gallery with dancing in the Great Dining Room.

Mrs Link (never 'Marjorie'), also remembered Mrs Maud Shimwell, W.K. Shimwell's wife, who as a young woman, was a stunning vision in blue silk, sitting by the fire in the Great Dining Room at a staff party. W.K. Shimwell (only ever known as 'WK'), became comptroller at the age of 26, a position he held until his retirement in 1965. He left school in 1908, aged twelve-and-a-half, and joined the regular payroll at Chatsworth as the bell-boy. His job was to sit by the bell-board (still on view to Behind-the-Scenes visitors), and when the bell rang in a particular room he had to run to find the valet to tell him that he was needed. He also ran the three-quarters of a mile to the Post Office in

Edensor with telegrams before a telephone was installed in the House. He moved on to the Estate Office in Edensor and showed such promise that when the 9th Duke went as Governor General to Canada, he asked the 21-year old WK to go with them to run their household staff at Government House in Ottawa. On their return to England five years later in 1921, WK was appointed comptroller, running the Duke and Duchess's London home at Carlton Gardens, and also Chatsworth and the Home Farm.

Duchess Evelyn, wife of the 9th Duke – and always referred to by Her Grace as 'Grannie Evie' – was a thrifty housewife, and when Mrs Tanner became cook at Chatsworth in 1924, Duchess Evelyn asked her to make nettle soup. So fearful of her were the gardeners that once all the nettles had been used up, they daren't tell her and continued to actively cultivate nettles so that the supply of nettle soup would not run dry. She also had an unusual method for dealing with death-watch beetle, hitting the wooden panelling with a hammer where she thought they were at work, to knock them out. My grandmother often spoke about her, and it was usually to make a remark such as, 'It wouldn't have happened in Duchess Evelyn's day…'

Mrs Tanner's daughter, Maud, started working in the Chatsworth Kitchen as vegetable maid in 1926, and was soon spotted by the young comptroller, WK, whom she was eventually to marry. From vegetable maid she progressed up the ladder to first kitchen maid and finally cook. She described the daily kitchen routine to Her Grace for her book, *The House: A Portrait of Chatsworth*:

> The first kitchen maid cooked for the school room and nursery, and the second kitchen maid cooked for the servants. The vegetable maid did the vegetables for the family. She did her own washing up. The scullery maids did the vegetables for the servants and washed up for the cook and kitchen maids. I got up at six, cleaned the cook's sitting-room and took her a cup of tea. Then laid the cook's table, set out all the knives and the other utensils in order, and saw that everything was at hand. I then chopped parsley and prepared other garnishes and then started on the vegetables. I worked till after lunch and had from 2pm to 5pm off. One girl was left on duty in the afternoons to watch the stock-pots. At this time there were six in the Chatsworth kitchens, and they ate in

the kitchen maids' sitting room. We had a man to clean the coppers. The cooking was done on gas, which was made at the gas yard near the kitchen garden till December 1939 when the House was connected to the main. One of the stoves was especially low for the big copper stock-pots, which were too heavy to lift, and had taps at the bottom to strain off the stock.

I never knew WK, but was very fond of his widow Maud, a strikingly good-looking woman even in old age.

When I was about to start my final year at university, Mrs Dean said that there was a job for me with the housekeeping team when I graduated, if I would like it. I said I would love to do it just for one year. So on 1st July 1977, after graduation, I came to work at Chatsworth and I have never worked anywhere else.

4

❧

Just for One Year

When I joined the permanent housekeeping team at Chatsworth, I was given a bed-sitting room on the 6th Duke's Bird Landing which overlooked a glass roof. There was no view but the room faced south so it was very light, with a vast window and fantastic red brocade curtains and tie backs, which were so old that I felt as though the 6th Duke might have chosen them himself. The Bird Landing is so-called because, following the Victorian fashion for stuffed birds and animals, it was lined from floor to ceiling with glass cabinets encasing all manner of animals and birds. At intervals, doors led off to what had once been guest bedrooms and one of these rooms had been turned into an office for Mrs Dean, which was very handy for the Orangery Shop, managed by the housekeeping department until 1978. Four bedrooms had been linked by inter-connecting doors to form a self-contained flat for Henry, the butler (who originated from Lismore Castle in Ireland), and another one was my bed-sitting room.

The room itself was about 21 feet long and 12 feet wide and with a ceiling about 15 feet high, and a drying room on the other side of the wall had been knocked through to form a tiny kitchen. Nowadays there is a bathroom too, but when I occupied the room there was a lavatory downstairs outside the Sewing Room and the nearest bathroom was 60 yards away at the far end of the Bachelor Corridor on what was then called the King's Landing. The Bachelor Corridor runs the length of the Dome Room, Great Dining Room and Sculpture Gallery, and provided several guest bedrooms for the 6th Duke's many bachelor friends, hence the name.

The King's Bathroom was installed for the visits of King Edward VII and later became the bathroom for the nursery. It was a wonderful affair, with the longest bath I have ever bathed in and pretty wallpaper of black and white figures: Victorian children, elephants and horses on wheels, birds' nests, and cats up trees. A visit to the bathroom at dead of night was not for the faint-hearted, as my torch-light glinted on the glass eyes of the animals and birds encased along the walls as I scurried along the Bachelor Corridor, hoping not to collide with the night watchman on his rounds. If royalty were staying, then the detectives used the nursery bedrooms and the King's Bathroom, and I had to forego my bath. Andrew Slater, the footman at that time, also had a flat on the Bachelor Corridor and once we got to know each other he offered me the use of his bathroom when the nursery was in use by the policemen or children.

The retired cook, Mrs Canning, also lived in a small flat on the Bachelor Corridor and as she could only get out with the aid of a walking frame, she was always pleased to have visitors. Any special shopping trip meant a visit to Mrs Canning afterwards to show her what I had bought, or if I was going out, she would enjoy seeing what I was wearing. If I was short of time I would sometimes creep as quietly as possible along the corridor to the bathroom in order to avoid her quavering call, 'Christine, is that you?'

For several months each year Miss Feeney would come to Chatsworth from Lismore Castle. She had been brought up on the Castle Dairy Farm, and the Dowager Duchess reminisces in her book, *Wait for Me*, that Mary's mother cooked all her family's food in an iron pot hanging from a chain over the fire. The 10th Duke's brother, Charles Cavendish, lived at Lismore Castle with his wife Adele Astaire, who was Fred Astaire's sister and dancing partner. Adele Astaire's mother taught Mary Feeney dress-making, and she made many of the curtains for Lismore, later coming to Chatsworth as well to do running repairs to the curtains or furnishings and to make new clothes for Her Grace. She was always terribly seasick on the crossing from Ireland but could never contemplate the idea of flying, so someone from the House would go all the way to Holyhead to collect her from the ferry. She was fantastic with a needle and thread and made all the new covers and copied the worn-out bed hangings when Chatsworth was being prepared for the 11th Duke and his family to move back into the House in the 1950s. I never knew her as 'Mary', only ever as 'Miss Feeney', and I used to see quite a lot of her as my bed-sitting room was directly above her Sewing Room. She was a devout Catholic and gave every appearance of being quite demure, but I remember one afternoon being invited down to her Sewing Room for a drink. I went expecting a nice cup of tea, and was rather taken aback when this sweet little old lady opened one of the cupboards, and out came two glasses and the Irish whiskey bottle.

The housekeeping team always prepared her bedroom for her before her visits and gave the Sewing Room a thorough clean. On one occasion Mrs Brindle, another character in the team, without thinking emptied the little bowl of holy water by the Sewing Room door. She went to fill it up from the tap in the lavatory next door, and Mrs Link said, 'You can't do that, Sarah! It's holy water, it's been blessed!'

'I'll give it a good blessing – she'll never know the difference!' retorted Mrs Brindle as she filled it up.

I was very touched on my first visit to Lismore Castle in 2011 to discover that her workroom there is still called Mary Feeney's room. The clerk of works, Dennis Nevin, took me to find her grave in the churchyard of the Catholic Cathedral so that I could pay my respects.

The furniture in my bed-sitting room was not my own, but belonged to the House. The loveliest piece was an enormous clothes press that was big enough to hold absolutely everything I owned. Inside the door, a small plate announced that the piece was made from the cedars in Chiswick Park. On my visit to Lismore in 2011, I saw a piece of furniture in one of the bedrooms that made me look twice. It was an enormous cedar wood clothes press and when I opened the door, the plate inside confirmed that it was the one I had last seen over 30 years before in my bedsit on the Bird Landing. There was also a very pretty oval table in my room, which was later found to be part of a set now displayed on the visitor route. It turned out to be a games table made by David Roentgen, German cabinet-maker to Marie Antoinette. A hidden button releases a spring, allowing a hidden drawer, writing leaf and two pockets to pop out on the unsuspecting, and I always enjoyed using it.

There was also a fireplace in my room and although open fires are no longer allowed in staff bedrooms, this was not the case in the 1970s, and I enjoyed many cosy evenings in front of a roaring fire. Gerard

Coleman, brother to Henry the butler, kept my coal-cupboard outside the Sewing Room topped up with the most enormous chunks of coal I have ever seen, and I was altogether very comfortable.

My early days at Chatsworth were spent working with the house-keeping team in the day-to-day maintenance of the House; cleaning, working in the Orangery Shop and selling tickets in the summer, and then spring-cleaning in the winter once the House had closed. In those days, ticketing was a very simple operation. One man sold tickets for the House and Gardens in a little hut like a sentry box at the Lodge end of the North Drive, one of the housekeeping team sold guide books in the North Entrance Hall; another sold tickets at the entrance to the Scots Apartments; and one of the House wardens sold tickets at the garden entrance at Flora's Temple.

Visitors progressed round the House in a different way from how it operates today. I have no recollection why it did not happen at the beginning of the season, but the House route changed in the middle of a very busy time of year, on 23rd June 1982. Instead of viewing the ground floor and then going up the West Stairs to the Sketch Galleries, through the State Apartments and back down to the Painted Hall, including an optional visit to the Scots Apartments, visitors instead viewed the ground floor and then went up the Great Stairs to the State Apartments. From there, the route followed the way the 1st Duke had intended, into the impressive Great Chamber (called the State Dining Room until 2006). This meant the visitors now arrived at the Scots Apartments very early on in their visit, and many of them took exception to being asked for an admission charge again so soon after entering the House. It took a particular blend of skills on the part of those on duty in that area to appease everyone. The new route did seem to make more sense, and the slog of going up the West Stairs was now replaced by the more gradual ascent up the Great Stairs, with the opportunity for a breather on the Mercury Landing (now the Carefree Man Landing).

In the 1970s the House was closed every Monday, which allowed us to get to grips with more time-consuming jobs, and also led to the launch of the Patrons Scheme in 1976, the forerunner of the Friends of Chatsworth Scheme we have today. On the Monday Patrons' afternoon, visitors were guided round the six principal private reception rooms and the afternoon always ended in the Library. Here Peter Day, the deputy librarian, would bring out some of the treasures and give a talk on them which gave a real insight into the art collection, and was always the highlight of the Patrons' day. There were no Patrons' tours in the winter when the House was closed, but they were invited instead to a series of winter lectures on subjects related to the collection, with experts being brought in to talk about subjects such as 18th century furniture at Chatsworth, Bess of Hardwick, Gems and Jewellery at Chatsworth, and the Devonshire Estate.

The Patrons Scheme ceased six years later when the House opened every day, and the Friends Scheme was eventually launched to replace it. In the early days of the Friends Scheme, one preview event involved the hiring of a coach to take the Friends on a tour of the Estate and up into Stand Wood. The Chatsworth land agent at the time, Derrick Penrose, was keen to help and urged the throng of Friends onto the bus so that they could make the most of their day. It wasn't until the coach delivered the Friends back down to the House an hour-and-a-half later that two of the Friends approached him to say in very broken English that they were German tourists who just happened to be standing at the Lodge when they were herded onto the bus. At the time, they couldn't think of the English quickly enough to explain who they were, but had really enjoyed their tour nonetheless.

At this time, the House used to close at the end of September, and the Chatsworth Horse Trials were held over the first weekend in October. The autumn colours were wonderful and it was always a lovely atmosphere. Princess Anne and Captain Mark Phillips came to compete one year but didn't stay until the end of the event because the rude Derbyshire crowd laughed at Mark Phillips when he came off his horse and fell into the moat at Mary's Bower and was drenched.

Autumn and winter are wonderful times of year for walking in the Park and woods, and an after-work walk in the autumn often gives fantastic opportunities to see the deer. There are two herds of deer (250 fallow and 200 red), grazing the 1,000 acre Park, and I vividly remember one walk southwards along the river bank when I stood by the top weir, at what my grandmother always called the Duck Pen Wood, to watch a red deer stag in the Old Park trying to lead his herd across the river. They were reluctant to cross and he spent several minutes trotting purposefully up and down in front of them. He then ran round behind them, but each time they shied away from the water at the last moment and scattered along the riverbank. Eventually he seemed to lose patience and plunged into the icy water and began to swim strongly at an angle across the river so that he swam more directly against the current, making a strange sight with his antlered head bobbing above the water. There was consternation amongst his harem on the shore as his wives ran anxiously up and down until he clambered safely out of the water on the far bank and turned to look at them. It seemed then that each one felt as though she must be the first to take the plunge and swim across to join him, and they were suddenly all in the water together and surging for the shore.

The housekeeping staff at that time was generally of mature years and drawn from the wider Chatsworth family. The team included Gladys Roderick (wife to George Roderick, gardener), Maud Fearn (wife to Maurice Fearn, forester), Gladys Hadfield, whose husband Joe worked in the Building Yard, as had Winnie Wightman's husband, Jim, before he died. George and Ada Jones also both worked for Mrs Dean, as did Norman and Sarah Brindle, Roy Andrews and Bill Rippon, and we had a lot of fun.

Mrs Marjorie Link ruled the roost. She gave every appearance of being a bit of a dragon, but she had a heart of gold and was always very kind to me. Her husband, Jim, was the younger brother of Bert Link, the head gardener before Dennis Hopkins. Jim also worked in the gardens and with Vic Adams, now a neighbour in Edensor, helped me when I first took an allotment up in the Paddocks, where the Kitchen Garden is now. Old Jim Link could remember my grandfather, Jack Tindale, judging horticultural shows when he was parks superintendent of Chesterfield Parks and Gardens.

I enjoyed the fresh air up in the allotment at the end of the day and the first year I had the allotment, decided to try my luck at the Chatsworth Horticultural Society's annual show, held at the end of August. The night before the show, I frantically dug up every carrot I had grown in an effort to find six that matched, by which time the tiny kitchen in my bed-sit was over-run with carrots. I had finally selected the magic six by midnight, and then had to think what to do with all the others piled up on every available surface!

There was consternation amongst the gardeners one summer's evening when I met Her Grace's maid, Maud Barnes, out with her little Jack Russell, Spot. I was on my way down to the House from my allotment with a basket over my arm.

'What have you got there?' she asked.

'Come and look! My first peas! Would you like to try some?'

Maud took some and enjoyed the delicious summer pleasure that is shelling a pod of fresh peas and eating them raw. Later, she went up to her duties in the House and mentioned the peas to Her Grace. It seemed that Her Grace was very partial to garden peas herself, and wondered why none were ready for the Chatsworth table, when her assistant housekeeper had managed to grow them in her first year of gardening.

Her Grace told me that George Roderick had been gardener to Lord Burton and was once given the job of taking birds' nests out of the ivy on the house wall. As he was up his ladder, he glanced in through an upstairs window and saw a housemaid making a bed, and that was how he met and fell in love with his wife, Gladys. They lived in Rock Villa in Edensor, where we lived from 1992 to 2006, and took in lodgers, a long-standing tradition for the occupants of that property. The first occupant of the Rock Villa, built in 1839, was Dame Wallace, whose lodger was the gardener Robert Aughtie. He kept a journal of his two years working in the Great Conservatory at Chatsworth, once spending a whole week cleaning the leaves of a cinnamon tree. Gladys and George Roderick were a wonderful couple, utterly devoted to each other and to the community in Edensor. Mrs Link and Mrs Roderick were so kind to me when I first started at Chatsworth in the summer holidays and taught me such a lot, not just about cleaning, but also about Chatsworth and what it meant to work at such a special place.

Bill Thompson was the silver steward and would be in the Great Dining Room every day in his green baize apron, dusting the silver with his chamois leather. He had a measuring stick marked out with the distance from the edge of the table for all the pieces, flatware, dishes, glassware and so on. Mrs Gladys Hadfield cleaned the ground floor along with Mrs Sarah Brindle (Sarah). Mrs Hadfield had lived at one time in the Hunting Tower before she moved to Pilsley, and Mr and Mrs Brindle lived in Edensor in Church View.

Mrs Brindle was a real character and the most kind-hearted person you could ever wish to meet. Some Americans were strolling through the village one day when she was in her garden and asked her if there was anywhere they could get a cup of tea. The village tea room was closed, so Mrs Brindle invited them inside her cottage to have a cup of tea with her. It was definitely a case of 'entertaining angels unawares', as they became great friends and invited her several times to stay with them in their palatial home in Hollywood, even sending her the airfare.

There have always been a number of housemen at Chatsworth, traditionally called 'odd men', whose role it was to turn their hand to anything: vacuuming, car parking, van-driving, chauffeuring, litter picking, coal scuttle filling, pheasant plucking – anything at all. Many were great characters, and several can easily be brought to mind, even after all these years. One such was Arthur Clegg, who had a penchant for philosophy and rather latched on to Peter Day, being the nearest thing to a philosopher he was going to find at Chatsworth. In his retirement speech of March 2003, Peter recalled the day he was safely locked in a lavatory cubicle in the gents' toilets, when over the wall came a question from Mr Clegg. 'Peter, are you a determinist, or do you believe in free will?' Peter said he had replied that he was not in any position to answer…

Mr Clegg spent his time as a houseman scrubbing the long service passage, or vacuuming the visitor route, and would sometimes be at the Lodge, where Her Grace found him at work one Christmas morning, not keeping a lookout for traffic but with his nose deep in a copy of *Advanced Algebra*. David Thraves was another houseman with unexpected interests. His principal role was to stoke the boilers, which consumed half a ton of coke a day in the winter months. He also kept the most amazing collection of classical music recordings and his knowledge of the subject would have put a Mastermind winner to shame.

At 22, I was very much the youngster of the team and decided that living and working in the House might not be a good thing if I did not get out and about to meet people. I joined the local Women's Institute, and the Cavendish Club (at that time called The Institute, or just the 'stute), but it was with the Cavendish Players, a new drama group, where I made most of my friends, amongst them Denise Spencer who, with her new husband David, had become the cooks at Chatsworth after Mrs Canning's retirement. The Institute was a great place to meet people and nowadays, as the Cavendish Club, it still serves the people of the Estate very well, with two bars, a billiard room and a large function room. There is also a gymnasium, opened on 12th September 1999 by the then High Sheriff of Derbyshire, retired Agent Derrick Penrose. It was instigated and paid for by His Grace, who was also in attendance at the opening, with Her Grace. She could never understand the need for a gym. 'If people need to lose weight, they should just eat less,' she said to me, 'and if they want to exercise, then why not go for a good walk?'

The Cavendish Club is the red-brick building at the north road entrance to Chatsworth Park, which has also housed the Estate Office since 1958. It was built in 1778 as a hotel by the architect Joseph Pickford, for travellers on the new turnpike road, and also for the convenience of visitors to Chatsworth, with 12 letting bedrooms and stabling for 40 horses. In 1912 it became the Institute, a working men's club for Estate workmen; women were not admitted until 1969. When I first used it eight years later, women were still not allowed in the snooker room, and were only allowed to pass through the 'spit and sawdust' bar to use the lounge area beyond. In 1912 the large hall attached to the Institute was built as a function room, and during the First World War, the hotel building was used as a convalescent home for soldiers and sailors. The Institute hall (now called The Cavendish Hall) provided a venue for parties, dances, concerts, staff parties, the Chatsworth Horticultural Society shows, badminton and more latterly, indoor bowls and even Zumba exercise dancing.

I also joined the tennis club and the swimming club (both built in 1975), and at the end of the day found it a great way to relax. A walk over the Crobs (the hill between Edensor and Chatsworth) for a game of tennis, then into the swimming pool to cool off, a drink in the 'stute and then a stroll back to Chatsworth again. I enjoyed taking part in several productions of The Cavendish Players, including *A Funeral Tea*, and *Mother Goose*. I also helped Joyce Fisher with the running of the Chatsworth Girl Guides, who met weekly in the Estate school at Pilsley. I attended Edensor Church regularly and soon became a member of the

Parochial Church Council and have been a member ever since, and secretary since 1986

Denise and David Spencer left after a year when David took the job of chef at Repton School, and in 1978 Diane Peach and her friend Marcia came straight from catering college in Leicester to replace them as cooks at Chatsworth. They also took over Denise and David's lovely two-bedroom flat in the main part of the House, with fantastic views across the Park to Baslow. Diane was only a couple of years younger than me and we became good friends.

Then Jean-Pierre Beraud arrived!

Jean-Pierre originally came to Chatsworth for just three months, and he wasn't very well received in the kitchen to begin with, as Diane and Marcia thought they could manage very well on their own without a Frenchman arriving on the scene to tell them how he thought things should be done. I got to know him well as we shared the television in the Staff Sitting Room, and I would practise my schoolgirl French on him, whilst he tried to learn English. Miss Bell, one of the teachers at Pilsley School, would come along after school once a week to give him English lessons in the Staff Sitting Room. He spoke no English at all when he arrived, and once at Chatsworth, all he learned was what came up in the Kitchen and Pantry. This caused great amusement, and he was often led astray by the staff. I remember him once describing someone to Her Grace, 'Eees a beet of a booger!'

Jean-Pierre had been 'found' by Lady Mosley, the Duchess's sister, who lived in Paris. Many years later, he ran a series of cookery schools for the public in the private Chatsworth Kitchen and in his opening introduction he would describe how he came to Chatsworth:

> I always wanted to be a chef and my mother told me this desire showed when I was four. After finishing school at fourteen I was an apprentice for three years in a restaurant near my home town of Palaiseau. I passed my diploma and then spent a few years gaining experience in some very good restaurants in Paris and Marseille. After eighteen months in Marseille I wanted to work in larger hotels and was told I had to speak another language, so in 1979 I came to the Portman Hotel in London, but soon realised my English would not improve as there were no other English speaking kitchen staff there! Through a restaurateur who was

a mutual friend, I met Lady Mosley, the Duchess of Devonshire's sister
who lives in Paris. After a brief talk we agreed I should meet the
Duchess who was looking for a chef. At this stage I could still not speak
any English, but I fell under the spell of Chatsworth and the charm of
the Devonshire family.

Marcia didn't stay for long, and Jean-Pierre remained and his English soon improved. His charisma and Gallic charm were much admired by the young staff living in the House. Here was someone of our own age to swim with, to play tennis with, and to go out with in the evenings when the work in the Kitchen was finished, and Diane, Jean-Pierre and I became very close friends. His brother and sister, Muriel and Richard, came to stay in July 1980, and we took them up to Pilsley Village Fair and well dressing, and I remember them having their photographs taken with the local policeman, the much missed Eric Yates.

I had come to Chatsworth for just one year in 1977, and as I was already in my second year, I started to think about whether I should look for something else. However, in the autumn of 1978 something was to happen that changed the course of my life entirely.

5

❧

Travels with Mr Painting

Galleries in the United Kingdom and abroad often request the loan of Chatsworth works of art for exhibitions and this has always been organised by the librarian. The appointment of a librarian dates from the 17th century and the time of Thomas Hobbes, the great philosopher, who served the Earls of Devonshire nearly all his life, acting as tutor to the 2nd and 3rd Earls, and arranging and cataloguing their Library. In the early 1800s, the 6th Duke employed John Payne Collier as librarian to catalogue a great collection of theatrical books he had bought, including rare Shakespeare items. Unfortunately, it was later discovered that Collier had been tempted to forgery when he added notes to Shakespeare's plays and passed them off as Shakespeare's own!

The 8th Duke's librarian was Sandford Arthur Strong, who started work at Chatsworth in 1895 and continued until his early death in 1904. He was the first librarian to pay serious attention to the collections of art as well as the books, and he initiated an extensive programme of systematic restoration. A death mask of Arthur Strong was taken, and is now kept in a wooden box in the Chatsworth strong rooms, although it used to be on a shelf in an old store room. I remember being frightened to death one day when I was tidying up and unsuspectingly opened the box, never guessing what the macabre contents might be. Arthur Strong's work was continued by his widow Eugenie until the 8th Duke's death in 1908, when she left to become the head of the British School in Rome. Francis Thompson was appointed librarian and keeper of the collection in 1921, and Tom Wragg joined as his assistant in 1934, taking over the position of librarian and keeper of the collection when Francis Thompson died.

For several years prior to my arrival at Chatsworth, plans had been afoot for a large exhibition to travel from Chatsworth to tour the United States in 1979. The exhibition was to be called 'Treasures from Chatsworth: The Devonshire Inheritance' and would include all genres of works of art collected over many years: paintings and miniatures, drawings, prints, books and manuscripts, gold, silver, gems and jewellery, furniture, costume, sculpture and ceramics.

However, in November 1978 the librarian and keeper of the collection, Tom Wragg, died suddenly, leaving his deputy, Peter Day, to handle the day-to-day running of the art collection and the final preparations for the exhibition. The deadline was fast approaching for the Ektachromes for the exhibition catalogue to be taken to the International Exhibitions Foundation in Washington for approval and then on to the Meriden Gravure Company in Connecticut, which was to produce the catalogue. Peter was too busy to be able to make the trip and as I had a reasonable knowledge of the House and its contents, I was asked if I would like to help.

Within a week of Tom's death I found myself on a train to London and queuing at the American Embassy for a passport visa. Hectic days followed, familiarising myself with all the detail of the exhibits – what a wonderful job!

Paintings to travel to the United States included old masters such as the popular painting by Cornelis de Vos, *Portrait of a Little Girl*, *The Holy Family*, by Murillo and two wonderful paintings by Sebastiano Ricci, *The Flight into Egypt* and *The Presentation of Christ in the Temple*. Also included was *View of London before the Fire* by Thomas Wyck, one of the most vivid views of London before the Great Fire of London in 1666, which destroyed the greater part of the city. The 11th Duke was a great collector of more recent works of art, and so two paintings by his artist friend, Lucian Freud, were also included, one of His Grace, and the other of Her Grace. Lucian Freud, grandson of Sigmund Freud, was one of the first guests to stay at Chatsworth after the 11th Duke and Duchess came to live in the House. He contributed an unfinished wall painting of an outsized cyclamen to the bathroom in the Sabine Bedroom and left his paints and brushes behind, thinking to finish the job off the next time he came, but never returned. The 11th Duke used to tell the story that when Freud's portrait of Her Grace was eventually finished he was invited along to Freud's studio to view it. On his arrival he found a stranger in the studio looking at the painting. The man looked rather morosely at the Duke as he came in and sat down and then asked, 'Do you know who that is?'

'Well actually, it's my wife,' the Duke answered.

'Well thank God it's not my wife!' the other man fervently replied.

Her Grace remembered going to sit for Lucian Freud in his studio for three hours every morning when she was in London. Freud took several months on the work and once told her, 'I had a wonderful night. I removed everything I painted yesterday!'

Another painting to travel to America was of Park Top, His Grace's favourite racehorse, painted by Susan Crawford. The famous jockey Lester Piggott rode Park Top to victory in the King George VI and Queen Elizabeth Stakes at Ascot in 1976.

One of the richest treasures of Chatsworth is the collection of Old Master drawings, mainly formed by the 2nd Duke. 53 of these drawings were taken on the American exhibition tour, including works by Leonardo da Vinci, Raphael, Titian, Veronese, Brueghel, Rubens, Van Dyck, Holbein, Rembrandt, and Degas.

My favourite manuscripts and books in the exhibition included an illuminated manuscript from Bruges, dated around 1470. It depicts fantastical creatures decorating the borders, and rich pictures of harp-playing monkeys, gorgeous butterflies and birds. I was also enchanted by an early manuscript called *La Vengeance de Notre Seigneur*, which is a traditional French mystery play written and painted between 1465 and 1468 for the Duke of Burgundy (1396-1467). Not forgotten were some of the letters received by the 6th Duke from such literary figures as William Makepeace Thackeray and Charles Dickens, and a letter from David Garrick to the 4th Duke.

The wonderful collection of gold and silver at Chatsworth was also represented, one of the most stunning exhibits being the 23-piece silver gilt toilet service originally made as a gift for William of Orange and Princess Mary on their marriage in 1677, and later given by them to the 1st Duke and Duchess of Devonshire. My favourite pieces were the gold ewer and basin made by Pierre Platel in London in about 1701; the ewer stands only 6¾ inches high, and the basin is only 10½ inches long, but they are absolutely exquisite and made of solid gold. Pierre Platel was a French Huguenot who, with his brother Claude, came to England as a page in the train of William and Mary, and was made a Freeman of the Goldsmith's Company in 1699. This gold ewer and basin is his masterpiece, with an elaborate engraving of the 1st Duke's arms on the basin. The American exhibition catalogue entry for the piece reads: 'The basin is associated with a ewer which, sadly, was stolen in 1978; the two together constitute Platel's masterpiece'.

The ewer was actually stolen from an exhibition at the Goldsmith's Hall in London and at the time its recovery seemed impossible. The catalogue entry went ahead without the ewer, and then miraculously, word came from the criminal underworld as to where the ewer could be found. It was proving impossible to sell as it was such an important piece and could easily be traced, so the thieves were planning to melt it down. Someone heard of this and was aghast at the thought of this masterpiece being destroyed, and did a deal with the police. The ewer was back at Chatsworth in time to be packed up for the American exhibition, and off it went. I took a phone call from the press to ask our reaction to the recovery of the piece, and I still have the cutting which reads, 'A spokesperson at Chatsworth today said, 'We are all thrilled to bits!' I wish I could have thought of something a little more creditable.

Gems and jewellery to travel to America included the Kniphausen Hawk, a 15 inch high silver and silver-gilt figure dated 1697, decorated with painted enamel and set with red garnets, amethysts, citrine quartzes, turquoises, emeralds, sapphires, and onyx cameos. The head can be unscrewed to expose a torpedo-shaped drinking tube, and when the Hawk was displayed for a time in the Berlin china cabinet that used to be in the space now occupied by the Old Master Drawings Cabinet, we angled the head so that the Hawk peered down greedily on all the anxious little finches painted onto the china.

The most amazing piece of jewellery was the *Devonshire Parure*, a set of seven pieces made by C. F. Hancock of Bruton Street, London, for the wife of the 6th Duke's nephew, the Countess Granville (1812-1860), to wear to the Coronation of Alexander II in 1856, when her husband represented Queen Victoria. The 6th Duke had attended the Coronation of Nicholas I in 1825, and so knew exactly what was required of a royal delegate. He offered money and promised the loan of the Devonshire plate, diamonds and gems, and his right-hand man, Joseph Paxton, was commissioned to act as an intermediary with Hancock's to create this stunning jewellery set.

Hancock made his reputation with the design for the Victoria Cross and for producing huge racing trophies. The gems used in the *Parure* had been collected by the 2nd Duke in the early 18th century and Hancock set these into a bracelet, a bandeau, a necklace, a hair ornament in the form of a comb, a coronet, a diadem, and a magnificent stomacher which the Duke's niece would have worn in the bodice of her dress. The more important of the diamonds were removed at a later date for setting in a more conventional tiara and for the American exhibition these gaps were filled with very fine paste imitations. The amethyst placed in the centre panel of the comb was taken to the jewellers in London for setting into its headpiece, and this was something entrusted to me when I went to get my visa at the American embassy. This amethyst is worked as an intaglio, where the craftsman has etched the design into the amethyst, rather than leaving it to stand 'proud' as in a cameo. It is absolutely amazing – about 2½ inches long, the most fantastic deep colour, and forming the central gem in the comb, being an inscribed portrait of the Sassian monarch, Bahram I, before his imperial succession in about 273 A.D. I had been instructed to take a taxi from London St Pancras to the jewellers but there was a bus strike and the queue for taxis was so long that I thought I would feel less vulnerable on the tube rather than standing waiting for a taxi, but I was still very relieved to get to the jewellers and to hand over my precious cargo.

Looking at the *Parure* makes one imagine the extravagances of the Coronation of the Tsar. The celebrations lasted a whole month during which time Lord Granville and his Countess attended many functions connected with the Tsar's consecration to his people; ceremonial entries, troop reviews, gala performances of opera and ballet, banquets in the Riding School, state balls and embassy receptions. All the guests seemed to have been determined to impress: Napoleon III's representative, his half-brother, Count de Morny, brought a private railway carriage for the journey from St. Petersburg, and Prince Esterharzy attended the coronation dressed in a velvet hussar's uniform, braided with pearls and sparkling with diamonds. His entourage even involved a gypsy orchestra to entertain his guests.

Furniture to travel to America for the exhibition included a beautiful marquetry coffer made in walnut, sycamore and rosewood, by Gerreit Jensen for the 1st Duke in about 1690, and also one of the 2nd Duke's Boulle cabinets, veneered with tortoiseshell and engraved brass. Ceramics for the exhibition included two of the Delft tulip vases at Chatsworth and a selection of pieces from the 1780 Berlin dinner service which originally belonged to Warren Hastings, the governor-general of India, who was impeached by the government in 1788 on grounds of corruption. He was eventually acquitted after a trial lasting seven years but his costs were so great that he was forced to sell much of his belongings including the Berlin dinner service, half of which was bought by his neighbour, the 1st Baron Redesdale. The service passed by descent to Her Grace's father, Lord Redesdale, who put the service up for sale in 1948. A particular feature of the service are the insects painted on the reverse of the plates to hide the blemishes caused during firing. These additions had always fascinated Her Grace, and so when the service came up for sale, His Grace bought it for her and they then endeavoured to keep the purchase a secret from Lord Redesdale as she thought her father would be aghast at how much money His Grace had paid for it.

Before my trip to America in early December, hectic days were spent familiarising myself with all the Ektachromes, and designing a family tree for the catalogue. One Saturday morning, a couple of days before I was due to leave, Peter and I were just about to finish work and go into Bakewell for a fish and chip lunch, when I had a message to ring the switchboard: 'Her Grace says, can you please go up to the Blue Drawing Room straightaway?'

I left Peter in the office and went straight there, to find Her Grace with Senator Edward Kennedy and his son – they were visiting Chatsworth and wanted to be shown round the House, so our fish and chips had to wait. Once the tour was over, Peter and I went into Bakewell for a late fish and chip lunch, and we both agreed that it was one of the most bizarre days I would ever spend at Chatsworth!

Involvement with the collections department also meant the occasional use of the department's car, the old Estate car that had belonged to the late Tom Wragg. Sometimes I would need it to take an object to

Kings of Derby to be photographed and suchlike, and the car often needed topping up with petrol before setting off. The Estate at this time had its own petrol pumps at the Estate Office, in the building that had been used as a canteen for the hospital, set up at the Institute during the First World War. Three underground tanks had been installed in the early 1960s, two for petrol and one for diesel, and the body of the pumps and most of the fittings were brass. The pumps delivered one gallon at a time up to a maximum of ten gallons before having to be reset. They were operated by the Club Steward, John Rhodes, and the process involved hand-cranking, so it took quite a while to fill up!

The trip to Washington with the Ektachromes was exciting, especially as it was my first visit to the United States and I was thrilled to be able to enjoy a bit of sightseeing, too. From Washington I went to New York by train, and the exhilaration of the city that never sleeps. It was just before Christmas, and the Lower Plaza outside the Rockefeller Centre had been flooded for ice-skating. The atmosphere was wonderful, with all the Christmas lights, the laughter, and a few snowflakes falling from the frosty night sky. Then I took another train to Meriden in Connecticut to visit the printing works that was to produce the catalogue. I received a warm welcome from the friendly staff there, especially Bill Glick, who gave me some wonderful bird prints to take home with me.

On my return to Chatsworth, I remained in the collections department helping Peter Day with the daily routine of the office and the preparations for the exhibition, together with some fascinating work cataloguing some of the old maps in the archive store. The exhibition was to open in Richmond, Virginia on 15th September 1979 and would then travel to Fort Worth, Toledo, San Antonio, New Orleans, and finally to the Fine Arts Museum of San Francisco.

Chatsworth frequently lends works of art to exhibitions, usually just the odd picture or drawing, but before the excitement of the American exhibition, there was also one of silver, gold, armoury and jewels at the Whitworth Art Gallery in Manchester, called 'Chatsworth Treasures', which ran from January to March 1979. Some of the exhibits loaned to Manchester were subsequently required for the American tour, so I was lucky enough to be involved with both exhibitions. I travelled in my own car, following the exhibits as they were taken to Manchester in a van with a police escort and changing forces as we crossed the county boundaries. I had been told by the police to jump the lights in Manchester if necessary to keep up with them, but I was very relieved not to have to do so!

The time came for the exhibits for America to be packed for their journey, and as the drawings were deemed to be too valuable and fragile to travel unaccompanied, it was decided that they must be carried by hand. I was delighted to learn that Peter and I were to be the couriers, and travel arrangements were made for mid-August, a month before the exhibition was due to open. August was also the month when the usual preparations began for the Chatsworth household to move to Bolton Abbey for the start of the grouse-shooting season on 12th August. Bolton Abbey and Bolton Hall have been the Devonshire's home in Yorkshire since 1753, in addition to the 30,000 acres of farms, woods, and heather moors. The Hall was once the gatehouse to the priory founded by Augustinian canons in 1150, and after the dissolution of the monasteries in 1539 the Abbey Church fell into disrepair. The gatehouse survived and was converted to a house in 1720, with Paxton adding the final touches in 1843, when the south wing was enlarged to make a drawing room, with a bedroom and dressing room above.

The move to Bolton Abbey required the kitchen and pantry staff to go too, along with the entire Chatsworth kitchen, right down to the pots and pans, extra linen and the *Bolton Silver*, a special service of silver taken from Chatsworth especially for the occasion.

In Mrs Canning's days as Chatsworth cook, she was of the opinion that it wasn't possible to buy sugar in Yorkshire, so a sackful was taken up from Chatsworth along with everything else.

So that I could say goodbye to Diane and Jean-Pierre before my trip to America, I drove up to see them for a long weekend, and it would be my first visit to the romantic Bolton Abbey in Yorkshire's Wharfedale. Bolton Hall, where the family stays, had been unaltered for years and it seemed quite bizarre to be staying in this little time warp, when in a few days' time I would be jetting off to America. Because the Hall was lived in for only part of the year, it was quite basic and the room I shared with Diane had no carpet, just a scrubbed wooden floor and a threadbare rug on which I slept in my sleeping bag. There was no ensuite bathroom – in fact, no bathroom at all, just a washbasin out on the landing for staff to share, and one lavatory. However, the kitchen was wonderful, and I shall never forget my first meal there.

'Would you like a steak, Christine?' asked Jean-Pierre, as I watched this master craftsman deftly prepare the tastiest steak I have ever eaten.

The following morning, I came downstairs to find one of Chatsworth's housemen, Walter Hancock, plucking grouse just outside the door. If ever Walter's name is mentioned, that is my abiding memory of him, either at Chatsworth or at Bolton Abbey, sitting with his legs astride a large bin, plucking grouse or pheasant and humming quietly as a soft cascade of downy feathers swirled around his head, settling on his grey whiskery sideburns and moustache.

The weather that weekend was glorious. On the Saturday morning we drove into Skipton to get supplies, and I remember eating my first kiwi fruit there. Then up onto the moors with the lunch for the shoot. The heather was in full bloom, the skylarks were trilling their breathless song, I was with my best friends, and all was right with the world. I have an abiding memory of driving with Jean-Pierre, crossing the moors in his left-hand drive Saab listening to Gerry Rafferty, and whenever I hear 'Baker Street' on the radio, I am transported straight back to that time.

The return to Chatsworth brought me back to reality and a new adventure. Due to the extreme value of the drawings, our insurers would not allow Peter Day and I to travel together in case the plane crashed, so Peter went out one day and I followed the next. The drawings had been packed at a transport office away from Chatsworth and sealed there by Customs and Excise, and the seals were not to be broken until the box containing them reached the other side of the Atlantic. The morning flight was from Heathrow, so I travelled down to London the night before and stayed with my friend, Doreen, in Clapham. I had given her address to the packers, who were to collect me by car the following morning and take me to the airport to reunite me with the case of drawings.

The next day I was sitting having breakfast with Doreen when she glanced out of the window of her first floor flat and noticed that there was a car parked outside with a man in a trilby reading a newspaper. It seemed like something out of a James Bond film, when at the appointed time, he folded his paper and came and rang the doorbell for me, and off I went into the unknown with a total stranger. At the airport I was given a large wooden box, which fortunately had a handle, and was told that on no account must I let the box out of my sight, or allow it to pass through the x-ray machine, or allow anyone to open it before I reached America. That was it. I was on my own, with several million pounds-worth of Old Master drawings in my hands.

The first hurdle was to get through to the departure lounge, where of course, everything is expected to go through the x-ray machine.

'I'm sorry,' I said, 'I can't put this box through the machine. I do have a letter here from Customs and Excise to say that they've sealed the box.'

'Oh, I don't know about that. Everything has to go through the machine.'

'Well, I'm sorry, but this can't. Would you mind checking with someone else, please?'

'You'd better come into this side room and I'll find my superior.'

A few minutes later, in the side room, 'Well, if we can't put your box through the x-ray machine we'll do a search instead. If you could just open it for us, please?'

'I'm sorry, I can't open it for you either, I don't have a key. It's been sealed by Customs and Excise. I do have a letter from them to say that they've sealed the box.'

'I'm not sure about that...'

Eventually, and after much perusal of the letter, I finally persuaded them to let me through to the departure lounge, only to find that the flight had been delayed by three hours. Everywhere I went, my large wooden box had to go with me in addition to my other hand luggage – in the queue for a cup of coffee, trailing round the shop to kill time, and into a very tiny cubicle in the ladies' room. I was very glad when the flight was called. At least my problems would now be over, or so I thought.

Because of the value of the drawings, the exhibition organisers had paid for us to travel first class, and because of the size of the box, I had a seat for me and one for the box of drawings. Computers like to keep things tidy and couldn't cope with 'a thing' and not a person occupying a seat and so I had one boarding card for Miss Tindale, and another one for Mr Painting. As we lined up to board the plane, I glanced down at the two cards again and wondered if I was going to have any more problems.

'I'm sorry, madam, Mr Painting will need his own card when he boards, so if you'd care to wait for him you can give him his boarding card and then you can both board the plane together.'

'There isn't a Mr Painting, I'm afraid,' I began. 'You see, it's this box I'm carrying…'

The flight to Washington DC was wonderful, and as I am nudging six feet tall, it was a great experience to travel first class and to have so much leg-room. If only the space in the aeroplane lavatories had been adequate for my box and me I would have had nothing more to complain about!

So much security. So much careful thought into transporting these drawings to the exhibition. I was met at Dulles Airport by someone from the Exhibition Foundation in an open top sports car to take the box and I across Washington to the secure unit where the treasures were to be stored prior to the exhibition. It was good to meet up with Peter again and we then had four wonderful weeks in America before the exhibition opened in Richmond, Virginia on 15th September.

Our first priority was to visit the Museum in Richmond, Virginia, to supervise the display of the exhibits and do the necessary press interviews to publicise the event, and as we had to liaise closely with the Exhibitions Foundation, we were initially based in Washington, where the Foundation was based. We had been given the use of an apartment in Washington that belonged to a friend of Taffy Swandby, who worked for the International Exhibitions Foundation, and we arrived at the apartment later that afternoon, very tired and hot, as Washington in August is always very humid. Wanting nothing more than a nice cup of tea, we were appalled to find that the whole apartment was over-run with cockroaches. They were everywhere, in the beds, in the shower, on the workbenches, on the floor, even in the fridge. We went straight out to a corner store and bought some tea bags and milk, which we put in the freezer as it was the only place that was cockroach-free. Our other purchase was a large one – as many 'roach motels' as we could manage. These are rather like matchboxes, opened to attract the cockroaches inside, where they are promptly poisoned. Having placed these strategically around the apartment, we went out for a meal and then slept fitfully when we returned, waiting for the cockroaches to drop on our faces as we slept.

Taffy said that she would drive us down to Richmond the next day, and with a 90 mile trip each way, we thought it would be quite a journey. Of course distance is nothing in America and this was considered just a quick trip down the road. The Museum was impressive, the people were very friendly, and we were made most welcome. It was good to see 'our' exhibits again, and to imagine how it would all look when the display was finished. We now had three weeks to wait until we were needed again, and so we went up to New York where we spent time with a friend of Peter's.

We did a lot of sightseeing together while she was at work, including a trip up the Empire State Building, where we had our photographs taken in Victorian costume. When we got back to England, we had this enlarged as a sepia photograph and I showed it to my Nan to see if she recognised anyone. Surprisingly, she said, 'I'm not sure who the man is, but the woman looks rather like me when I was your age.'

We also showed the photograph to Her Grace. I said, 'Peter and I have just come across this photograph, Your Grace, and wondered about putting it in the 'Bygones Exhibition' in the Theatre. Do you have any idea who the couple might be?' She studied it closely for a moment and then looked up, laughing, and exclaimed,

'Christine, what *were* you doing?'

Peter and I also took a helicopter trip over New York circling the twin Trade Centre Towers and viewing the other buildings of Manhattan, fantastic from the air. We enjoyed picnics and concerts in Central Park, and a trip on the subway up to Harlem to visit The Cloisters, which seemed strangely anachronistic in the middle of so much modernity. They are genuine cloisters, built in the Middle Ages and brought from France, Italy and Spain to be reassembled in Fort Tryon Park. The exhibit I remember most was the amazing 'Hunt of the Unicorn' tapestries, which reminded me of the four Devonshire Hunting tapestries made around 1430 and now at the Victoria and Albert Museum in London after they went to the government in lieu of death duties. Peter made some other visitors look at us rather curiously when he announced, 'Look at these, they're rather the like the ones we've got at home!'

I also went off on my own for a week to explore the eastern seaboard, travelling up to Newhaven by train to visit Yale University, and then on to Boston, with its Quincy Market, the Boston Tea Party Ship, and the magnificent Maritime Museum. I then continued by bus to Cape Cod and Provincetown, which I thoroughly enjoyed, although just before I left the weather was quite stormy as I caught the tail end of a hurricane. From Cape Cod I travelled back to Washington DC for another week on my own, staying in another flat belonging to one of Taffy's friends, this time cockroach-free, which gave me a wonderful opportunity to get to know the city. On one evening, I went out with Taffy and her friends to the Wolf Trap open-air theatre, where we ate a lovely picnic before enjoying a spectacular performance of Carousel.

When Peter and I returned to Richmond for the exhibition opening, it had been arranged for us to stay with people from the Museum but there had been a misunderstanding, and the person I was supposed to be staying with thought I was coming the next day, so there was nowhere for me to stay. Peter was staying with the Governor of Virginia and when they realised my predicament, he and his wife offered to put me up, which was another amazing experience, to be staying in a wonderful colonial home. Our time there also allowed for more sightseeing, this time in historic Virginia. We made that visit with Warwick McCallum, a picture restorer who had worked on the preparation of the paintings for the exhibition and who had come over for the opening. Peter hired a car, which turned out to be an enormous Cadillac with a long leather bench seat for all three of us in the front, so we rode in style to explore the area. We included a trip to Colonial Williamsburg, where we bumped into Lord and Lady Hartington, also over for the exhibition opening and taking the opportunity to do some sightseeing themselves.

All too soon, the grand opening of the exhibition was over; it was back to Washington, and then home to England, and to reality.

6

✦

Estate Life

As the butler Henry's family grew, the flat he occupied on the Bird Landing was no longer suitable and he moved with his wife, Joan, and their two children, Ann and Henry (now under-butler), to a cottage in Pilsley village (their sons Patrick and Seamus were born later). This left the flat free for me to move into. I now had a lovely kitchen, a comfortable sitting room, two bedrooms, and beautiful views across the Park towards Edensor. Of course, it was still on the Bird Landing with all the stuffed birds and animals, so it was a case of 'turn left at the kangaroo' for trips to the bathroom.

Although there were stunning views from the sitting room, my bedroom overlooked the coal yard where a vast heap of coke lay ready to feed the boilers, which consumed half a ton of fuel a day during the winter months. Not long after moving into the flat, I was awakened by the sound of someone shovelling coke, and the next night the same thing happened. This continued for a week and then stopped, before starting again a couple of weeks later. I thought I had better tell Eric Oliver, the comptroller, what I had heard, and he told me he already had his suspicions that coke was being pilfered by one of the security staff whenever he was on nights. Inevitably, this led to disciplinary action in which His Grace had to be involved. He subsequently confided to Eric that he had gone through the whole disciplinary process in a state of confusion, since his first thought had been that Eric Oliver was talking about cocaine!

A few years ago, I discovered that my sitting room had been used as a staff bedroom during the Second World War when Chatsworth was occupied by the staff and students of Penrhos College in North Wales.

The 10th Duke offered the girls the use of Chatsworth when he heard that their school building was to be taken over by the Ministry of Food, and he wisely thought that the girls would probably take greater care of the House than soldiers would. The House carpenter, George Maltby, was the man responsible for packing everything away in just eleven days so that Chatsworth was ready for the invasion of the 300 girls and their 27 pianos, and the 10th Duke and Duchess moved to Churchdale at Ashford-in-the Water to make room for them. Mr Maltby famously said on a television programme in the 1970s, 'Ah were t'last person to see t'ninth Duke o' Devonshire!'

'Were you really?' exclaimed the interviewer.

'Aye. Ah screwed t'lid down on 'is coffin!' he replied.

The pupils and teachers of Penrhos College spent the duration of the war at Chatsworth, sleeping in the State Rooms, the Great Dining Room and some of the corridors. After the war the school returned to its proper home, but there were regular reunions at Chatsworth until the closure of the school in 1995, the last reunion being in March 1996. The one thing they all used to mention was how cold they were and how long it took them to dry their hair in front of the only two fires allowed, in the North Front Hall and the Chapel Passage. If their hot water bottles fell out of bed during the night in winter time they were often frozen solid by morning.

Chatsworth was fired upon by a German plane that mistook the River Derwent for the River Wye at Bakewell, where it had intended to attack the DP Battery works, where submarine batteries were manufactured. During the attack on the House, a bullet came in through a window and embedded itself in the wall of one the school mistresses' bedrooms. The irony was that the mistress in question was the German mistress, Fraulein Brandenburg, whom the girls nicknamed 'Brandy'. Her bedroom was the one that subsequently became my sitting room on the Bird Landing. The girls called the embedded bullet 'The Brandy Bullet' and Fraulein Brandenburg charged them sixpence each to come and view it, the proceeds being given to the Red Cross. It's a great pity that the bullet has long since been removed.

The now retired comptroller, John Oliver, wrote of the event in one of the Chatsworth staff newsletters. He recalled that the attack happened early one evening in the summer of 1941 when he and his two brothers,

Arthur and Joe, and young Jimmy Link, the son of Bert Link, were playing on the grass near the Stables, where they lived in staff flats. They saw two low-flying twin-engined aircraft flying south between the west front of the House and the river, and so low that the children could see members of the crew. They waved to them, thinking they were British, but when they opened fire, the children beat a hasty retreat to the north arch of the Stables. The aircraft scored several hits on the north and west facing walls of the 6th Duke's wing and were later shot down over Lincolnshire by the RAF.

In another staff newsletter, the incident was remembered by Mrs Margaret Wylde (née Beecher-Bryant), a pupil on duty as a school air-raid warden on the day of the attack. She wrote:

At the time we were in the Lower Sixth and were sleeping in the Alcove Bedroom, which was approached by a two-storey windowless spiral staircase. We became 'air-raid wardens' to all the younger dormitories. When on duty, we slept on the roof, or under the 'Birds' as look-outs, learned how to operate the stirrup pumps, and had lectures in the Theatre about mustard gas and bombs. Our most important job, presumably to free the Upper Sixth who were reading for important exams, was to be in charge of the younger girls in an emergency. As air-raid warden, whenever Sheffield was bombed I took my charges down to the beer cellar, where we stayed until Sheffield's all-clear siren sounded. We heard the German bombers and the bombs but thankfully were not attacked until the summer of 1941 when, while the whole school was in evening prayers in the Painted Hall, enemy planes strafed the building. The noise, like falling glass and china, was terrific and then there was real panic as the girls in the choir stalls fell onto those below. Eventually I got my lot down to the safety of the cellars. We had been very fortunate as the mistress who should have taken prayers, and who usually raced through 'Lighten our Darkness', was off and we had the long-winded Deputy Headmistress instead. Otherwise, at the time of the attack we would all have been out in the grounds after prayers, walking or playing tennis.

Old Penrhosian, Nancie Park, now living in Edensor, added that 'After the attack, the comptroller, W.K. Shimwell, picked up some of the girls' black woollen swimming costumes that had been left out to dry and found them riddled with bullet holes.'

John Oliver remembered another incident, in 1943, when they were playing in the Gardens near the bottom of the Cascade and heard a zipping sound in the beech trees, which they later discovered was caused by machine gun bullets. At the time, Beeley Moor was used as an Allied training area prior to D-Day and it was assumed this was where the bullets had come from. A few years ago, a bullet found in the lead parapet over the south east door at Chatsworth, was sent to a ballistics expert who confirmed it was of an American calibre, slightly smaller than the British ·303. Visitors to Chatsworth are told of a bullet that became embedded in one of the tables in the Library which was also shown to have come from the same source.

Living in the House in my early days at Chatsworth was Stefan, a young Swiss man from Zurich, who was an apprentice cabinetmaker. Diane, Jean-Pierre, Stefan and I enjoyed many evenings together, and walks in the Gardens when the visitors had left, hunting for each other in the maze and playing in the Willow Tree Fountain. On 20th October 1979, Their Grace's younger daughter, Lady Sophia, married Antony Murphy, and the four of us were thrilled to be invited to the wedding reception. It felt so grand to be announced by a Master of Ceremonies, and presented to the Duke and Duchess and the happy couple in the Painted Hall, before going up to the Mercury Landing (now the Carefree Man Landing), and into the private apartments. The large marble bath that is now in the Grotto was on the Mercury Landing at this time and had been filled with ice and bottles of champagne, and every time we turned round our glasses were refilled. It was a lovely afternoon, with a perfect ending as I swept down the staircase on the arm of my handsome Swiss companion.

Not long after this, on the beautiful evening of 21st May 1980, a fire broke out in Diane's flat at Chatsworth, situated on the north side of the building. It was discovered when she went back to the flat from the House Kitchen for something she'd forgotten. Fortunately she had the presence of mind to close the door behind her before raising the alarm, but the fire had still managed to take quite a firm hold. I had just driven from the House to the Cavendish Hall for a WI committee meeting, and as I opened the car door, I heard the old air raid siren wailing out its devastating warning from the top of the Theatre tower. I jumped back into the car and drove back at break-neck pace, stopping only at the Prince of Wales's tree opposite Edensor village to pick up Bill Jones, a retired houseman. He had been pottering in his Edensor garden when he heard the siren and had thrown down his hoe and run down to the gates, knowing that if he waited by the tree someone would stop for him. I shall never forget the sickening stomach-lurch I felt as we rounded the bend at Sandy's Turn and the House came into view. There had been false alarms before and Bill and I were hoping that this would be another, but the ominous plume of dark smoke rising from the roof told us the awful, inevitable reality.

At that time we only had a basic fire team in place, which had been formed during the firemen's strike in the 1970s, and they managed to tackle the blaze until the fire brigade arrived. There was molten lead dripping off the roof, and the House team worked together with the fire brigade to try to limit the damage. The whole Estate and villagers within earshot of the siren came to see if they could help, and of course the fire brigade was fantastic. Once the fire was subdued and it became a matter of damping down, Mrs Dean and I made countless cups of tea in our kitchen, in the old Confectionery, and carried them upstairs to the thirsty fire crew, who stayed the night to make sure the fire would not break out again. A shocked Diane stayed with me in my flat on the Bird Landing and we went up to see the fire crew after midnight, as she wanted to thank them. The acrid smell was awful, there was no light apart from our torches, and we discovered a fireman, fully clothed and still in his boots, dozing in the empty bath!

We finally got to bed at about two in the morning, but were up again at 5am to prepare the House for our visitors arriving at 11.30am. The only casualty was Jean-Pierre, who had broken the glass on the fire alarm and cut his hand quite badly in the process. Whilst we were waiting for the ambulance to arrive the Duchess sent me up to the private West Front Hall to get a jacket for him, and I remember running up the steps in the North Front Hall and through a curtain of water falling straight through the archway from the firemen's hoses up above. As the fire was contained quickly the fire damage wasn't too severe, but the water-damage was longer-lasting and it wasn't to be until the winter of 1999-2000 that the staining on the stone walls around the archway was finally cleaned away. This work was done by Paul

Giudicci and his team, who cleaned all the stonework and statuary in the North Front Hall.

Diane's parents came to visit her that weekend, and she, Jean-Pierre and I walked with them up through Stand Wood to the Hunting Tower, where we sat on the cannons and looked down at the House below. I don't suppose it had been the first fire at Chatsworth, but we hoped it would be the last. Two days later, His Grace wrote an individual letter to everyone who had been involved in the fire. Mine read:

Chatsworth, 23rd May 1980

Dear Christine,

I write to offer you my most heartfelt and fervent thanks for all the marvellous work you did when the fire took place on Wednesday evening. The Duchess tells me that it was really tremendous to see how you and so many others on the Estate were on the scene of the fire in a matter of minutes of the hooter sounding. Without any shadow of doubt, without your prompt and extremely efficient work the damage would have been far greater. I understand the Fire Brigade arrived reasonably quickly, but without you being on the scene before they got there, heaven knows what might have happened. As it is, thanks to you and your companions, the damage is relatively slight. I am only sorry I was not at home, as it must have been a real inspiration to see such loyalty displayed to the House and all it stands for. Thank you very much indeed.

Yours sincerely,

Devonshire

On 5th November that year, the Duke held a fantastic bonfire party for all the Estate staff which ended with a marvellous fireworks display, the finale of which was a huge framework reading, 'Thank you from Chatsworth'.

Earlier that year, Peter Day was programmed to give a talk about Chatsworth to the Beeley Women's Institute, but at the last minute was unable to go, and he asked me if I would step in. I rather nervously rang the Beeley WI programme secretary, Janet Robinson, to explain the situation, and to offer my services instead of Peter. 'I'm quite happy to come, but am afraid I haven't got a projector for my slides, so it will have to be just a straight talk. Will that be all right?'

'Don't worry about that,' she reassured me. 'My son has a projector, and I'm sure he won't mind coming along for the evening to help you out.'

The evening duly arrived and all went well. Mrs Robinson's son was Clive, who had lived in Beeley all his life, and was then in partnership with his brother and parents, running the dairy farm at South Oaks Farm, which was tenanted from the Chatsworth Estate. When I met him that evening I realised that we had met before, when I was about 15 years old, and had seen him in the village shop. I was fetching something from the shop for my Nan and apparently I went back to Nan's and asked who the lad was. It seems that Clive did the same when he went back to the farm and asked who the girl might have been that he'd seen in the shop. It took us long enough to get together, but thanks to that meeting at the WI, we finally started going out in 1980.

The following year, in October 1981, Mrs. Dean retired after 13 years' service and I was offered the post of Housekeeper.

Clive and I were still great friends with Diane and Jean-Pierre, and the four of us enjoyed many evenings out together. Diane and Jean-Pierre had finally become an 'item', just after Jean-Pierre had agreed to go to America to work for a businessman in New York and the Bahamas. Wishing to honour his agreement to work as arranged in America, and also anxious for the longed-for professional experience that it would bring, Jean-Pierre went off to his new job, leaving a wistful Diane behind. She was delighted when, not long afterwards, Her Grace asked his employer if Jean-Pierre could be spared for a few days so that he could cook for The Queen and Prince Philip, who were coming to Chatsworth for the weekend. So keen was Her Grace that Jean-Pierre should be at Chatsworth for the royal visit, that she agreed to pay his airfare.

I vividly remember Her Majesty's visit on this occasion, and when she was due to leave, the House staff were asked to assemble in the private West Front Hall. We stood there, chattering nervously, and then fell silent when Her Majesty came round the corner and down the stairs. She shook hands with us all, and we dropped a curtsey or bowed. I was lucky enough to be one of the members of staff whom Her Grace presented to The Queen, so Her Majesty actually had a few words with me, though for the life of me I could never remember what they were!

My lasting impression of her was how diminutive she was, how interested in us she seemed to be, what a lovely smile she had, and the brilliant intensity of those bright blue eyes. Straight after work I dashed along to the farm to tell Clive's family all about it, and greeted his brother with, 'Shake the hand that has been shaken by Her Majesty! I'm never going to wash it again!'

'I'll soon make you change your mind,' cried Frank, as he dropped his muck fork and heartily shook my hand!

I think Jean-Pierre found this return visit to Chatsworth unsettling, because he didn't stay in America long after that, but returned to England to become a 'catering trouble-shooter' for Chatsworth. He had a great passion for food, for life, and for Chatsworth, but I think that sometimes he found that things moved too slowly for him. Yet his achievements were remarkable, and he transformed the Devonshire Arms at Bolton Abbey into one of the finest country house hotels in the country. Her Grace remembered his arrival at Bolton Abbey in an old staff newsletter: 'When we took the Devonshire Arms at Bolton Abbey in hand, Jean-Pierre was chef there for some months. There were no proper pots and pans, but he didn't wait for a budget from the directors, but dashed to Leeds and bought a *batterie de cuisine* on my personal account!'

Diane had moved out of the House by this time and was living in the Guide Cottage in Edensor, a tiny one-up-one-down cottage tucked underneath the Church. It had originally been the infant department for the village school that used to be on the village green until the 1950s. After the school closed, the cottage was used by the Chatsworth Girl Guide Company and made an excellent base for night-hikes by the Girl Guides until the floor became unsafe to use and the building was refurbished as a small dwelling.

In 1983 when the Devonshire Arms at Bolton Abbey was successfully up and running, Diane moved from the Guide Cottage to Rose Cottage in Edensor, she and Jean-Pierre became engaged, and Jean-Pierre returned to Chatsworth. For his next project he was asked to help save the Farm Shop, which was then making a loss and facing closure. He laid the foundations of what it has become today, with visitors travelling great distances to buy the excellent, varied produce, especially the locally-sourced meat. Her Grace had a wonderful anecdote about a lady she met in the Farm Shop who asked, 'When I drive through Chatsworth Park I see the lambs have four legs, but when I unpacked my whole lamb for the freezer the other day, it only had two – can you tell me what happened to the other two legs?' I'm not sure exactly how Her Grace answered that one, but probably explained about the shoulders…

After successfully turning around the Farm Shop, Jean-Pierre then took over the catering for visitors to Chatsworth, and established the Carriage House restaurant, which is now recognised as one of the best in the class of 'Restaurants Attached to an Historic House Open to Visitors'. At the same time, he also managed to run the House Kitchen and preparation of food for Their Graces, and established popular cookery schools. These continued for several years after his death under the direction of his assistant chef and close friend, Michael Kokuciak.

In 1982, a flat above the restaurant in the Stables became vacant, and I moved up there, with much greater freedom to come and go than I had found living in the House, and it was also much handier for my allotment in the Gardens. In those days, only one man was on Lodge duty all night and he would periodically lock the gates to make his rounds, so if I was a few minutes late home I would have to sit outside until he'd finished his rounds before I could get in again. There had also been the odd occasion when Clive had been locked in, and had then been obliged to scale the gates, like a latter-day Joseph Paxton. In the Stables, I had a vast living room, a big kitchen and three enormous double bedrooms, and much easier access for visitors to come and stay.

Walks up in Stand Wood were a great temptation, and I would borrow my parents' dog whenever possible to go for long walks in the woods behind the House. Mum and Dad would often come over for the weekend, and although my father had not been well for many years and found the stairs up to the flat difficult, he said it was always worth the effort for the wonderful views. He must have spent hours sitting in what he called 'the snake pit' on the terrace below the 11th Duke's greenhouse in the Gardens, where the Cavendish Snake is marked out in pebbles from the Crumbles beach at Eastbourne (made to a design by Dennis Fisher), or on the Salisbury lawn listening to the band at weekends. In the early part of the year he liked to sit at the sitting room windows in the flat, to watch the antics of visitors trying to park on the muddy ground below. He also liked to watch the birds from the window and once saw a sparrowhawk fly in to take a blue tit feeding on our bird feeder.

The Stables flats had originally provided accommodation for grooms and other horsemen, and in one corner of the Stableyard, horse feed was stored in a granary. One of the doors on the corridor leading to my flat (which is now an office), still has '1st Postillion' painted onto it. With the horses long gone, the spaces provided accommodation throughout the first half of the 20th century for Chatsworth families such as the Links, the Barnes's, the Jones's and the Olivers. In the covered ride underneath the flats there was some space for residents' cars to be parked, but the rest was filled with items no longer needed, but never really put away tidily anywhere else. The north east corner, where the restaurant kitchen is now situated, was the blacksmith's shop, where Bob Hutchinson from Beeley was the last incumbent, together with Wolfgang. They were no longer shoeing horses, but doing running repairs as they came up, a job now undertaken by Paul Neale in his workshop in the House.

Wolfgang had been a German prisoner of war working at Green Cowden Farm where Clive's father had also worked during the war, and had stayed in England after the war and married a Bakewell girl. After he retired from the smithy at Chatsworth, he became a warden in the House, and it wasn't until another German-speaking warden was engaged that it was realised how scant had been Wolfgang's knowledge of the House. He drove a green and cream Triumph Herald with reckless disregard, especially on the bend between the Estate Office and the Cuttings. It was always tempting to take to the wrong side of the road just in case Wolfgang was coming the other way, swerving across the road as he hurtled round the corner.

In an old staff newsletter John Oliver remembers what life was like in the Stableyard when he was growing up in the 1950s. 'Harry Turner was the storeman. One of his jobs was to ring the bell at 7.30am for the start of work and then again at 12.00pm for lunch, 12.45 for the restart and then 5.30pm for home time. In those days there were up to 15 joiners and other trades, and at 5.25pm all the men would line up on their bikes, the first one with his hand on the gatepost, the second with his hand on the first one's shoulder and so on. Eventually there was a very long line of men waiting for Harry's bell. When the bell finally struck it was like the start line at Brands Hatch racing circuit as the host of men rode down the hill.

One team of men worked in the stick yard, cutting logs and chopping sticks all day. It seems strange now to think that so many sticks were needed, but the house was then heated by coal fires and coke-fired boilers and so the demand for sticks was enormous. The logs were cut by Sam Bond who operated a great pendulum shaft driven by a turbine and belts, which swung back and forth while Frank Beresford pushed the logs through the saw. The men who chopped the sticks tended to be the ones who were no longer fit enough to carry out their original trades. They would sit in a big circle by a roaring fire with their chopping blocks in front of them and a huge pile of logs at the side chopping and talking all day. As young boys, we would creep onto the roof of their shed and put a sod of turf over the chimney and then run away to watch from a distance as the old men came tumbling out of the shed coughing and cursing.'

One evening in my flat in the Stables, I had a phone call from the switchboard to say that His Grace had asked me to go with Clive down to the display greenhouse in the Gardens. When we got there, His Grace was with his house guests, including Harold Macmillan and Lord and Lady Hartington. We discovered that His Grace wanted us to see the night flowering cactus, which was really amazing. Canon Bob Honner, Vicar of Edensor and Beeley, had also been summoned from the Vicarage at Edensor to see the blooms and he apologised that his wife Alice wasn't feeling well and so was unable to come. His Grace immediately said that Canon Honner must take a flower home for her, and started to take one off, whereupon Bob Honner said, 'Oh no, don't pull it to pieces, Your Grace!' but the Duke replied, 'Well they'll all be gone by morning anyway, so it won't matter – in fact, let all the ladies have one!' and he gave all the ladies present a flower to take away. I pressed mine carefully, but it didn't survive.

Harold Macmillan was a regular visitor to Chatsworth, especially in his later years as he was the great uncle of the 11th Duke, having married Dorothy Cavendish, daughter of the 9th Duke of Devonshire. Her Grace used to tell the story that she once came across him shuffling along a corridor muttering, 'The trouble with this house is that you need to throw a double six to get out!'

On the road across Beeley Moor from Hell Bank Plantation towards Screetam Farm there is an ancient stone finger post, and beside this on the evening of 23rd April 1983, Clive asked me to marry him. It was a glorious evening and the sun was just setting over the distant hills above Bakewell and Youlgreave. We had been on our way to visit my grandmother, who was convalescing at my parents' house in Chesterfield after a bout of 'flu, and so we carried on to see them, full of our exciting news. They were all three delighted, and over the next few days we began planning our wedding for the autumn.

Sadly, my Nan died less than a month later, on 16th May. I took a phone call at work from her neighbour to say that she had collapsed at home, and when I arrived in Beeley ten minutes later, she was unconscious. She had been down to the village shop, stopped to chat to neighbours on the way home, and when I arrived, she was sitting in her chair by the window with her jacket still on. It seemed she had felt the need to sit down for a moment, and then had a stroke. I travelled with her to the hospital in Chesterfield where she died a few hours later from another massive stroke, never having regained consciousness. She had been so independent and so full of life that it would have been a bitter blow for her to have made a partial recovery and ended her days in a twilight world of frustration. Her liveliness and forthright manner were sorely missed by her family and by the community in which she lived, and it was a marvellous tribute to her that Beeley Church was packed for her funeral, with standing room only.

The following month we were in Edensor Church for a happier occasion when Diane and Jean-Pierre were married on 4th June 1983, and later that year, on 15th October, Clive and I were married in Beeley Church. Of course the cows had to be milked before we could get married, so Clive worked on our wedding morning and Mum and I took the dog for a walk in Stand Wood. The ceremony was at 11.30am and I was determined not to be late, but just after Mum and the bridesmaids had left for the church, and Dad and I were about to leave the Stables flat with our friend John, the top button popped off Dad's shirt, and I had to stitch it back on for him. I was in such a hurry that I pricked my finger, so then I was worried that I would be dripping blood on my wedding dress.

'Put a plaster on it!' said Dad.

'No!' I cried, 'I don't want a plaster on my finger, do I?'

Eventually we got away, travelling in style in John's vintage Speed 6 Bentley, in which both Clive and I had navigated many times on vintage car rallies with him up and down the country. As we drove through the wind and rain to Beeley, I suddenly heard the church bells ringing and realised that they were peeling for me! It was the most amazing feeling. The Chatsworth gardeners had made a beautiful job of my flowers and the church flowers, and a friend of my mother's played the organ. I had made my own wedding dress and the page boy outfits and my mother-in-law had iced the three tiered wedding cake I had made myself, so it was very much a home spun affair. Her Grace came in a wonderful bottle green jacket and hat, and sat with my mother. It all felt so much like a traditional country wedding with a packed church, and kneeling on the white bride's kneeler made by my great-great-grandmother, Sarah Burdekin.

As we left the church, following the Beeley tradition, the village children were waiting by the gate and as we passed through Clive threw them the pocketful of coins he had remembered especially for them. After the reception at the Red House Hotel in Darley Dale everyone went back to the farm for cups of tea and to see the wedding presents, and then we set off on our honeymoon, making a detour by Beeley Church to lay my bouquet on Nan and Granddad's grave. We spent the first night at the Devonshire Arms at Bolton Abbey and when we were shown our room, there was a bottle of champagne on ice for us and a card with compliments from Her Grace, who had been talking to my mother before the church service and asked where we were going for our honeymoon. When I thanked her for it on our return from holiday, she said, 'Oh, I wondered afterwards if I did right to phone them – I thought the last person you wanted to be reminded of on your honeymoon was me!' My mother-in-law was touched that Her Grace took the time to call at the farm whilst we were away to have a look at our wedding presents, as she had been unable to do so on the afternoon of the wedding – something very typical of her to do.

On 22nd November 1984, our son Philip was born in the local maternity hospital, Darley Hall (now a care home for the elderly), and my own GP, Mike Chadwick, delivered him. Apparently it was his day off, but he still came down to deliver our baby when they rang him from Darley Hall to say I was in labour. It was such a comfortable maternity home, with excellent food, and as baby Philip had an infection, I even had a room to myself with lovely views up to the wood behind the hall. I had visits from many friends bringing chocolates, gifts for Philip and so on, but when Jean-Pierre came, he brought me four bottles of Guinness. He said they would do me more good than the traditional bunch of flowers.

I had been uncertain how the arrival of a family would affect our life at Chatsworth as I did not want to give up my job, but also didn't want to be a full-time working mother, and of course our flat went with my job. Eric Oliver was the comptroller at this time and he said that as they didn't want to lose me from the Chatsworth team it would be all right if I worked part-time until my family was older. I felt that I had the best of both worlds, although I returned to work much sooner than I would have really liked, starting back in January 1985 and working five mornings a week. Luckily my Mum and Dad could take care of Philip for one morning; Clive took him to the farm on another morning for Grandma to look after him, and Doreen Motley, a friend living in the Stables, had him for the other three mornings.

Doreen worked on the Chatsworth switchboard for many years, and was married to Glyn, one of the Lodge security men. She had stopped work to have her own daughter, Mandy, three years earlier and was more than happy to look after Philip, and Mandy always called Philip her 'part-time brother'. We often used to meet Her Grace in the Stable courtyard first thing in the morning when I was taking Philip round to Doreen's, and she loved to say, 'Hello, Philip' to him so that she could hear his lisped two-year old's reply, 'Mornin' Grace!'

Doreen went back to work at Chatsworth as telephonist once Mandy was older and Philip went to play school. Doreen is a very unpretentious person but an absolute fount of knowledge and the perfect person to be responsible for the switchboard, where so much knowledge is required about so many things – who needs to be contacted if sheep have got out onto the road going through Baslow, or through Beeley,

Above: The Burdekin family at the funeral of Tom Burdekin in 1902.
Top row l-r: Samuel, Polly, Thomas, Melissa, Joseph, Nellie, George.
Bottom row l-r: Alice, Emily, Mary (widow), Annie Muriel (my grandmother), Sally.

Below: Sarah Burdekin, née Grafton, 1815-1910, pictured here with her horse, Kit.

Above: My great-grandmother,
Mary Burdekin, née Wilton
[died 1932].

Right: My grandmother, Annie
Muriel Tindale, née Burdekin
[1892-1983].

My grandfather, John Edward Matthewson Tindale (1892-1964) in the uniform of the Northumberland Fusiliers.

Peter Day and I taking a break from the preparations for the Treasures from Chatsworth Exhibition in August, 1979, when we donned costume to have our photograph taken in the Empire State Building in New York City.

James Paine's Mill in the 1930s when it was tenanted by descendants of the Burdekin family.

Paine's Mill today.

Norman Villa, built for Clive's great-great-great-grandfather, William Strutt in 1840 at a cost of £1200. I always imagined sitting in the tower with a good book, but sadly the only access is through a tiny window on the roof.

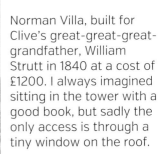

Rose Cottage, Edensor. The house is actually semi-detached, and the half we occupied is to the right of the photograph.

Rock Villa, built in 1839 and our home for several years.

Philip and Michael in the garden at Rose Cottage
with their older cousin, Trevor.

Our wedding at Beeley Church, 15 October 1983.

Left to right: Ed Robinson, Janet Robinson, Clive Robinson, Christine Robinson, Eric Tindale, Jean Tindale.

Attendants: Liz McKenzie, Trevor Robinson, Matthew Gray, Carol Robinson.

Christine and Clive Robinson with Deborah, Duchess of Devonshire,
at our wedding, 15th October 1983.

Above: The party held for staff, pensioners and tenants from all the Devonshire Estates to celebrate Lord Burlington's 21st birthday, which took place at Chatsworth on 6th July 1990. The 11th Duke and Duchess and their grandson, Lord Burlington, greeted the 3,000 guests below the Cascade before the party began.

Below: A party held for family and friends took place on the following evening. The Inner Court was transformed by a fully sprung dance floor with a star-studded canopy stretched above it. The housekeeping team were kept busy for almost a month beforehand supplying tea for the workmen.

Above: Members of the Derbyshire Constabulary inspecting the view of the stage from the auditorium before the start of the Tercentenary party in 1994.

Right: Hunting Tower flying the Tercentenary flag.

Above: Deborah, Duchess of Devonshire at the party in 2000, in costume as the Empress of Palmyra. Behind her stand the 11th Duke and their granddaughter, Lady Jasmine Cavendish.

Facing Page, Top: Judy Coggins (assistant housekeeper) and her husband Dick, dressed as Mrs Hackett, housekeeper of the 1st Duke of Devonshire, and the artist Antonio Verrio, who painted her image onto the ceiling of the Great Chamber.

Facing Page, Below: Clive and I with Peter Day at the 2000 party.

Above: The 11th Duke and Duchess of Devonshire at their
Diamond Wedding party in 2001.

Below: Staff dressed in uniform at the Diamond Wedding party in 2001
(front row, 4th from left, John Oliver, comptroller; 5th from left: Helen Marchant
private secretary to the 11th Duke of Devonshire)

Lord Burlington with Lord James at his christening,
at Chatsworth, 3rd March 2011

Above: The horseshoe-shaped table in the private dining room, specially constructed for Eric Oliver's retirement dinner in 1996.

Below: The Dilettanti dinner in the Great Dining Room in 1994. Ian Fraser Martin and Sean Doxey position the potted vine; head gardener, Ian Webster, looks on.

Above: Tulips from the Chatsworth gardens fill the Great Dining Room on the occasion of the farewell dinner for Simon Seligman and Paul Cottrell.

Below: The private dining room set for a visit by HRH Princess Anne at the time of the 11th Duke. Food arrives hot via a service lift behind the screen.

Above: Janet Bitton and I on the West Sketch Gallery. Janet has been deputy head housekeeper at Chatsworth for four years, and is also a key member of the Christmas team. Her artistic talents play a huge part in delivering the Christmas theme each year, and as the illustrations in this book demonstrate, she is a most gifted artist.

Left: The Chatsworth Violin, painted by Jan van der Vaardt (c.1653-1727). Even from a short distance it is a most effective illusion. Only the knob on which the violin 'hangs' is real.

or through Pilsley; who to contact if a wall is knocked down by a car; who to contact if a sheep gets run over in the Park; all the opening times for the House, Gardens and Farmyard, the admission prices for events, the finer details of the Friends of Chatsworth Scheme. People even ring up to ask what the weather is going to be like, or what colour the leaves are. Once, someone phoned to ask for directions to the House, not from somewhere nearby but from their home in Leeds, and they couldn't even work out how to get to the motorway from their house! When Sir Cliff Richard gave a large outdoor concert at Chatsworth a few years ago, John Oliver (who succeeded his brother Eric as comptroller in 1996) decided that he would surprise Doreen, who is a keen fan of Sir Cliff, and took him into the switchboard to meet her. She was so taken aback, that she couldn't think of anything to say to him, but he was perfectly charming and I don't think Doreen will ever forget the experience.

Juggling family life and work was sometimes a challenge, but when great opportunities came along, my family usually rallied round to enable me to take them. When Her Grace received a letter from the Marquis of Lansdowne at Bowood House in Wiltshire asking her to bid on his behalf for a painting at a local auction, she asked Peter Day if he could sort something out. The sale was at Snitterton Hall, a late medieval house near Matlock that was sold in 1985, together with much of its contents. As one of the paintings was of a previous Lady Lansdowne, the Marquis was keen to acquire it for the Bowood collection and as Peter couldn't get to the sale, he asked me to act for him. On the day, I dropped Philip off at the farm and spent a wonderful afternoon at Snitterton Hall. I bid successfully for the painting and that evening I had a phone call from the Marquis to thank me for my efforts.

With the arrival of Philip, family life and the pattern of work continued very happily and I felt I had the best of all worlds. I could become more involved with Clive's work on the farm, I had a wonderful husband, an adorable son, a rewarding family life, and Chatsworth – I could not imagine a happier combination. We were fortunate, also, that our two families got on so well together. Our Christmases were always great family occasions when, with my parents, Clive's brother Frank and his family, we all got together on Boxing Day at South Oaks Farm with Clive's parents in Beeley.

It was a terrible shock when, in October 1986, Clive took a phone call one tea time up in the Stables flat to say that my father had suddenly died. It was just before his sixty-second birthday. He had been ill for many years, but a bout of 'flu had confined him to bed and this had very quickly developed into double pneumonia, with fatal results. Clive phoned Peter Day, who fetched Clive's mother so she could put Philip to bed, and Clive and I went over to Chesterfield to collect my mother and the dog. It happened so suddenly, so unexpectedly, and without the chance to say goodbye to him and it seemed impossible that such a lively mind had gone. We still talk about him such a lot and although Philip wasn't even two when Dad died, he talks about him as though he knew him, and Michael, who wasn't even born then, still feels he is real to him.

It was hard to leave the stables flat, as I had so many happy memories of Dad there, but when Diane and Jean Pierre moved out of Rose Cottage, it seemed the right thing for us to ask if we might have it, as the stairs at the Stables were especially awkward with a baby. Rose Cottage is a lovely house, with a large garden and enormous kitchen, a very small dining room and sitting room, two bedrooms and a box room, and at that time the bathroom was downstairs. We moved there in May 1987, and on 9th April 1988 our son Michael was born in Chesterfield, making our family complete.

In September 1992, Rock Villa, farther up the lane in Edensor, became vacant. It had more space for our family, and we spent 14 very happy years there. It is one of only two houses in the village which display a date of construction on the outside of the building, in this case, 1839. Whilst we were living there we came across a book called *A Gardener at Chatsworth*, which describes three years in the life of Robert Aughtie, taken from his diaries. In 1848, Aughtie was employed as a gardener at the Duke's house in Chiswick, but was moved to Chatsworth on an exchange programme operated by Joseph Paxton, who managed both gardens. Aughtie lodged with Dame Wallace in Rock Cottage, later known as Rock Villa, arriving there from London on 10th April 1848. He described Edensor as, 'A place consisting of newly built stone cottages of very pretty design … arrived a day sooner than my landlady expected so slept with Peter, her son, who is to start for Chiswick tomorrow. Found a nice clean room but very thinly furnished.' I later discovered that the cottage is listed in the Estate plans as comprising a 'house place, kitchen, dairy, closet and two bedchambers'.

We were blissfully happy in Rock Villa with our wonderful little family, but were made to count our blessings when the unthinkable happened – Jean-Pierre was killed in a tragic traffic accident in the Park on 13th October 1996, aged just 40. I wrote in my diary:

Tuesday October 15th: Our wedding anniversary. It makes you think. I went to see Diane yesterday afternoon, and we fell into each other's arms. Jean-Pierre's photo is up in the kitchen. Her parents Stan and Mary Peach, are staying with her, and we had a cup of tea and talked about the old days and reminisced about our walks up into Stand Wood and the happy times we all shared when we were living in the House together.

Thursday October 17th: Everyone is still in a great state of shock. It will be Oliver's sixth birthday tomorrow, and without his Daddy. The Prince of Wales has sent a lovely bouquet of lilies and a note to Diane offering his condolences and memories of Jean-Pierre.

After his death, Deborah Duchess wrote a moving tribute to him in the staff newsletter. The following is an extract:

Jean-Pierre fell in love with Chatsworth, or Shaswors as he used to pronounce it with his French accent and his lisp…he told me once that he was having difficulty with somebody and he was longing to discuss it with the Duchess. He compared it to if you wanted to see God – you had to get St Peter's approval, so he said one day he decided 'why go to St Peter when he could go straight to God'!

From the day he arrived we were reminded of what good food is. I had to act 'cabbage' and everything else till he learnt enough English for us to communicate the essentials to each other…

After the disaster, among the marvellous letters I received was this from Peter Day:

'Cookery is an art but not so much a fine art or an applied art as a performing art like dancing, acting or singing. It is of the moment and then gone, and has to be spot on. I was struck by this, even awe-struck, in Jean-Pierre's case when one evening staff and their families were invited to see the big table in the Great Dining Room with all its silver

and special decorations ready for the great dinner for the Society of Dilettanti, to which His Grace was host. There amid all the wide-eyed admirers strolling round the table was Jean-Pierre and his family – only a minute or two before he had to go down to the kitchen to cook this mighty meal in prospect! I think I vaguely thought everything would somehow have been prepared days in advance. But I realised then with a shock how much Jean-Pierre's work (or art) was like going on stage for a great performance and giving his audience an evening of pleasure, a transport of delight – something to get right on the night, every night. In his case his whole life and character were like this, immediate and direct, all passion with no side, front, or anything else to come between him and others. Everyone who knew him knew that storms were followed instantly by sunshine. Jean-Pierre could not have been more at one with the lively art of which he was a master and memories of him will never be other than vivid.

7

⊷

Keeping House

My early days as housekeeper seemed fairly straightforward, with the pattern of the years following on like clockwork. It is an enormous house, with 297 rooms, 3,426 feet of passages, 18 staircases, 359 doors, 2,084 lights bulbs, 7,873 window panes and with a visitors' route over half a mile long. Up until the late 1980s, the House closed at the beginning of October, just before the Horse Trials, after which the housekeeping staff would take a week's holiday before the deep cleaning began. We always started this deep clean in the Scots Apartments, then moved into the State Apartments, followed by the ground floor, the North Wing, and finally, all the staircases. Now that the House closes just before Christmas, re-opening in March, the length of time available for the deep clean is drastically reduced. The cleaning is now done by several teams working in different areas of the House simultaneously, and we also have to slot in any alterations, refurbishment, or restoration as we go along.

At the start of the deep clean the glass and ceramics are carefully wrapped, packed into boxes and moved to a collection area within the group of rooms to be cleaned. Items too large to be moved are covered with dust sheets, fire grates are black-leaded, brasses cleaned, steels burnished, and then the grate is covered over. Portable tower scaffolding is then erected in the room to give access to the areas impossible to reach from steps.

Special vacuum cleaners, which are carried strapped to the hip of the operator, are used to remove dust and debris. We find this method much more effective than using brushes on their own, which would just transfer the dust from one place to another. Soft dusting brushes waft the dust into the nozzle of the vacuum cleaner and in this way we can clean delicate items like the intricate carvings of the State Apartments. These beautiful fish, game birds, fruits and flowers were carved by a local carver, Samuel Watson, together with Lobb, Young and Davis, a team of carvers from London engaged by the 1st Duke between 1692 and 1694. Once the high areas have been cleaned, the scaffold team moves on to clean windows, mirrors and the huge doors. In earlier times we used scrunched up newspaper and methylated spirits to clean windows and mirrors, but not any more. The windows now have a film applied to the glass that prevents ultraviolet rays from fading the furnishings. We dare not use anything that may scratch this film, so soft cloths alone are used.

The scaffold team moves from one room to the next, each having been prepared for them, and other members of the housekeeping team move in behind to finish cleaning and polishing furniture, washing ceramics and glass and polishing the floors.

Most of the ceramics are washed every year during the course of the deep clean, but no items are actually immersed in the water as the shock of going into hot water could cause a crack to become a break or the glue in an old repair might soften and become a break again. A few pure soap flakes are placed in a bowl of hot water and a well-wrung cloth is then used to gently wipe the piece before it is dried with a soft cloth. If the china is intricate, then soft paint brushes are used to dislodge the dirt from the crevasses. The Delft tulip vases require special attention. They were made around 1690 to cater for the craze for tulips at that time in Holland. They are elaborate multi-tiered pots, each tier having four or more holders which were intended for a variety of flowers, not just for tulips.

Glass is washed in a similar way, including the magnificent chande-liers, of which there are 13 on public display throughout the route. There is a product available which can be sprayed onto a glass chandelier and the dirt just drips off along with the spray, but we prefer to dismantle them tier by tier, so that we can check on the maintenance of all the little brass pins that hold the glass droplets in place and replace any that are becoming black and brittle. It is a skilled job, taking two people up to two days on some of the larger pieces, and requires the utmost concentration as well as a certain agility, given the height of some of the chandeliers.

In 1996 Her Grace decided that it was time to refurbish the Great Dining Room and to replace the ivory watered silk that had been hung on the walls in 1964. This had suffered water damage during one winter and had become badly stained. The damage had been caused by water from melting snow on the roof above. The water ran into the gutters and then froze again, resulting in further snow melt being unable to drain away down the downspout, finding its way instead through the ceiling and down the walls below. Since then capillary heating cables have been laid on the roof so that they can be switched on if there is any risk of a severe frost. It was an unfortunate fact that no matter how lovely the Bohemian ruby glass, silver or ceramics looked on the table, or how magnificent the paintings on the walls, it was always the stain on the watered silk that drew the visitor's eye.

An interesting anecdote concerns one of the paintings in the Great Dining Room by Daniel Mytens, which shows a family group including Christian Bruce, widow of the 2nd Earl of Devonshire and her family in 1628. This lady established a charity for young apprentices to help them to buy their own tools, a charity still active today, and providing young people on the Estate with a small bursary when they go to college, or for apprentices who come to work at Chatsworth, assisting with money towards their tools.

For the Great Dining Room walls, Her Grace selected a red striped cotton fabric that has worked really well and gives the room an added richness. It needed 131 yards of this to cover the walls and it took two seamstresses 468 hours to do the work. In addition to this work, David Walters of Sudbury in Suffolk was commissioned to make a copy of the silk brocade curtains that were disintegrating and were making the newly decorated room look rather shabby. Each of the five windows needed 32 yards of brocade and then 185 yards each of the edging and fancy braid specially commissioned from Heritage Trimmings of Derby, all of which had to be hand sewn onto the brocade. Finally, the drop braids for the curtains and pelmets were added, at a cost of £203 per yard (in 1996), and with 109 yards being required in all.

One of the great satisfactions of the project was that it was all accomplished 'in house'. The housekeeping team stripped the chandelier and cleared the room of furniture; the joiners removed the old fabric from the walls and re-lined them with board; the House painter and decorator redecorated the room; the textiles department hung the new fabric on the walls, edged it with 355 yards of gimp braid, and then made the new curtains; the electrician rewired the chandelier, and the housekeeping team reassembled it. One of the problems faced by the textiles team was that although the paintings came out of their frames, the frames themselves are part of the fabric of the room, so all the material for the walls had to be carefully fitted around them.

When we dismantled the chandelier we took a lot of very careful photographs and drawings as it was going to be some time before it was put back together again. This was before the days of digital photography, which is a great help with projects like this today, when we photograph and label everything as we take it down. Dismantling the chandelier also allowed us to count the component pieces, all 2,763 of them – it was good to find none left over when we came to reassemble it. The chandelier chain was covered with an ivory silk sheath, which I took home to wash. I put it into my ironing basket when it was dry, and I kept my mother guessing for some time as to what it was when she offered to catch up with my ironing for me and found a very long cummerbund of silk with hooks and eyes running the entire length of it.

The Great Dining Room looked absolutely stunning when it was finished and when the House reopened an American visitor was overheard remarking to her husband, 'I don't often say this Sam, but when I look at this table, I feel quite outclassed!'

The furniture is mostly only polished once a year during the deep clean as over-polishing can cause damage to carved pieces and the polish tends to become lodged in the carved areas. Dusting gloves are always worn to prevent finger grease from marking the woodwork, unless Boulle furniture is being cleaned, when no gloves or cloths are used at all. Boulle furniture incorporates elaborate pierced brasswork with an inlay of tortoiseshell and the use of dusters or gloves can cause great damage as fibres of material can snag on any slightly raised piece of brass and cause it to lift and come out. The cost of repairing these pieces is phenomenal, so every care is taken to ensure that such damage does not occur.

Visitors are always keen to know what happens when things go wrong and if we ever have any breakages. In fact, the team is very careful and accidents are rare. Unfortunately, when accidents do happen, however, they can be quite catastrophic. This has only happened once in my time at Chatsworth, when a clock was pulled off the top of a desk, crashing onto the floor with devastating consequences. Two of the housekeeping team had been taking dust sheets off a desk, and had tugged rather too hard so that the very heavy clock underneath had been dragged off the top of the desk and onto the floor. The clock was most decidedly broken and the individuals concerned, who were usually so careful, were in floods of tears. Of course Peter Day, as keeper of the collection, had to be informed, and he in turn had to tell His Grace. His Grace decided to write letters to the two women, telling them not to worry and that accidents did sometimes happen, and they were not to think any more about it. This resulted in even more tears as everyone was so touched by his thoughtfulness.

The leatherwork on the walls of some of the State Apartments was last treated over 30 years ago when we used saddle soap to prevent it from drying out. No one working at Chatsworth at that time had ever needed to treat the leather, so we had been wondering what to use. The Estate clerk of works at the time, Bob Getty, had recently come to Chatsworth from Hatfield House where he had been a joiner. He suggested using saddle soap and gave us Hatfield's home-made recipe, which we used to great effect in the State Apartments. We measured six parts of lanolin to two parts of soft soap with two parts of milk into an old saucepan, which was gently heated on the gas stove in the Confectionery, and then the resulting paste was sparingly applied with a soft cloth to the leather of the State Apartment walls. The effect of all that soft lanolin on hands that had been black-leading a grate in the morning was quite remarkable.

Tapestries, curtains and soft furnishings are cleaned with a vacuum cleaner, using a layer of gauze in between the machine nozzle and the fabric itself. This acts as a buffer to prevent the vacuum nozzle rubbing against the delicate fabrics while still allowing dirt to pass through the mesh into the machine.

We were all delighted when, after Christine Thompson's arrival as seamstress in 1983, the much-needed conservation of the tapestries could begin. Christine had been working in a little haberdashery shop in Skipton, where she also took in orders for curtains and had made some for the Devonshire Arms Hotel at Bolton Abbey in 1982. Her Grace was so taken with her work that following the retirement of Miss Feeney, Christine was offered a full-time position at Chatsworth, together with her husband John who took on the job of French-polisher and clock-winder. They moved into Diane's old flat up in the attics, which had been refurbished following the fire of 1980, and I can remember seeing their furniture arriving. As the housemen carried it upstairs, I was surprised that it was all so modern – John was a French polisher, and I had expected it all to be antiques. I said so to John but he said, 'Oh no! We wouldn't want second hand furniture!' John and Christine and their two daughters quickly fitted into Estate life and Christine went on to become personal maid to Her Grace when Maud Barnes retired, in addition to her role as seamstress. They have now retired to a lovely Estate cottage in Baslow village.

The tapestries had received some attention in previous years, but sometimes thread had been used that had not faded at the same rate as the original, leaving some areas that were brighter than others. In other instances, nylon thread had been used to effect a repair and this had cut into the tapestry, causing it to split. Further problems arose where worn and holed patches of tapestry had been glued onto the hessian backing to prevent further spread of the hole, and the glue had become hard and brittle. Some of the trees in old tapestries look quite blue instead of green which is because blue and yellow were mixed together to make the green dye for the wool, and the yellow fades more rapidly, leaving the blue behind. Enquiries were made about having the tapestries conserved professionally, but the sum involved was enormous and in any case, there was a twelve-year waiting list before work could begin. Not to be beaten, Christine Thompson took herself off to Blickling Hall in Norfolk, where she was able to learn from the National Trust's textile conservation centre about how to conserve the tapestries, and together with help from the textile conservation team at Hatfield House, she was able to set up a tapestry conservation centre here at Chatsworth. This meant that our own tapestries could be conserved at a fraction of the cost and without a lengthy wait.

The tapestries were sent away to Blickling to be washed and on their return were mounted on the wooden work frames made in our own Joiners' Shop. A team of highly skilled volunteers then worked under the supervision of the textile team for countless dedicated hours to complete the conservation. Once the repairs were completed, the tapestries were backed with a layer of wadding and a layer of cotton and then re-hung, but not in the traditional way with a nail straight through the tapestry into the wooden batten. Instead, Christine, who thus earned the nickname the 'Velcro Queen', stitched one half of very broad Velcro tape onto the tapestry, nailed the opposite tape to the batten and then married the two together. Now, in the event of a fire the tapestry can be pulled off the battens and carried away to safety.

All the tapestries in the House have now been conserved with the exception of those in the State Drawing Room, and conservation work started on these in the winter of 2013. They were woven at Mortlake around 1635 and the pictures on them are after the cartoons of biblical scenes by Raphael (1483-1520), now in the Victoria and Albert Museum. It is thought that they were probably part of the original decoration of the room but were subsequently cut down to fit into the spaces, and the 6th Duke replaced the mouldings round them in around 1830.

The deep cleaning of the House always feels like a juggling act with at least six balls in the air at any one time, and we may well drop at least one of them. I am always convinced that the House will not be ready for opening but it always is, and it is amazing how everyone rallies round in the last fortnight to achieve the unachievable. My recurrent nightmare every year before we open, is that I am going round the route in the morning with my keys, locking doors, switching lights on and putting ropes up, making sure the House is ready for visitors. In my nightmare, there is always something to delay me and I find myself being overtaken by the public, who then gain access to everywhere they shouldn't and complain because the lights aren't switched on!

Winter time when the House is closed is also the opportunity for special conservation and restoration projects. Mrs Dean once spoke of the time when the Gibbons brothers worked to restore the painted ceiling in the State Bedchamber, and she was aghast to discover that they had brought their own primus stove and kettle to brew their tea whilst they worked. 'I was horrified!' she recalled. 'I thought, My God, the damn place will go up in smoke with all that wood! They were funny, those old boys. They were living in Bakewell and I was told that even when they went for a glass of beer they sat at separate tables. They were very odd. We nearly had words!'

When I joined the Chatsworth housekeeping team, the closed season was also the time for making marmalade to be sold in the Orangery Shop, and so a large delivery of Seville oranges signalled the start of the work. This took place in the Confectionery, now the staff canteen in the House. At that time there was a huge table in the middle of the room and a gas stove on the east wall on which all the meals used to be prepared for the staff working and living in the House when the Solymossy sisters were in charge – it's hard to imagine it now.

It is always interesting to see how other historic properties approach the same problems, and opportunities to meet to do this are always welcome. One such opportunity was in April 2005 when I attended a 'Dust Conference' at the British Library, much to the amusement of my family and colleagues, who all thought it would be as dry as…dust! However, it proved to be fascinating. The first day was spent visiting Hampton Court Palace and Knole, the wonderful Tudor mansion at Sevenoaks in Kent, where we discussed the particular conservation issues faced by these two properties. Tests at Hampton Court Palace had shown that the parts of the room with the most visitor traffic had the most dust, and at Knole we learned that a damp atmosphere causes the dust to stick more firmly to objects and is much more difficult to remove. Knole have tried to address the problem of damp affecting their prized King's Bed by enclosing it in a glazed box, which allows visitors to view the room, but enables the light and humidity to be controlled. The restoration project took 13 years to complete at a cost of three million pounds. The second day of the conference was based on the findings of a research project at the University of East Anglia, funded by the Leverhulme Trust and in partnership with the National Trust, English Heritage and Historic Royal Palaces.

The problems highlighted were very similar to those we face at Chatsworth: cleaning can cause damage to fragile surfaces, but so can the cementation of dust, so objects do still have to be cleaned. We also need to be aware of the visitors' perception of dust – if they're viewing a castle dungeon, the dust and cobwebs add something to the atmosphere, but on a visit to a stately home it's not something they would want to see.

The most intriguing part of the day for me was the discussion on what dust actually is and how it behaves; for example, I learned that dust particles are larger in the winter months because of the more fibrous nature of winter clothing. It was fascinating to hear from an architect working with the Antarctic Heritage Trust that even after a year enclosed in a visitor-free environment and at sub-zero temperatures, the artefacts in Scott's sheds in the Antarctic are still coated in dust! More food for thought was the discovery that the more activity there is in a room, the more dust is deposited. It led me to think that if we exhausted our Chatsworth visitors with a long walk around the Park before they entered the House, they would jig about less, so there would be fewer particles shaken off their clothing; or that if they were sprayed with a jet of air as they crossed the threshold, any dust particles would be blown away; or perhaps if they arrived naked there would be hardly any dust deposited at all!

Although the basic daily housekeeping routine remains essentially the same, we are guided by such expert bodies as the National Trust and the British Library in the care of historic objects within a sensitive environment, and so there have been some changes in our approach to the task. We have also sent some of the housekeeping team for training at Windsor with the experts advising the Historic Royal Palaces. When I first started working for Mrs Dean, the handling of books always involved wearing cotton gloves to prevent finger grease from damaging the leather surfaces, but now, following advice from experts in the conservation world, we never wear gloves when dusting the books as the lack of manual dexterity might mean that pages could become damaged. Perhaps counter-intuitively, it has been decided that the finger grease is likely to do more good than harm.

When the books on the visitor route are cleaned every winter (and there are 17,500 in the Library and Ante-Library alone), they are carefully taken off the shelf and dusted using a fine pony hair brush, dusting from the spine towards the edge of the page so that dust is not driven into the spine. In the Ante-Library, where there is a greater accumulation of dust due to the visitors passing through, we have laid a strip of dark brown cotton along the top of the books that can be taken off and cleaned regularly throughout the year, thus avoiding the heavy accumulation of dust on the top edges of the books.

For many years Chatsworth has been open to visitors every day, and since 2001 the open season has run from mid-March to late December. This has had a considerable impact on how we undertake the deep cleaning of the House, and we can no longer simply work our way through from one end of the House to the other. I always put together a schedule of winter work that starts in the second week of November with the preparation of the State Apartments ready for the deep clean, and the work then progresses room by room. At the same time, the deep clean also starts in the Scots Apartments and the Sketch Galleries so that the work in all of those rooms is completed by the time the House closes fully at the end of December. In the New Year, the Christmas decorations are taken down and then the deep cleaning of the ground floor, staircases and North Wing can begin.

The period when the House is closed also provides the opportunity to clean the storage spaces not on view to visitors. Before the arrival of Christine Thompson and the formation of a textile team, the housekeeping department was also responsible for the care of the fabrics in the collection. One day during the deep clean, my deputy, Judy Coggins, and I were going through a very dark and dingy room on the Kitchenmaids' Landing to sort through a pile of boxes of old passmenterie – bobbles for curtains, braids and so on. I opened one cardboard box, dirty and neglected, and held together with a bit of very old string. Inside, we found some yellowed tissue paper that I carefully lifted to one side, and there lay the most beautiful baby dress, which would probably have fitted a child about two years old. The pattern seemed almost modern, in a purple and white design and with wonderful handmade buttons and tiny fastenings. Together with the dress was a pair of little red leather shoes, and attached to them was a label reading, 'Shoes worn by William Cavendish ("Can") died 1834. Sent to Chatsworth by Miss Egerton 1925.' It was such a poignant find and one that brought a tear to my eye, for although the skirt had a deep hem to be let out, the little boy had died before he was able to outgrow his dress.

Another find in a cupboard in the old Servants' Hall was an object which had us puzzled for ages. It is a circular wooden board with a rectangular piece at the bottom edge of the circle. The circle is covered with small holes in straight lines marking the points of the compass, and the piece at the bottom has four rows of small holes in straight lines, and the word Fortroendet across the rectangular section. There are several strings from the centre of the circular piece with bone and lead pegs attached to the end of them, and on the back is a very old label with water-damaged writing, although part of it is distinct, with the date, 1636. Was it a game? Was it a lace-making device? Was it an abacus of some sort? The points of the compass were the clue, as we found out when we went on a family holiday to the USA in 1996 and visited Jamestown on the coast of Virginia, where they had a replica ship of that which first travelled across to the New World centuries ago. Costumed 'sailors' guided us around the ship, and I was amazed to spot, hanging on a peg, a replica of our wooden board back at Chatsworth. The guides were delighted to explain that it was a Traverse Board, an early aid to navigation, used together with a sextant by those early travellers to find their way across the Atlantic. They would have marked the direction in which they were travelling with one set of pegs on the circular part of the board, and with the other set of pegs they would have kept a tally of how many watches they had followed on that course. The next puzzle was how did it come to be at Chatsworth? We have yet to find an answer.

The housekeeping team is now also responsible for the cleaning of the Theatre, office spaces, corridors, mess rooms, attics, and also the bookings and cleaning of service flats in the House and Stables used by conservators, photographers, film crews, staff at the country fair and so on. The team also does the twice-weekly turnarounds of the five holiday cottages on the proximate Estate: the Hunting Tower, Swiss Cottage, Russian Cottage, Park Cottage and Gardener's Cottage.

Besides Christmas opening, Behind-the-Scenes tours and the like, Chatsworth hosts many other events and gatherings to bring extra money into the Chatsworth House Trust in order to provide money for special projects. We have hosted flower festivals for NAFAS (National Association of Flower Arranging Societies) on several occasions over the years, the most impressive one being a 'Flowers in Celebration' event held in September 1994 to link in with the Tercentenary of the Dukedom in that year. Two of the displays took the form of floral carpets in the

Chapel and in the Painted Hall which involved a total of 76 people working on trestles set up along the office and service passages. Following the tradition of Derbyshire well dressing, flower heads, lichen and tiny cones were inserted into trays of foam that had already been pricked out with the design and were then assembled in the Chapel and Painted Hall, like a giant jigsaw puzzle. As they were working on these trays, we noticed – just in the nick of time – that they had misspelled the Cavendish motto, *Cavendo Tutus* as 'Cavando'. The Flower Festival was an absolute triumph for the women involved, including Inge Hanford, who has been a friend of mine ever since.

NAFAS flower festivals move from one location to another, and rather than wait another ten years for the possibility of the organisation returning to Chatsworth, we decided to create a flower festival ourselves, and this proved so successful that it has now become a regular event. In that first year we had a competition to come up with a title for the event, which was won by our CEO's wife, Sheron Reynolds, with 'Florabundance'. We have engaged the services of renowned flower arranger and demonstrator, Jonathan Moseley, who works with the gardeners and local volunteers to design, install and maintain the displays for the House. The housekeeping team work closely with Jonathan on the designs, advising what can go where, bearing in mind the fragility of some of the historic artefacts and how the flower arrangements will be watered. On installation day we make sure that the 60 or so volunteers don't get lost in the House, that they are safe, don't go up ladders without the necessary training, don't eat or drink on the visitor route and so on.

Chatsworth supports charities by offering the use of the Gardens or Park as a venue for sponsored rides or walks, and the House for other events. We have enjoyed some wonderful occasions over the years including a Blue Peter 'Bring and Buy' sale, coffee mornings, talks, fashion shows and concerts. These mostly take place in the Painted Hall, which has excellent acoustics. The housekeeping team is always involved in the preparation for these events, supervising rehearsals, taking coats on the night and so on. I remember a rehearsal many years ago when Holymoorside Choral Society were giving a concert in aid of Guide Dogs for the Blind. The rehearsal was going well, but there was a constant tapping that was decidedly off-beat. The conductor called the choir to order and asked whoever was tapping to stop, as they were out of time. The rehearsal began again, accompanied by the irritating tapping, and when the conductor stopped the rehearsal again, the tapping continued. Then he realised that it was the guide dog sitting with one of the singers, vigorously wagging its tail against the metal balustrade!

Chatsworth has hosted many different events over the years, including one in July 1999 for the Derbyshire Constabulary. This involved a champagne reception followed by a full house tour for 400 people, and it was a beautiful evening for guests to spill out into the Inner Court and listen to a fantastic steel band whilst they enjoyed the reception.

We had a coffee morning in November 1994 for the Mayor of Chesterfield's Charity appeal and Chesterfield Rotary Club. A lady Labour councillor was celebrating her 60th birthday and asked if it would be possible for her to sweep down the Great staircase in evening dress, on His Grace's arm. Not only did the Duke agree, but he also arranged for a bottle of champagne to be waiting for her at the bottom of the staircase!

I often recall that when I first announced to my friends that I had decided to work at Chatsworth, many of them were less than enthusiastic. 'You must be mad!' one of them cried. 'Who'd want to live in the middle of the countryside where nothing ever happens!' exclaimed another. 'You'll be bored to death in no time!' bewailed a third. Granted, some of the work is routine, but it is also extremely varied and we never know quite what the next day is going to bring.

My current office is in the old Steward's Room. It looks out across the north drive so that the Steward could slip out quickly to receive guests at the front door. Previously my office had been in what was originally the Bake House next to the Confectionery, and is now a staff locker room. One morning, I opened the office door to see a huge mounted head of a Jacob's sheep ram on my desk. Its twisted double horns rose magnificently from his shaggy locks and his baleful yellow eyes fixed mine with an accusatory stare. Resting against him was a little note that read, 'Her Grace thought you would know how to clean this for the Farm Shop'.

What I thought was going to be a routine morning, organising the preparation of the House prior to the arrival of visitors, or perhaps making a start on the timesheets, or thinking about Christmas, which is my usual default job, was not to be. As ever, Chatsworth had presented a new challenge. Taxidermists were contacted regarding the safe cleaning of the ram's fleece – pure soap, and not too much of it. The horns needed some titivation, so I went up to see Margaret at the Farmyard and Adventure Playground to find a bottle of hoof oil. The wooden base board polished up nicely with good old beeswax polish. By the end of the day the ram was ready to go back home and I paged our van driver, Trevor McDowell, to take him back to André at the Farm Shop where he now gazes down imperiously on those entering the butchery department.

Something a little different happened in December 2005, when Peter Sinclair, editor of the Historic Houses Association magazine, asked me if I would write a review of the new and much-expanded edition of the *National Trust Manual of Housekeeping*. Her Grace had done so for the first edition in 1991, and I felt it a great privilege to be following in her footsteps. It was a pleasure to write my enthusiastic endorsement of the immensely helpful, if rather unwieldy, collection of information and advice.

Such a variety of tasks are all in a day's work and they certainly spice up our daily routine. I don't think I have ever spent a single day at Chatsworth where I have been 'bored to death'.

A wonderful opportunity presented itself in the summer of 2011 when the 12th Duke asked me if I would go to Lismore Castle later in the year to meet the housekeeping team and have a look at what they were doing. I needed no second bidding! Lismore Castle is a fairy-tale castle in County Waterford in the Republic of Ireland, and I had long wanted to go and visit, having heard so many stories about it from Henry and Miss Feeney.

Clive took some annual leave in the October and we flew to Cork and hired a car so that we could explore the area in addition to getting to know Lismore. Having left Manchester airport quite early in the morning, we arrived at our bed and breakfast accommodation by late morning and dropped our things off before driving the two miles into the town of Lismore. We had lunch in one of the cafés on the main street, and on hearing our English accents, the friendly proprietor asked if we knew Chatsworth. As soon as we admitted where we were from, she fetched out a copy of Her Grace's book, *The House,* and asked me to sign it! She wouldn't hear of us paying for our lunch, asking only that we sent her a postcard from Chatsworth on our return home, which of course we did. Everywhere we went in the town over the next few days we heard nothing but praise for the Devonshire family.

There is no distinct view of the castle from the centre of Lismore town, but the approach from the Knockmealdown Mountains is stunning. Crossing the 5th Duke's seven-arched bridge into Lismore, there is a dramatic view of the castle on its rocky outcrop, towering above the Blackwater River a hundred feet below. The castle was built in 1185 by King John on the site of a monastery founded by St Carthage, and the Cathedral in Lismore town is dedicated to the saint. It was later bought by Sir Walter Raleigh, who subsequently sold it on to the 1st Lord Boyle. Lord Boyle later became Earl of Cork and it was his descendant, Charlotte Boyle, who inherited Lismore on her father's death in 1753, along with Bolton Abbey, Devonshire House, Burlington House, Chiswick and Londesborough. Charlotte was married to William Cavendish, son of the 3rd Duke of Devonshire, and so all this wealth and property ultimately came into her husband's family. Sadly, she never became Duchess of Devonshire since she died before her husband inherited the Dukedom.

Lismore Castle at this time was a ruin, and remained so until the 6th Duke of Devonshire began restoring it in 1812 with the architect William Atkinson, using stone brought from the Estate quarries in Derbyshire for the dressing stone. Joseph Paxton then added to the south and east wings and the interiors were fitted out by Crace and Pugin. In 1932 the castle was given by the 9th Duke to his younger son, Charles Cavendish, as a wedding present on his marriage to Adele Astaire, dancing partner of her brother Fred. As there were no surviving children from the marriage, on Charles's death, it passed back into the Cavendish family, although Adele was allowed to remain there for the rest of her life. The 11th Duke used to visit every February at the start of the salmon fishing in the River Blackwater, and both the Duke and Duchess would go again in April.

Denis Nevin (the late Joan Coleman's brother), looks after the castle and the Estate, and he and the housekeepers, Patricia and Norma, could not have made Clive and I more welcome. I felt such a strange affinity with Lismore and Denis; we discovered that we had both started working for the Estate in the same year and knew the same family members and guests of the family who had been entertained at both Chatsworth and Lismore. He was delighted when I recognised so many people in the photographs in some of the rooms; it was as though our professional lives had been running on twin paths, both serving the same family, but not knowing each other for all those years.

The castle gardens are also quite magical, and we had a wonderful time exploring them and enjoying the open air sculpture exhibition, including pieces by Antony Gormley and David Nash and the new art gallery that was built within the shell of the castle's long-derelict West Wing in 2007.

The Lismore Estate runs to 10,859 acres, with a further 618 acres of forestry, and now also includes Careysville, a large house situated 16 miles upstream of Lismore on the River Blackwater, which is reputed to have the finest salmon fishing in Ireland. Careysville used to be rented by the 10th Duke during the 1930s, and he bought it when it came up for sale after the war. In her memoirs, Deborah Devonshire describes how her father-in-law, the 10th Duke, was an expert fly-tier, and explains his method like this: 'Once the flies were ready, he lay in the bath imagining he was a salmon, while Edward, the butler, pretending to be a fishing rod, jerked them over his submerged head. The ones the Duke judged most attractive were used on his stretch of the Blackwater in County Cork at the start of the salmon fishing season.'

Clive and I were enchanted by Careysville. It is the most wonderful place. It has a fishing hut by the river that used to be the cricket pavilion at Chatsworth, complete with a wood-burning stove and veranda for picnics by the riverside.

As the number of events at the House increased over the years, so did the demands on the housekeeping team and, like Mrs Dean before me, I needed an assistant to help me. I have been fortunate in having the support of three deputies over the years, together with a fantastic team of housekeeping assistants, from Mrs Link and her colleagues, right through to the present day.

Judy Coggins first came to work as a member of the housekeeping team in 1982, and then became assistant housekeeper. When Judy retired to North Wales, Marjorie Bateman took over the role. I had known Marjorie and her husband Barrie, who worked in the greenhouses, since my early days at Chatsworth. I first got to know her properly when we both volunteered for the church cleaning rota, and were given a slot together. Every six weeks or so, Marjorie and I would put the world to rights as we cleaned the church, and every Tuesday, Marjorie also helped out at the village shop in Edensor. Once her children were at secondary school, I invited her to join the housekeeping team. She was a fantastic worker, utterly dedicated to Chatsworth, and a great member of the team. When Judy decided to retire as assistant housekeeper I offered the job to Marjorie. She was perfect for the role, outwardly quiet and unassuming, yet tenacious for what she thought was the right thing to do. Judy had been a stalwart support and a good friend, and whilst I perfectly understood her decision to retire, I knew I was really going to miss her.

Luckily, when Marjorie announced her retirement, Janet Bitton applied for the position and I was delighted to appoint her. She had first joined the House guiding team in 2007 and helped out with housekeeping when the House was open. Like Marjorie and Judy before her, Janet has been a wonderful assistant and a true friend to me and to Chatsworth. She has revealed a wealth of talents, not least an artistic flair that finds expression in the annual extravaganza that is the 'Chatsworth Christmas'.

8

⚜

Birthday Parties

B irthdays are an excuse for a party in any family, and the Cavendish family is no exception. There are elaborate celebrations for special birthdays, but impromptu parties are always welcomed. Such an occasion took place in 1991 when Her Grace celebrated her 71st birthday. It happened to coincide with the viewing of the recently opened tea room at the Stableyard and staff were invited to see the new facility and to enjoy a cup of tea and a scone. Her Grace was there, not expecting any surprises, but when everyone was present, Jean-Pierre made a dramatic entrance carrying a cake decorated with 71 flaming candles. A spontaneous rendition of 'Happy Birthday' followed, and it was a truly memorable afternoon.

Some birthday parties are just for family, like the one on 1st January 1988 when His Grace celebrated his 68th birthday with a lunch in the Painted Hall for 123 guests. Then, of course, there are the jaw-drop-pingly amazing, out-of-this-world parties that Chatsworth does so very well, like coming-of-age parties.

When the 11th Duke's grandson, William, Earl of Burlington, came of age in July 1990 the Duke held two magnificent parties at Chatsworth to celebrate the event. The first was for all Estate staff and their families, pensioners and tenants – not only from the Chatsworth Estate, but from all the Devonshire estates – some 3,000 guests in all. It is a family tradition to hold a 21st birthday party for the heir to the title, and my parents-in-law could remember going to a similar party organised for the 12th Duke when he came of age in 1965.

Friday, 6th July 1990, was a balmy summer's evening, and between 8pm and 8.30pm we listened to music by the local band, Rhodian Brass, as we queued on the path across the Salisbury lawn, waiting to be greeted by the family at the foot of the Cascade, before entering the wonderful marquees that had been erected for the buffet supper. The party concluded with a magnificent firework display by the Cascade at 10.30pm. The band of the Worcestershire and Sherwood Foresters was there to provide the musical entertainment and to beat the Retreat, along with their regimental mascot, the Derby Ram known as 'Private Derby', resplendent in his dress uniform of a scarlet coat with Lincoln green and gold facings, emblazoned with the regiment's main battle honours and a replica of his India Mutiny Medal and General Service Medal with the Northern Ireland clasp. On his forehead, he wore a silver plate embossed with the regimental cap badges, and on the tops of his horns, a pair of silver protectors to prevent accidental damage to his two handlers, the Ram Major and the Ram Orderly. Since the first Private Derby, there has been a succession of rams serving with the regiment, usually presented in whichever part of the world the regiment was serving, but since 1912 it has been the tradition for the ram to be provided by the Duke of Devonshire from the flock of Swaledale sheep at Chatsworth. Each new ram is trained to the halter at Chatsworth before he is presented. The ram comes back to Chatsworth each year for his annual shearing, and when his marching days are over, he retires back to Chatsworth to be much admired at the farmyard and adventure playground.

On that July evening, once Private Derby and his regimental band had beaten the Retreat at Lord Burlington's party, coaches provided by the Estate arrived at 11pm to return all the guests to Baslow, Pilsley and Edensor, whilst the staff who had travelled from Lismore and East-bourne were accommodated at Earnshaw Hall, one of Sheffield University's halls of residence, and Bolton Abbey staff travelled back to Yorkshire by coach that evening. The Chatsworth staff and pensioners had organised a collection for a birthday present for Lord Burlington, and within the month he had sent a handwritten letter to everyone who had contributed to the gift.

The next day, Saturday 7th July, a second party was held for Lord Burlington's family and friends, with 250 attending a dinner, and a further 800 coming to the dance afterwards. The marquee company began work on 18th June and worked all the daylight hours fitting a marquee and a fully sprung dance floor above the Inner Court and members of the housekeeping team were kept busy going to and fro with enormous pots of tea to keep the workmen happy. In addition to the Inner Court marquee, other tents needed to be built outside, including a vast marquee covering part of the South Lawn to provide the dining area. This was lined with black silk and studded with fairy lights to resemble the night sky, and stage painters had decorated either side of the marquee with Arcadian scenes. The doors at the end of the marquee opened on to the Gardens, where there was a firework display at 1am and a ballet tableau on a stage that had been built over the Canal Pond between the statuary. The Prince of Wales lent his Arabian tent as the sitting out area for the disco. The inside of this tent was truly amazing with colourful hangings, carpets and low tables, and it afforded a great recovery space for those who had been tossed by the bucking Bronco! A separate marquee provided the space for chefs to cook the food for the guests, and then became the rest area for staff after 11.30pm, as up until that time food was available for them up in the Carriage House restaurant.

Chatsworth staff were on security duty in the private rooms of the House, and members of the housekeeping team were involved in attending to coats in the North Entrance Hall as guests arrived and left, and also in providing refreshments for the chauffeurs who were using the coach drivers' room. It was a wonderful opportunity to gaze at the fabulous gowns and jewellery of the guests; one lady arrived in a stunning scarlet off-the-shoulder dress, but we discovered later that she had not actually been invited to the party, but had come along with the photographer she was dating at the time. I think she thought that her own fame would carry it off, and although she was allowed in, Her Grace had the *mot juste* when she said to her, 'How clever of you to know we were having a party!' Her Grace wore a magnificent fuchsia pink Balmain silk ball gown she had also worn for her son's 21st party, 25 years before!

Breakfast was served to the guests and staff at 4am, and the last guest didn't leave until 7am. We were 'dead on our feet', but wouldn't have missed any of it for the world. It was then a case of all hands to the pump to get the House ready for opening again that day. The marquees from Friday night were still in the Gardens and as the Duke and Duchess thought it would be a pity to waste them, the Gardens were opened to visitors free of charge that day and local charities were invited to use the marquee space to sell their goods. All in all, a wonderful weekend.

In 2010, Her Grace celebrated her 90th birthday and as this year also saw the re-opening of the Scots Apartments from the Leicester Landing (renamed as the Guest Bedrooms), an exhibition celebrating her life and achievements was held throughout the rooms and proved hugely popular. We also decided to launch the year of her 90th birthday with an Easter trail in the House for children to follow, with the number of chocolate eggs in various nests around the House all adding up to 90 in total. However, we had to re-think the idea after only two days, replacing the chocolate eggs with foil ones as so many were eaten that Her Grace would have been only two years old in no time!

As both Her Grace's birthday and the annual staff party always fall in March, the Duke decided to have a really special staff party to mark the occasion, and this was held on 5th March 2010. For the first time, it was decided to theme the party, so guests were given the option to dress up if they wished to, the theme being 'Ascot Best'. Everyone made a great effort and there were a lot of very colourful hats, and even a jockey and a horse, which on closer inspection turned out to be my deputy, Janet Bitton and her guest. The entire Stable courtyard had been covered with a marquee for speeches and dancing, with horse racing (betting tickets provided) in the main restaurant. It was a really fun evening, with dancing to The Casablanca Boys and DJ Steve Massam and the presentation of the 10 year long-service awards. The 25 and 40 year service awards used to be presented at the annual staff party, but they are now presented privately at Chatsworth instead.

About a month before the party, I was sitting in my old office off the Confectionery eating my lunch at my desk, when the Duke came in to see me.

'Hello, Christine! Oh! You're eating your lunch, I'll pop back later!'

'No, it doesn't matter, Duke, what can I do for you?' I replied.

'I'll come back in half an hour, don't worry,' he said, and off he went. I then had the next half hour to wonder what he wanted. He duly reappeared and said that he and the Duchess had thought it would be nice if several long-serving members of staff gave their reminiscences of Her Grace at the staff party, and would I consider being one of them?

I felt it was such an honour to be asked, and was delighted to be able to pay tribute to someone I admire so much. Other members of staff to provide their memories of Her Grace were Simon Seligman from marketing, André Birkett from the Farm Shop, Margaret Norris from the Farmyard, Julia Hubbard from the switchboard and Ian Turner, the farm manager. I had the uncertain pleasure of going first, but at least it meant that I was able to enjoy what everyone else had to say. A couple of days after the party I received this handwritten note from the Duke:

> Dear Christine,
>
> Thank you so much for your lovely contribution to the celebrations of my mother's 90th birthday in the Stables on Friday.
>
> You set the tone perfectly and I know that your remarks were much appreciated by my mother – and by everyone else as well.
>
> Sincerely,
>
> Stoker Devonshire

At one time, the staff parties were held in the House, in the Theatre, the Sculpture Gallery, or in the Great Dining Room, but the first staff party in a form similar to those we know today was held in March 1959, when presumably the event had grown to such a degree that it was no longer practical to hold it in the House itself. This new party format in 1959 was for all staff, but not for pensioners, and was held at the Institute (now the Cavendish Club and Cavendish Hall). Grosvenor Caterers supplied the food and the entertainment was provided by the Ken Simmonds Casino Players Band, the Foxhill Singers and a conjuror, Kenneth de Courcey. Arrangements were made for Institute regulars, such as retired staff and tenants not eligible for the party, to use the land agent's office on the first floor for dominoes, cards and games, and the Social Bar for their drinks. These regulars were listed as including my great uncles, Sam and Joe Burdekin.

These early staff parties at the Cavendish Hall involved dancing, with dances like the Valeta, the St Bernard's Waltz, and the Gay Gordons, followed by a buffet, the presentation of the long service awards, and then a disco until 1am. I was always fascinated at the lightness of the dancing from some of the old farmers who attended, like Ken and Margaret Finney and Margaret's sister, Bobby, and her husband Brian, all from Calton Lees. Depending on who was staying at the House, Their Graces would bring guests along to the party, and

I recall a couple of occasions when Prince Charles came with them, unannounced, which caused quite a stir. When I received my own long service award for 25 years' service on 14th March 2003, Henry Coleman received his pair of silver candlesticks for 40 years' service. He was private butler to Their Graces and so highly thought of by the Cavendish family that they all came along to the party to see him receive his award, which made it extra special for the rest of us too.

Over the years, staff working during the 'open season' as guides and in the shops developed such a fondness for working at Chatsworth that many came back year after year, and it seemed unfair that they weren't eligible to attend the annual staff party in March, which was for permanent staff only. This led to the introduction of a second staff party for seasonal staff in November every year. In 2001 when the House stayed open until late December it seemed unnecessary to continue the practice of two parties, and so we introduced one large party every March, held in the Stables. However, in 2012 the Stables complex was opened to the public in January, so the staff parties were moved to the Dome at Buxton.

The staff party in 2014 was also a celebration of the Duke and Duchess's 70th birthdays. In addition to the wonderful meal and venue, we had a fantastic surprise when the Duchess took to the stage and announced that she would like us all to share the Duke's birthday present to her. This was that the live band playing for the whole night would be Jools Holland and his 20-piece Rhythm and Blues Orchestra, complete with guest singers Marc Almond and Melanie C. What an evening we had!

These fantastic parties were wonderful for all those involved, and the more remarkable for being the continuation of the strong tradition of hospitality shown by the Dukes of Devonshire to their staff. The form of these the parties has changed over time – in 1780 there were so many staff that the 5th Duke held a series of parties that consumed 136 gallons of ale, 261 pounds of beef, 264 pieces of bread, 44 pounds of cheese and 100 clay pipes!

9

❧

Behind the Scenes

When the House closes to visitors, it is then possible to get on with all the jobs that are impossible to achieve during the open season. In addition to the deep clean, there is also the opportunity for restoration, conservation, plumbing, wiring and security upgrades. Over the years the projects have been extensive, and although some of them might not have been immediately obvious to the visitor, they have still been incredibly important. Most recently, the Master Plan of the 12th Duke is the ongoing achievement of an exciting ambition to take Chatsworth firmly forward in good heart into the 21st century.

Much of this work has been possible due to the setting up of the Chatsworth House Trust in 1981, after the eventual settlement of the death duties faced by the 11th Duke following his accession to the Dukedom in 1950. With the sudden death of the 10th Duke of Devonshire, His Grace had been obliged to pay 80 per cent of everything he owned in death duties. It was a crippling tax, from which many country houses did not survive. Land was sold, works of art were sold or went to the nation in lieu of death duties, Hardwick Hall was given to the National Trust, and eventually, after 17 years, the debt was paid. The 11th Duke was then able to consider ways in which Chatsworth would be able to survive any future uncertainty, the Estate having previously faced similar, crippling death duties in the earlier part of the 20th century. His Grace sold works of art from the family collection and the money raised formed the endowment for the Chatsworth House Trust which, after three years of negotiations with the government, took over the running of Chatsworth in March 1981 on a 99-year lease. This charitable foundation helps to ensure, for the public benefit, the preservation of the House, its essential contents, the Garden and the Park, and the Duke and Duchess pay a full market rent for the part of the House in which they live. The annual income from the endowment together with the income from visitors to the House and Garden pays for the upkeep of the House and also enables purchases of new works of art and a programme of conservation and restoration to keep the House and Garden in good order.

The ceiling paintings of the State Apartments had suffered damage over the years from leaks in the lead roof above. Melted snow would freeze in the gutters so that fresh snow melt could not run away and would find its way instead through faults in the lead work and cause damage to the ceilings below. Once a six figure sum had been spent on renewing the 1.3 acres of lead work on the roof, the programme of conservation of those ceilings could begin.

This work was tackled by Pauline Plummer and her team and involved the surface cleaning of the painted surface, fixing the areas of flaking paint and cleaning the dirt from the surface of the old varnish. Next, the old varnish was taken off, together with any earlier retouching that had disguised, sometimes very crudely, previous areas of loss or damage. This resulted in areas of bare plaster where there was no paint left at all. Pauline and her team then had to paint over the gaps and fill in the missing pieces of the painted surface, creating a representation of how they thought the artists would have left it 300 years ago. It was painstaking work, at impossibly back-breaking angles, but ultimately with absolutely stunning results.

The painted ceiling in the Great Chamber was painted in 1691-2 by Antonio Verrio, and depicts the *Return of the Golden Age, with Vices destroyed by their opposing Virtues,* which was a reference to the blessings of the reign of William and Mary. One of the three Fates, Atropos, seen cutting the thread of life with her shears is, in reality, a portrait of the 1st Duke's housekeeper, Mrs Hackett, with whom Verrio was at odds, although no one knows why!

In addition to the restoration of the State Apartments, Pauline and her team also worked their way through the other painted ceilings of the House: the Chapel, the Sabine Room and the Painted Hall. Once this was all complete, Pauline decided that it was time to hang up her painting smock and retire.

Since Pauline's retirement, Brian Cardy has been the restorer for other projects, such as the cleaning and conservation of the Painted Hall walls in 2005-6. These paintings depict scenes from the life of Julius Caesar on the east wall, and his graphic assassination on the north wall. They were painted in oils by Louis Laguerre and his assistants in 1694 on lath and plaster, over timber studding attached to the stone walls. As Brian's restoration progressed, it became increasingly obvious that a narrow strip of original plaster along the bottom edge of the paintings on the east and north walls had been cut away, replastered and repainted, probably in 1834 when the 6th Duke added new galleries around the walls to provide access between the Oak Stairs and the Great Stairs, after replacing the original horseshoe-shaped lower section with a single flight of stairs at the south end of the Painted Hall. At the same time the 6th Duke cut out two sections of the north wall paintings at each side of the *Death of Caesar* to create arched entrances from the Oak staircase through to the newly installed galleries.

In 1911, the 9th Duke replaced the lower fight of the Great Stairs yet again and took down the 6th Duke's gallery that obscured the view of Laguerre's painting on the east wall, and rebuilt the west gallery. The last recorded restoration of the wall paintings took place in 1936, when the ceiling was found to be collapsing due to death watch beetle damaging the beams above. Major structural work was necessary to re-attach the lath and plaster ceiling, followed by the restoration of the ceiling paintings by Mr Constantine of Sheffield City Art Galleries, and subsequently by Pauline Plummer and her team.

Brian Cardy's work was begun in January 2005 using a team of six conservators, who cleaned about two-thirds of the east wall before House opening. The remainder of the work was finished in 2006, when visitors were able to see first-hand what was happening on closed circuit television and begin to understand how some of the admission money was spent.

In addition to the painted walls and ceilings, the Chatsworth House Trust has enabled the restoration of other works of art, including the carvings in the State Apartments, which were first worked by local craftsman, Samuel Watson, and the London carvers, Lobb, Young and Davis, and which were completed in the very early 1700s. Years ago they fell prey to extensive damage by woodworm, and although the carvings are carefully vacuumed and brushed during the annual deep clean of the House, it was not sufficient. One busy Spring Bank Holiday, a piece of carving fell from an overdoor narrowly missing a visitor passing underneath, and alerted us to the fact that something needed to be done. Consequently, in the following winter of 1991, Neil Trinder conducted a major programme of work, surveying and consolidating these carvings. Neil took extensive photographs of all the carvings and carefully examined each section, strengthening weak areas with glue and replacing them so that although some of the pieces were actually hollow where the worm had eaten them away, at least they were made safe against future degradation.

Another programme of conservation was carried out on the hand painted Chinese wallpaper of the Scots Apartments. When the paper was first installed in the 1830s, birds and flowers from left over pieces of paper were cut out and stuck on top to give a three-dimensional effect, and over the years some of these had fluttered down off the paper and needed to be re-affixed. During the process, as the conservator cleaned areas of the paper, she again provided a written assessment and photographs so that we now have something by which to compare the condition of the wallpaper year after year.

Further restoration work inside the House has included the conservation of the Gumley mirrors in the State Apartments, which began in November 1998 and was completed just in time for House opening in 1999. These mirrors were commissioned by the 1st Duke of Devonshire when he built the suite of State Apartments at Chatsworth during the rebuilding of Bess of Hardwick's Elizabethan house in the late 16th and early 17th centuries. The 1st Duke was hopeful that King William and Queen Mary would visit him at Chatsworth and was determined to have a suite of State Apartments grand enough in which to receive them, and so the south front of the Elizabethan house was rebuilt in order to achieve that. Sadly for the 1st Duke, William and Mary never came to visit, and it was Queen Victoria who was actually the first monarch to stay at Chatsworth. The furnishing of these State Apartments was just as important as their architectural appearance, and the two magnificent pieces of mirrored glass were a demonstration of the wealth and taste of the Duke. The two pieces were made by the best craftsman of the day, John Gumley, who had produced similar pieces for the royal palaces. He etched his name into one of the Chatsworth mirrors, together with the date of their completion: 'John Gumley, May 17th 1703'. Each piece of plate glass is surrounded by over 300 pieces of blue and plain glass set in an intricate pattern depicting rosettes of flowers and the coat of arms of the 1st Duke and Duchess of Devonshire. Over 300 years the wooden framework had become dry, brittle and damaged by woodworm, and pieces of glass had dropped off.

The Chatsworth House Trust requested three quotations for the restoration as it was likely to be expensive, but as there were very few people capable of doing the job it was agreed that Patricia Jackson and her team from West Dean College in Sussex would come to Chatsworth and work on the mirrors over two winters. It was impossible to take the mirrors away as they were too fragile and could not even be laid flat, as the weight might have caused the glass to fracture. Sean Doxey (then House clerk of works) and his team made special easels for them to be lowered onto so that they could be dismantled piece by piece and the delicate patterns traced onto a huge sheet of tracing paper on a large table put up in the room. Missing pins were replaced and some old pieces of glass were re-silvered and new ones made to replace those that were missing. This involved bringing an elderly gentleman in North Wales out of retirement, since he was the only man that Patricia knew who would be able to achieve the exact shade of blue required to match the original pieces. An added complication was the fact that the old method of silvering a mirror involved the use of mercury, a highly toxic substance, so careful risk assessments had to be completed to ensure there were no accidents. The account books at Chatsworth tell us that the two mirrors originally cost the 1st Duke £100 each and to have both of them conserved cost the Chatsworth House Trust £80,000.

In late 1993 an ambitious textiles plan was begun to make new curtains for the private dining room (and later, for the Great Dining Room). The original curtains of dark red silk damask were installed by the 6th Duke in around 1830, and in 1993 David Walters of Sudbury in Suffolk was commissioned to recreate this original fabric. Over two years, he succeeded in producing an almost exact copy and the textiles team then had the daunting task of making the curtains for the four windows, plus all the swags and tails to a greater depth than the originals. Each curtain was edged with a wide border of red satin, the join being covered with an elaborate four-inch-wide red and gold braid, specially woven by Nottingham Braids, based in Derby. The whole curtain was then lined and interlined before being bound with narrow gold braid. The entire project involved half a mile of machine stitching, 310 yards of hand-sewing, and the weight of drapes for each window was 64lbs. Her Grace invited all the people who had been involved in the project to tea in the private rooms at Chatsworth, including the designers and weavers from Suffolk and the braid makers from Derby, who were thrilled to see their handiwork in place. The lady who did the actual weaving had retired, but as she was the only one who knew how to work the particular loom required to do the job, she had agreed to do the work. Although she had woven fabrics used in prestigious buildings all over the world, it was the first time she had ever seen the finished project installed, so she was delighted to do so at Chatsworth.

Activity behind-the-scenes has never been confined to the inside of the House, and in sharing Chatsworth with visitors throughout my working life I have always found it of interest to pay attention to work in hand outside as well as indoors.

The area behind the Carriage House Restaurant was known as The Paddocks for many years because it was the area where the carriage horses would be turned out to graze at night. In the 1950s the area was no longer needed for horses, and instead became the location for growing vegetables, fruit and cut flowers for the House. Chatsworth's original kitchen garden at Barbrook, whose walls the young Joseph Paxton had scaled in 1826, ultimately became the current caravan site. Between 1991 and 1993 the Paddocks was developed into a more formal Kitchen Garden with a view to opening it up for visitors, and it has proved to be one of the most popular areas of the Gardens. My old allotment was lost with this new development, but as I was living in Edensor by then I now had my own garden for growing vegetables. Her Grace had a lovely little garden shed with its own veranda erected up in this 'new' Kitchen Garden, with the intention of sitting up there to do her writing, well away from the distractions of the House.

Around the same time, a programme of restoration of Flora's Temple took place between November 1992 and March 1993. The Temple was originally built as a Bowling Green House in the 1st Duke's gardens to the south-west of the House and was moved to its present site on the north east corner of the House in 1765. The Derbyshire weather and acid rain took a heavy toll over many years, causing spalling and erosion on the columns, balustrades and blocks. The lead work on the roof was also a worry and the whole building was suffering from rising and falling damp. The repair of some of the stonework and introduction of some new pieces was carried out by H & W Sellors Ltd from Bakewell, and MacDonalds of Leicester installed the damp course, whilst Norman and Underwoods of Leicester renewed the lead work on the roof. The sculpture of Flora had been situated in the 1st Duke's Rose Garden and once she had also been conserved by Paul Giudici, a stone conservator from Wales, she was moved back to Flora's Temple, with the help of Tony Dore from the farms department and his tractor and front loader.

Impressive conservation work on the Chatsworth waterworks has also taken place over the years, and the Cascade House was restored in the early 1990s. The plan had originally been to just replace the lead capping on the stepped roof, but when the lead was removed it was discovered that the stone underneath had crumbled away, so that had to be replaced, which more than doubled the original estimated cost. The Cascade House was designed by Thomas Archer, the architect of the north front of the House, who also designed the Temple, which was completed in 1711 with carved embellishments by Samuel Watson. The Cascade House has marvellous views down the hillside and across towards Edensor, and the intention of the 1st Duke was that whilst his visitors were admiring the view, a gardener would go behind the building and turn on a tap feeding water to the holes in the floor of the Cascade House so that guests were taken by surprise.

The work on the Cascade House was followed during the winters of 1994-6 by the restoration of the cascade steps. These were built in 1696 to the design of a French hydraulics engineer, Grillet, who had produced the decorative waterworks for Le Notre and Louis IV in France. Grillet designed the Chatsworth Cascade so that each set of steps was placed in such a way that a different sound was made as the water flowed over them, but only six years after it was originally installed, it was taken up and re-laid to give a longer and steeper run of steps. The 6th Duke re-laid it yet again in the 1800s to line it up with the House, and had a tunnel built under it in the mid-1800s for the coal road. This ran under the Cascade, giving access to the boilers for Paxton's Great Conservatory without the activity being visible from the House. The north end of this tunnel has also been completely rebuilt as there had been major subsidence due to blocked drains.

The Cascade was restored using 35 tons of new stone from Stanton Moor Quarry to replace the old worn slopes and it took 10,000 man-hours to rebuild the 24 steps and to restore the waterworks on the Cascade House to their full effect. Carl Wragg did the carved dressing of the stone, attracting the attention of the media as the project drew to a close. A film crew came to record the work and to interview the person who had been doing such a fascinating and unique job.

'What has it been like, Carl, to be involved with a project like this?'

'Well, it were a bit monotonous…' was Carl's response.

In the years since the accession of the 12th Duke and Duchess in 2004, visitors and staff alike have grown accustomed to the new acquisitions of sculpture and the sculpture loans in the gardens, but it was actually the 11th Duke and Duchess who began that trend in 1991, when Dame Elisabeth Frink's *Warhorse* became the first important sculpture to be added to the gardens for 150 years. There was a lot of discussion beforehand about where it was to be sited, as it was so large and heavy that the sandstone base had to be put in place well in advance of the bronze sculpture being carefully lowered into position. Her Grace stood on the roof with a two-way radio whilst the team in the garden stood with another, together with a life-sized cardboard cut-out of the sculpture so that she could direct them, 'Left a bit, right a bit, no, let's turn him round!'

The horse was first placed at the south end of the Canal Pond, and I always thought it rather rude that the horse should be positioned with its bottom facing the House, but I was told that it was because he is a war horse, and needed to face outwards so that he could be on the lookout for any invaders. Her Grace even had a couple of trees pruned so that he had a clear view down the valley.

A great deal happens behind-the-scenes at Chatsworth, both inside and outdoors, but we had never really considered using that as a means of income. However, all that was set to change!

On 6th November 1994, six different WI markets in Nottinghamshire joined together to celebrate their 75th anniversary in a special day at Southwell Minster School, with market stalls, demonstrations and exhibitions. The day proved to be so successful for the 75 members taking part, and so lucrative that they were left with an excess of funds. They then wondered how they should use the money, as the WI is not supposed to be a profit-making concern. They decided to use the proceeds to benefit as many members as possible, and that whatever it was spent on should be educational but also fun at the same time. A letter was written by the WI committee to Her Grace to enquire into the possibility of a Behind-the-Scenes tour for 75 to 100 people, and the committee subsequently came to Chatsworth to discuss the idea with Simon Seligman, then the House education officer. In this way our Behind-the-Scenes events were born and have been hugely popular ever since. That first event was held on 15th May 1995 for 75 people and we offered four different activities, with the group being divided equally and moving between the sessions, with a leisurely lunch in the middle of the day. I presented four separate talks about housekeeping, Christine Thomson spoke four times about the work of the textiles department, and Simon Seligman gave the group an illustrated talk about how the House was run. Dennis Hopkins, the retired head gardener, took four tours of the greenhouses, including the care of the vines which had been one of his first jobs when he started work at Chatsworth as a boy in the 1930s. He was given a pair of scissors and told to thin out the grapes – a job he continued doing until the end of his career, still using the same pair of scissors.

The whole event was so successful and provided such positive feedback, that we decided to explore the idea of running similar tours for general visitors, which could be booked in advance either by a group or by individuals. However, following the experience with the Nottinghamshire WI, we decided that four sessions was rather a lot to fit in and did not leave sufficient time in the day for participants to explore the House and Gardens afterwards. It was therefore decided to offer three sessions: a talk, a tour, and a demonstration, and we ran free testing days with staff to provide feedback before we launched the idea properly. I remember going down to the Old Park in one such group on 4th December 1995 with the now retired Domain Supervisor, David Robinson, and we had the most wonderful time. It had snowed quite heavily, lending a magical atmosphere to the whole morning as we trod through virgin snow and looked out for signs of badgers and deer. The snow had drifted up against the trees, and David made us really think about some of the old oaks that had been there since before the Spanish Armada. This 190 acres of Old Park is the only part of the Park that is not generally open to visitors, so that the herds of red and fallow deer can have somewhere sheltered to graze and breed. Since the 1950s, fallen trees have been left to lie where they fall, providing a habitat and food for insects, invertebrates and birds.

In the years since those first Behind-the-Scenes tours, many different days have been planned for various groups, giving a valuable insight into the managing of a House like Chatsworth, and they have all proved to be a great success. Housekeeping demonstrations have been part of the portfolio of events since the outset, and when I first told my family that I would be doing a demonstration about housekeeping, Michael, aged eight at the time, looked perplexed and said, 'But there's nothing to it, Mum! You just pick up a duster and find someone to give it to!'

Fate provided us with something new to talk about when, in the winter of 1998, a surprise discovery was made in the passage outside the Joiners' Shop. Access was required to some built-in cupboards in order to install sprinkler systems in the locality, and Sean asked me for the cupboard keys. I had never had the use of the cupboards and, as it turned out, neither had the joiners, plumbers or the electricians. As no keys could be found, the six cupboards were broken into and what wonderful finds lay inside – a vast array of 19th century copper and pewter moulds all wrapped in newspaper dated 1939. It would seem that in their haste to prepare the House for the arrival of the 300 Penrhos College girls and their 26 pianos, the Chatsworth staff had only two weeks to clear everything away, and so the bulk of the Kitchen paraphernalia was wrapped up in the newspaper of the day and locked into the built-in cupboards just outside the Kitchen. When Chatsworth was occupied once more as a family home in the 1950s, the 11th Duke and Duchess very sensibly had a new kitchen installed beneath their private dining room so that food had at least half a chance of arriving hot at the dining table. What had been the old Victorian Kitchen became the Joiners' Shop, and no one ever needed to go into the cupboards again until nearly 60 years later.

We had a wonderful time in the housekeeping department going through the boxes, making an inventory of the contents and then packing them all away again, this time in acid free tissue paper. Some items were mundane: an old glass milk bottle and an old empty jar of Robertson's marmalade, whilst others were more interesting, like the empty tin of Mazawatee tea. I looked into the history behind some of the more unusual objects to spice up my Behind-the-Scenes tours and discovered that the name Mazawattee tea was registered in 1887 by the four sons of John Boon Densham, owners of the tea firm called Lees and Densham. The name came from the Hindi word for luscious, and the Ceylonese word for garden, and for 50 years Lees and Densham were leaders in the tea industry, largely through their advertising success. They had a long term contract with all the major railways which enabled them to place large advertisements on virtually every platform in the country.

There was also an old can-opener with a bull's head business end and a handle made from cow's horn and I found out that tinned food actually arrived in Britain in the 1840s, when housewives were advised to open the tins with a hammer and chisel! Subsequently specific tools were made, one of the earliest being of cast iron in the shape of a bull's head.

There were several cups made from horn, which feature in a painting in the art collection of the Steward, where he stands filling one of the horn cups from the tap on the barrel that used to trundle on its little trolley the length of the table in the Servants' Hall so that staff could draw off their daily ration of beer. On one side of the trolley is painted 'The Servants' Hall, Chatsworth', and on the other side it reads, 'Be merry and wise'.

Box upon box of small copper pattie-tins and pastry moulds were carefully unwrapped, together with pewter moulds and sorbetières. The ice cream moulds were beautiful, and in all shapes and sizes – peaches, figs, roses, asparagus shoots, lemons, oranges and pineapples. It was obvious they were a mould for something, but it was pure guesswork what that something might be, until I showed them to Ivan Day, the food historian, who I had asked to make an Elizabethan banquet for our Christmas displays one year, not long after the discovery of the '1939 Cupboard'. He took one look at the little pewter moulds and said immediately, 'They're ice-cream garnitures'. He explained that there would have been one each for all the ladies at the dining table, and a larger mould to the same design that the gentlemen would have shared. It was good to find out what they were for, and Ivan was also a great help in explaining what some of the other objects were too. I became fascinated by the way in which the Victorians made their ice-cream, and was lucky enough to help Ivan make ice-cream on a couple of occasions: once when he was doing a food and drink programme for Radio 4, which we recorded entirely in the Chatsworth cellar copper store, and even made our ice-cream down there; and on another occasion for a programme about the royal progress of Queen Victoria via the food she ate at grand country houses, in which Chatsworth was the dessert course. On this occasion, Ivan made the sorbet swan he had told me about many times, using an ice cream mould of his own in the shape of the swan.

Ivan told me that the sorbets and ice-creams would have been made in the Confectionery, or Still Room, not the Kitchen, as that would have been too hot for making ices. The cream and sugar would be placed inside the sorbetière, which would have been turned back and forth inside a wooden ice pail containing ice and salt, the salt being added to the ice to make the temperature drop. Every now and then the Still Room maid would have lifted the sorbetière lid and stirred the ice-cream with the spaddle, and then put the lid back on and continued turning. Each sorbetière had its own made-to-measure spaddle, which is a long wooden-handled spoon, the bowl of which is made of pewter and has a curvature made to exactly fit the shape of the corresponding sorbet-ière. After about 40 minutes the ice-cream would be ready, then coloured if necessary, before being packed into its mould. In the case of the swan, when it was ready to be served it would have been turned out of its mould onto a platter in the Still Room and then carried up to the Dining Room. In the time it took to carry it there, hoar frost would have formed on the surface of the ice so that a feathered swan was presented at the table.

In our cupboards we also discovered some tiny little Victorian vegetable scoops for shaping garnitures for soup, and a real puzzle of a spoon about three inches long and with a circular bowl of about an inch diameter containing four holes, which we pondered over for ages. Whilst we were making our inventory of all the objects, almost everyone working in the House visited the Confectionery at some point every day to see what we had uncovered, and they were all foxed by the little spoon – until Michael Kokuciak, the cook came in. 'Oh!' he exclaimed straightaway. 'I see you've got a quail egg separator!' We all wondered why we hadn't thought of that before!

Another unusual item was a set of small copper balls, each comprising two halves, one half with a small spout at the top. We had no idea what these were for until Ivan Day told us that they were called 'ballettes'. He explained that the cook hard-boiled as many eggs as were needed, and then used a cutter about the size and shape of a Polo mint to cut shapes from the hard-boiled egg white. Next, using a different cutter, small discs were cut out of the hard-boiled egg yolks about the size of the hole in the middle of a Polo mint. Each disc of egg white was then filled with a smaller disc of egg yolk and the inside of each half of the ballette was lined with these. Pâté was then packed into each half and the two halves were clipped together to form a complete ball. Finally, aspic jelly was poured in through the central spout and then left to set, after which the ball of stuffed hard-boiled egg and pâté could be removed and served at the dining table as a starter, with one or two ballettes for every guest. What an enormous amount of work!

Behind-the-Scenes tours always used to include a visit to the Theatre roof, which has extensive views across the Estate, taking in the Coronation Wood to the north, which was planted in November 1953 to mark the coronation of Queen Elizabeth II. There are two blocks of plantings, depicting the letters E and R, originally made up of light coloured sycamore on a background of dark Norway spruce. After 35 years, the letters were no longer clearly defined, so both plantings were felled in 1989 and the wood was replanted using purple (copper) beech and Lawson cypresses for the background. One American visitor on a Behind-the-Scenes tour noticed the plantation from the roof of the House and made the observation, 'Gee, I didn't know the TV series was so popular in England!'

In addition to providing the funding for restoration projects, the income from visitor admission and from Chatsworth House Trust investments enabled other purchases to be made, such as the Gainsborough painting of Georgiana, the famous wife of the 5th Duke of Devonshire, which was purchased on 13th July 1994. In its day it was the most famous painting in the world, having been stolen, cut down and at one point, disappearing for many years. One day in spring 1998 Peter Day was searching through the archives for a particular letter from the 7th Duke in order to answer an enquiry, when he came across a sequence of letters regarding the sale in 1876 of this same painting. The 7th Duke's daughter, Louisa, went to view the painting at Christie's and tried to persuade her father to buy it, but even after several letters of persuasion he only allowed his picture dealer to bid up to £2,500 for it. Straight after the sale Louisa wrote to her father, 'The picture has gone for £10,650! I am glad it has gone for such a preposterous price, for it would have made it folly for you to buy it.'

This was then the highest price ever paid for a picture, bought by a young Bond Street dealer, William Agnew. The painting had quite a history, as many years prior to its sale, it had been cut down in size by an earlier owner, to fit above a fireplace (or so it is thought). The fame now attached to the painting following the astounding amount it had fetched at auction, prompted the notorious international crook, Adam Worth, to plot to steal it, planning to blackmail William Agnew into putting up a bond to secure the release from prison of Worth's brother. On the night of 25th May 1876, Worth employed another thief, Joe Elliott, to act as a look out whilst he climbed on another accomplice's shoulders, wriggled through the gallery window and cut the picture off its stretcher. Using the end of the velvet cord which kept back the crowds who had flocked to see the painting in Agnew's gallery, Worth then daubed the picture with paste onto which he fastened paper and then, having rolled it in the correct way, face side outwards, he lowered the picture through the window and scrambled out the same way he had come in. Despite a series of demands from the thief and the receipt through the post of strips of canvas from the painting, Agnew's refused to accede to Worth's demands and the story petered out.

However, in 1901, following a tip-off and the payment of a reward, the painting was recovered for Agnew's by Pinkertons Agents in Chicago and Morland Agnew, William Agnew's son, was there to identify it. He wrote,

> *Two minutes sufficed to convince me that it was the Duchess. It makes me weep to see how the canvas has been cut. It is, alas, much mutilated, the outside having been cut away to enable the thief to pack it more*

easily, but the face, which is of wonderful beauty, is unhurt, and, mutilated as it is, the picture is still of immense value and of the highest interest.

Once it had been recovered, Agnew's sold the portrait to the American millionaire collector Pierpont Morgan and it remained with his descendants until its sale at Sotheby's in July 1994, when it was bought by the Chatsworth House Trust, restored to its former glory, and brought back to Chatsworth, where it belonged. In the summer of 1998, Peter was able to show the letters to the visiting daughter and son-in-law of the Pierpont Morgan descendant, whose death had precipitated the portrait's sale and its return to Chatsworth.

Other important paintings purchased by the Trust have included a painting of William III, bought in December 2009. It had long been recognised that Chatsworth needed a portrait of King William, who had granted the first Dukedom of Devonshire, (and for whose anticipated royal visit the State Apartments had been created) and so the purchase of this missing link has made the telling of the Chatsworth story much more visual for our visitors.

Winter is the time to prepare for the season ahead, not only for objects on the visitor route, but also for other commitments. In 1997 Her Grace was getting ready for a talk she was due to give at Hardwick Hall about her memories of it after it had been given to the National Trust in lieu of death duties in 1959, but whilst the Duke's grandmother, Duchess Evelyn, was still living there. She invited a few people along to give feedback on the talk and I remember enjoying it very much. It was held on a snowy afternoon in the Stag Parlour. Amongst those attending were Judy Coggins, Mavis Cooke (another member of our team), Maud Barnes (Her Grace's lady's maid), and Her Grace's elder daughter, Lady Emma and Lady Emma's daughter, Stella and her husband David. It seemed bizarre to have Stella jumping up to make tea for us, and Her Grace gave a fascinating lecture, making us laugh when she talked about the dog races they used to have in the Long Gallery at Hardwick when they were visiting Duchess Evelyn.

In the autumn of October 2005 the Prince of Wales asked if we would consider hosting Prince William for a couple of weeks so that he could have some work experience on a country estate. It was a great pleasure as well as a privilege to have him working with us, and he certainly came across as a delightful young man. He came for two weeks, staying in the Hunting Tower, and he spent time with different departments on the Estate: helping in the Gardens, making sausages in the Farm Shop, making mince pies in the Carriage House restaurant, checking wildlife with the game keepers, working in the Farmyard mucking out, and with the joiners in the House. His time with the joiners coincided with a charity ballet in the Chatsworth Theatre for a local charity, Helen's Trust, which provides care at home for terminally ill patients registered in one of five local practices in Baslow, Bakewell, Eyam, Hope and Tideswell. Helen's Trust had arranged for dancers from the Bolshoi Ballet to perform *The Golden Spinning Wheel*, an original ballet with music by Dvořák, on two consecutive nights. However, when the dancers arrived two days before the performance, they announced that the stage was not long enough for the principal dancer, Alexander Voitugue, to make his first leaping entrance, and the stage would have to be extended. All day the joiners and Prince William trooped up and down the stairs to the Theatre with the wood for the stage, passing through the Orangery Shop as they did so. We noticed several people give a second glance to one of the young men, wood across his shoulders, walking through the Orangery, before shaking their heads. It couldn't be him… could it?

One event we used to look forward to every summer was the 11th Duke's Heywood Hill prize giving. His Grace was the major shareholder in the London Bookshop, Heywood Hill, and in late June 1995 he inaugurated an annual award of £10,000 from his own pocket for a lifetime's contribution to the enjoyment of books. The presenter of that first prize was Sir Tom Stoppard, and the prize-winner on that occasion was the octogenarian biographer and novelist, Patrick O'Brian, who, by a happy coincidence the week before, had been awarded the CBE for services to literature. Other winners have included Michael Frayn and Jane Gardam, and presenters have included P.D. James, John le Carré and J.K. Rowling. The event, which entailed lots of preparation, was always quintessentially English, with marquees on the South Front lawn, tea and sandwiches, Pimms, a local jazz band and the brass band from Lady Manners School in Bakewell… and the weather was always perfect!

Our younger son Michael played the tuba in the Lady Manners School brass band and in 2002 when J.K. Rowling presented the prize, the children were told that she had agreed to autograph any of her books they would like to bring along. She was endlessly patient with them, even when some brought not just one, but half a dozen books. Michael has a lovely comment above her signature in his book, 'Cool glasses Michael!' which made his day. She presented a signed broomstick before she left, which has been exhibited in the House on numerous occasions, and also another to be used to raise money for Pilsley fair which was won by the Chatsworth plumber's son.

10

≼

Dining at Chatsworth

Chatsworth, what a grand place to dine! And yet not always very grand, for in the 'old days', when I was living in the House before we were married, impromptu meals for friends and family were commonplace, although my friends always found it strange that they didn't just ring my front door bell, but had to wait while the Lodge man rang through to summon me to escort them up to the flat. Once I moved from the bedsit to Henry's old flat, the view out across the Park was always much admired and I remember many occasions when one could see the deer grazing on the west side of the river above the Cedar Bank. One morning I was enjoying breakfast, looking out across the Park and thinking how lucky I was to have such an amazing view from my breakfast table, when there was a sudden crack of rifle fire and one of the deer I had just been admiring fell to the ground. It was a shock but I understood that however beautiful they look, the deer need to be culled in order to maintain the overall fitness of the herd. There is a limit on how many deer can be healthily sustained in a finite area of parkland...and of course, the venison sells well at the Farm Shop.

Not long after Jean-Pierre came to live in the House he decided to have a fondue party in his little flat and Diane, Andrew the footman, Maud, Her Grace's ladysmaid, and Clive and I joined him for a hilarious evening. Always the perfect chef, no matter what the event, Jean-Pierre produced magnificent food, seemingly without any effort.

The 11th Duke and Duchess loved to entertain, and I remember an occasion when the Italian ambassador was a guest at Chatsworth, and Her Grace received a phone call from Home Farm to say that a favourite

Shetland pony had gone into labour. The Duchess was then dressed for dinner in her Balmain ball gown, but she went off in her blue Mini Clubman to see the birth for herself, returning just in time for dinner.

Politicians, family members, artists, actors, musicians, television celebrities, members of the royal family – Chatsworth has played host to them all, and all with equal flair, attention to detail, a sense of grandeur and warmth of welcome.

In 1994, His Grace decided to invite friends from The Society of Dilettanti (a club he belonged to that had been founded in 1743), to dine at Chatsworth. The dinner was to take place on 6th October, with 34 to be seated at the dining table. At that time the table in the private dining room was unable to accommodate that number of guests, so His Grace, ever mindful of not wanting to make extra work for his staff, asked if we would be able to do something for him in the Great Dining Room, although he knew that at that time, the table in the Great Dining Room was not large enough either. However, underneath the Theatre stairs were the leaves and base of a spare table that was considerably longer, so we fetched it out to have a look at it. Two days before the dinner party, the joiners and housemen assembled the table in the Painted Hall before the visitors arrived, that being the only indoor space large enough to house it, and Her Grace came along to see the work and to make sure that it was comfortable and at the right height. Once the table passed muster, it was taken down, polished, and moved to the Great Dining Room, replacing the existing table.

We knew that the old tablecloth from the Great Dining Room was neither long enough nor wide enough and as Her Grace was keen that the cloth should hang nearly to the floor, we laid two identical cloths on the table and overlapped them. Then the lightest amongst us crawled the length of the table stitching the two cloths together. Once that was done, another cloth was laid over the top of them both to hide the join, and then Stella Mellors, the private housekeeper, and Barbara Burchby, the gardens secretary, stitched swags of ivy around the table sides. Next, the table had to be laid, and the unfortunate silver steward, Ian Fraser-Martin, had to try to reach the centre of the table to place the enormous silver candelabra in position. White socks were quickly found for him so that he could pad about on top of the table in his stocking feet to position the heavy silver with his customary precision.

Finally, the gardeners brought in a magnificent potted vine as a centrepiece. It was planted in a huge moss-covered pot and the gardeners tied extra bunches of grapes onto it with raffia. Her Grace was so excited with the effect that she sent for His Grace's sister, Lady Elizabeth Cavendish, to come across from Edensor to view the table. I was told to send for Clive and the boys to come and admire it, and Jean-Pierre had to summon Diane and their boys to see it, together with others in the House. The table looked truly magnificent. The lucky guests dined from Sèvres porcelain for the first course, silver for the main course, and Berlin china and gold plate for the pudding. We all heaved such a sigh of relief when the whole evening had been a success but the Duke had enjoyed it so much that he invited the Roxburghe Club to a similar event the following year, so we had to do it all again.

About a month before the Dilettanti party we had been sorting out the contents of some old dustsheet cupboards, where I had found a pile of table napkins in amongst them. The napkins appeared to be in good condition and with the forthcoming dinner party in mind, I sent three dozen away to the laundry to see what could be done with them. They looked amazing when they came back, the silky soft linen shining and showing off the pattern in the damask of the fabric to full advantage. The Cavendish snake and coat of arms were in each corner and also in the centre of the napkin. Each napkin had an embroidered laundry mark in one corner, including the number 72, the number in the set (and I had found all 72 of them), and the date, 1872. I couldn't wait to show them to Her Grace and to ask her if they would be suitable for the dinner, but she declined saying, 'Well, they are lovely Christine, but I can't bear the thought of ladies wiping their lipstick on them!'

Another magnificent party was held in the private dining room on 28th February 1996, when Clive and I were fortunate enough to be invited. The occasion was a retirement party for Eric Oliver, the comptroller of the House. He had moved with his family to Chatsworth in 1939 at the age of eight from Ashford-in-the-Water, when his father began working for the 10th Duke of Devonshire. Eric started at Chatsworth in 1945 as an apprentice joiner and ultimately became head house carpenter in 1962, then assistant comptroller, and finally comptroller when Denis Fisher retired in 1979. Eric was asked to invite whoever he liked to the party, from within the immediate House staff and his own family, but what he did not know was that Her Grace had asked the joiners to make a horseshoe-shaped table instead of the traditional long dining table. I don't know how they managed it, but somehow they did so without Eric finding out, so that it was a real surprise for him when he entered the private dining room on the evening of the party. Of course Her Grace asked for the table cloth to be wide enough to almost touch the floor, so it became the challenge for the housekeeping team who had only rectangular cloths that could not be cut as they were all historic fabrics.

Chatsworth is renowned for its camellias and the Duke wins prizes every year for the magnificent blooms produced in the glasshouses, so it was an inspired idea for Their Graces to ask the gardeners to bring in a magnificent potted camellia to be the centrepiece at Eric's dinner, placed on a plinth in the middle of the horseshoe. The food, of course, was excellent, with Jean-Pierre producing a starter of poached egg and watercress sauce, followed by noisettes of lamb with mushroom mousse and a green salad, and chocolate fondant with pistachio ice-cream for pudding. As Her Grace was anxious that the private kitchen and dining room staff should be able to attend the dinner themselves, Jean-Pierre arranged for the Carriage House restaurant staff to do the cooking and the waiting on, so that he and Diane, and Henry the butler and his wife Joan could enjoy the dinner with everyone else. The hardest thing of the whole evening was persuading Henry to sit down – he said it just didn't feel right for him to be sitting down in the dining room where he was usually waiting at table!

I remember that evening with such pleasure. It was such a tangible illustration of the closeness between the family and their staff, that we should sit down at the same private family dining table and enjoy a wonderful evening together. It was something really special and, I imagine, probably not commonplace in other stately homes.

The same family spirit was evident when the 11th Duke and Duchess gave a dinner for Pauline Plummer to celebrate her completion of the programme to clean and restore the paintings that cover the walls and ceilings of nine major rooms and staircases at Chatsworth. Pauline began the work in 1985 and it has actually involved cleaning and restoring 25,000 square feet of paintings. All those who had helped Pauline in this vast project were invited and it was a very happy occasion. The invitation Clive and I received from Her Grace was as follows:

31st January

We are giving a little dinner in honour of Pauline Plummer to mark the sixteen years of restoration work she and her team will have completed.

This will be on Thursday 22nd February, 7.45pm for 8pm, dress informal. My husband and I do so hope you will join us. We know it would give Pauline great pleasure if you could be here.

It was a lovely evening, with circular tables placed in the private dining room, and the dinner served from a buffet table at one end of the room. Following the first course, His Grace announced, 'Let's all change places for the remaining courses! It will be much more fun as we'll be able to talk to more people.' It was great fun, but led to huge confusion as we tried to keep track of our cutlery and glassware between our old and new tables.

There is a history of private parties for staff at Chatsworth, illustrated by an entry in the 6th Duke's diaries where he notes that the completion of the North Wing and new Great Dining Room was finished just in time for the arrival of Princess Victoria in November 1832. He recorded that on 18th October, a 'cooked rehearsal' took place so that he could be certain everything would go according to plan. The diary also records that following Her Majesty's visit, there was a special party for those who had been involved in the building work:

Thursday 1st November 1832 Happy day. Grand dinner in the banqueting room for masons, gardeners etc. Charles Taylor the singer came and diverted them extremely.

Friday 2nd November 1832 A delightful ball at night for the servants.

In 2010 two longstanding members of staff, Paul Cottrell and Simon Seligman, left Chatsworth and the Duke and Duchess held a dinner party for them, this time in the Great Dining Room. I recall finding it strange to sit on the chairs in there – it seemed wrong to sit on the historic furniture! The dinner was held on 12th May 2010, and began with a champagne reception in the Library. It is a lovely room, warm and welcoming, especially when the fire is lit, and with such a small, intimate group, the atmosphere was relaxed and cordial. Disposable cameras were handed to everyone, and we had fun taking lots of photographs, which were then turned into keepsake albums for Paul and Simon.

Dinner comprised spring herb and vegetable terrine, followed by fillet of sea trout with Jersey Royal new potato cake, asparagus and samphire salad, and then lemon and white chocolate mousse and home-made chocolate truffles. The Great Dining Room table looked wonderful, as the gardeners had dressed the table and mantelpieces with marvellous vases of tulips. The public were able to see the preparations throughout the day and to see that the House is still used as a home, rather than having the atmosphere of a showcase museum. After dinner, we had highly entertaining speeches from the Duke, Simon and Paul, before moving to the Sculpture Gallery, which was lit entirely by candlelight and looked enchanting.

A house like Chatsworth affords the perfect setting for family parties and entertaining and on many occasions some of the staff are lucky enough to be invited. With the arrival of the 12th Duke and Duchess it has been lovely to revive the tradition of family christenings in the Chapel at Chatsworth, and Clive and I have considered ourselves very fortunate to be invited to the baptisms of the Duke and Duchess's grandchildren. The Duke and Duchess's son, Lord Burlington, was christened in the Chatsworth Chapel in 1969, and so it was no surprise that Lord Burlington's own children should be baptised there as well. His sister, Lady Jasmine and her husband Nicky Dunne had also had their son Cosmo baptised there, just after the Duke and Duchess came to live in the House.

Not long before the event, I asked the Duchess what they were going to use as a font. 'Oh, of course, there isn't one in there,' she said. 'Never mind, I expect the Duke will have a silver dish or something we can use.' In the event, it was decided to use the vast William Tanqueray silver gilt wine cistern, which measures about 17 inches by 32 inches, stands 27 inches tall, and weighs a staggering 52½lbs. Underneath, it has the maker's mark, 'David Tanqueray London 1718', and it is engraved with the arms of Richard, 3rd Earl of Burlington. It was inherited by the 5th Duke of Devonshire from his grandmother, Lady Dorothy Savile, wife of Richard, 3rd Earl of Burlington. It looked amazing when placed on the table for the baptism, and the reflection of the water on the highly polished sides of the cistern had a mesmerising effect on the baby, who was as good as gold.

On 24th October 2009, Lord and Lady Burlington's daughter, Lady Maud Elizabeth Cavendish (born 25th March 2009), was also baptised in the House Chapel, and again on 16th April 2011 there was a double baptism when Lord and Lady Burlington's son, James William Patrick Cavendish (born 12th December 2010), and Lady Jasmine and Mr Dunne's son, Reginald Thomas Drew Dunne (born 11th October 2010), were both baptised by the Venerable David Garnett, priest in charge of Beeley and Edensor. The Duchess loves music and had invited Joe Clark and the Derbyshire Singers to perform at the baptism, accompanied on the organ by their regular instrumentalist, Roger Briscoe. The effect in the Chapel was magnificent.

There was a merry tea party after the service, themed along the lines of Alice in Wonderland, with delicacies such as the Caterpillar's purple cucumber and cream cheese sandwiches, the Mad Hatter's afternoon tea sandwiches, Cheshire Cat pinwheels, nonsensical chilled pea soup, the Mock Turtle's lobster mousse, Dormouse lemon curd meringues, the Queen of Hearts tarts, chess board biscuits, the Mad Hatter's chocolate and raspberry popping candy canes and Through the Looking Glass lolly pops. The children of all ages loved the chocolate fountain with fresh strawberries and marshmallows, and the enormous teapot, continually steaming away with dry ice inside it.

Deborah, Dowager Duchess of Devonshire, was a keen fan of Elvis Presley and had visited Graceland and had been given an Elvis telephone by her grandchildren, which gyrated to the King belting out 'Jailhouse Rock' whenever there was a call. This led to her interest in meeting people who had actually met Elvis. Tom Jones was one such and he and his family were invited to tea one afternoon when he was performing in a concert at Chatsworth. Donna Presley (Elvis's cousin) came to Chatsworth when she was in England for the opening of the musical, *Jailhouse Rock*, together with the star of the show, Mario Kombou.

OK Magazine was there to record them enjoying tea with Her Grace, and knowing that one of the housemen working in the housekeeping team, Terry Orwin, was also a keen Elvis fan, Her Grace invited him to join the group. Everyone was highly entertained when the magazine's photograph described Terry as the Duke of Devonshire. I don't think they could quite believe that a Duchess would invite a houseman for tea, just because he was interested in Elvis. How little they knew of the Devonshires!

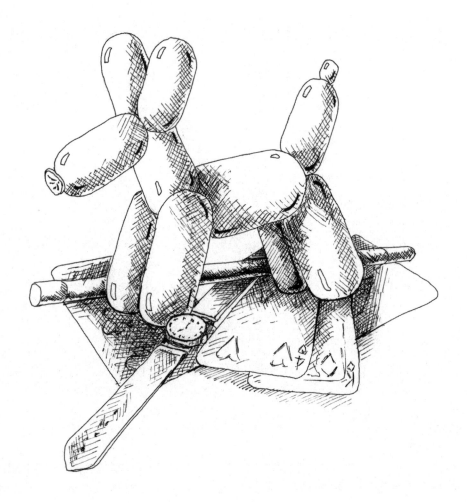

11

❧

Weddings and Anniversaries

Deborah and Andrew Cavendish, who were to become the 11th Duke and Duchess, married on 19th April 1941 in the church of St Bartholomew the Great in London; the reception was held at the Duchess's parents' home in Rutland Gate. The windows had been blown out during an air raid two nights before, so Mary, Duchess of Devonshire, arranged for camellias to be sent from the Chatsworth greenhouses, and Lady Redesdale hung strips of grey and gold wallpaper at the windows instead of curtains. Rationing meant that no icing was allowed for the cake, so it was covered in chopped nuts and cased in white cardboard.

Fifty years later, in 1991, the Duke and Duchess decided to celebrate their golden wedding anniversary at Chatsworth, with not just a party for their family and friends, but with a fantastic party for every couple in Derbyshire who had been married in the same year. They placed invitations in the local press, expecting that a few hundred might respond, but some 3,700 people qualified and attended the party! The afternoon tea party was held in a vast marquee, with a gold colour theme and Her Grace looked magnificent in a sparkling golden jacket. It was a snowy afternoon but the guest couples queued happily along the west drive, waiting to be greeted by the Duke and Duchess and presented with a boxed commemorative plate especially commissioned from Crown Derby.

A collection by Estate staff and pensioners enabled the purchase of trees and shrubs for the Golden Grove in the Gardens at Chatsworth, and the Duke and Duchess planted some of them at a ceremony on 29th November 1991. This was timed to coincide with a private visit by the

Prince of Wales, who on the Sunday of that weekend watched members of the Derbyshire Federation of Young Farmers plant 50 trees in the Park on the group's National Tree Day to mark the golden wedding.

Ten years later, on 19th April 2001, the Duke and Duchess celebrated their Diamond Wedding and another large party was planned with, once again, local residents married in the same year being invited to apply for tickets. However, due to a country-wide outbreak of Foot and Mouth disease, the party had to be postponed until later in the year. Instead, the Chatsworth staff gathered in the Painted Hall on the day to congratulate the Duke and Duchess, and Roger Wardle, the Chatsworth land agent, presented them with a crate of Double Diamond beer.

The public celebration took place on 27th September, with an amazing wartime themed afternoon tea party, and every guest received their own 'ration book' as they arrived. The cover of the ration book had the name filled in as 'Devonshire', the initials A & D, and the dates 1941-2001; inside the booklet were photographs and text with details of the wedding, and also what had happened at Chatsworth during the war. The centre pages of the book listed 'Today's Rations', which included a selection of sandwiches, hot and cold savouries, cakes and scones. There was tea and a champagne toast. The programme for the afternoon also included the New Squadronaires Orchestra, and a Dame Vera Lynn performer. Three days before the party, on 24th September, the Rotary Clubs of Derbyshire presented the Duke and Duchess with the *Devonshire Rotary Diamond*, a garden sculpture created by Tony Pickering, which was placed in the Kitchen Garden, where it spins in the wind.

The marriage of Lord and Lady Hartington's daughter, Lady Jasmine, to Nicholas Dunne took place at St Carthage's Church of Ireland Cathedral, Lismore on the evening of 25th July 2003. The Duke's Lismore agent at the time, Michael Penruddock, wrote about the occasion in a staff newsletter, describing Lismore Castle as having been decorated with 40 white flags, each 18 feet high, strapped to the battlements and turrets to give a the castle a realistic medieval appearance.

The first night of the newlywed's honeymoon was spent in a tent on the banks of the Blackwater River a few miles upstream from the castle. The tent was decorated by Lady Jasmine's mother, and was magnificently furnished with a neo-Gothic Pugin bed, and an old Victorian washstand, water bowl and jug. A roaring fire was lit just outside the tent to welcome them, and the following day they swam in the river and cooked themselves bacon and eggs for breakfast.

So that the rest of the Estate could celebrate their marriage, the couple held another party at Bolton Hall in Yorkshire for the Bolton Abbey staff and some members of staff from Chatsworth, who travelled up by coach. Clive and I were fortunate to be invited and we strolled on a beautiful, balmy summer's evening down towards the river and through the stone gateway that reveals the first proper view of the Priory, with the peaty brown water of the River Wharfe babbling in the distance as it swirled around the stepping stones. Lanterns led the way from the car park all the way down to the Hall and flags fluttered from its battlements.

We were greeted outside the Hall by the Duke and Duchess, Lord and Lady Hartington, and Lady Jasmine and her husband, and enjoyed a glass of champagne on the lawn before going through a marquee to the dining area in a second marquee. The first marquee had been erected as a sheltered area for the reception in case it was wet, but we were lucky with the weather on that fine evening. The walls of the marquee were lined with black and white photographs of the wedding at Lismore, so we could share in the experience even though we had not been there.

When it was time to eat, we made our way through to the main marquee, finding seats at long trestle tables. Clive and I were pleased to find ourselves seated with the vicar of Bolton Priory, and with Nick and Jo Wood, together with some of the staff from Lismore. The marquee was erected in such a way that it only had two sides, the other two sides being right up against the deep herbaceous borders, so that it seemed as though the flowers were actually part of the marquee. There was a delicious barbecue buffet, followed by marvellous puddings, served from the buffet with the help of Lord and Lady Hartington's grandchildren.

We were just enjoying our coffee, when there seemed to be some kind of disturbance amongst three of the waiters who had been working so hard throughout the evening. Their raised voices made us feel rather uncomfortable, not wishing that such an unpleasant thing would spoil the evening for Lord and Lady Hartington. The disturbance continued, until one of the waiters suddenly broke into song. He was answered in song by a second waiter and then the third joined in, and it was at that point that we realised that it was a carefully orchestrated performance that had deceived us all completely! The performers were amazing, and once they had finished the little 'opera', they went around the tables doing close magic tricks with cards, cups, coins and so on. We were sitting so close to them, but had no idea how they managed to trick and thrill us with every move. All too soon the evening was over and it was time to get back onto the coach. We arrived back home in the small hours, still excited by yet another fantastic Chatsworth party.

In March 2007 Lady Jasmine's brother, Lord Burlington, married Laura Montagu in a beautiful chapel at Laura's family home near Chester. In the following September there was a party at Chatsworth for the Chatsworth Estate staff, pensioners and tenants, together with those from Bolton Abbey, Lismore Castle and Compton Place, so that they could all have the opportunity to meet the new Lady Burlington, the future Duchess of Devonshire. It was a spectacular party held over two evenings on the South Front lawn so that all staff would be able to attend, partly because there would not have been room for everyone to go on the same night, but also because someone always has to work on security, the switchboard, car parking and so on, and those on duty on the first night could attend on the second.

It was a warm evening, even though it was September, and we enjoyed a leisurely stroll along the Broad Walk, admiring the row of flags fluttering up on the roof and lining the path up to the Cascade House, and smiling at the statues sporting scarlet blindfolds. We enjoyed meeting old friends at a champagne reception on the South Front lawn where marquees had been erected in case of rain, and these were lined with photographs of the wedding in Cheshire. Music from various jazz bands entertained us whilst we enjoyed a delicious buffet meal, served within crimson marquees with a good view of the staged area where the family were seated.

After the speeches there was more music and the opportunity for some to have their palms read in the two gypsy caravans that used to be taken on holiday by the Duke and Duchess, when the Duchess and the girls would sleep inside, whilst the Duke and Lord Burlington slept

The door providing access from the Library to the gallery above. Paddy Leigh Fermor, friend of the 11th Duke and Duchess, provided amusing titles for the false book spines attached to the door viewed in the image below.

Above: The Chatsworth salvage team in a 'book evacuation' drill in the early 1980s.

Right: The Chatsworth fire team in the office yard at Chatsworth in the 1980s. The housekeeping team had the dubious privilege of stitching the reflective tape onto their trouser legs!

The Great Dining Room, before and after refurbishment. (Image above shows Christine Thompson, Sean Doxey, Tony Hubbuck and Matt Oliver)

Above: A behind-the-scenes tour visiting the Joiners' Shop, originally the Kitchen in the 6th Duke's Victorian North Wing.

Left: Items from the copper store 'lost' for nearly 60 years and rediscovered in 1998 when a sprinkler system was installed in the Joiners' Shop.

Right: Christine Thompson, the seamstress who initiated the programme of tapestry conservation still ongoing at Chatsworth.

Below: With help from a team of volunteers, tapestry conservation progressed on custom-built frameworks in the Chatsworth Theatre, until the workshop was relocated to rooms off the Kitchen Maids' landing.

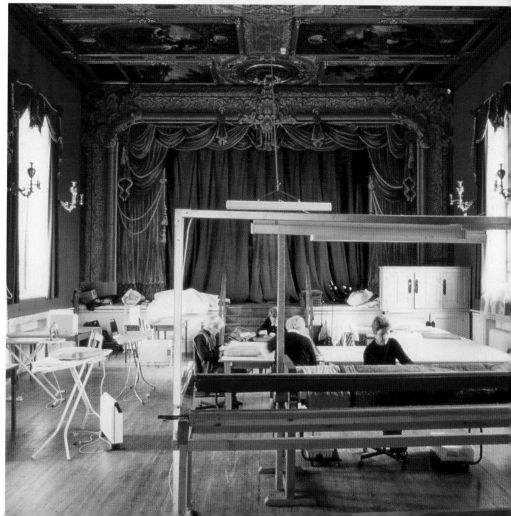

Above: The Antiques Roadshow in the private West Front garden in 1996.

Right: Talking to my first behind-the-scenes group in 1996 in the Stag Parlour at Chatsworth. The painting behind me was often mistaken for a Lowry, but is actually by Helen Bradley, from her book, *And Miss Carter wore pink. Scenes from and Edwardian Childhood.*

Above: Her Grace and Eric Oliver chat together as Estate children pose for a photograph in the North Front Hall before the Children's Christmas party in 1992.

Below: Our eldest son, Philip, stands next to Father Christmas and waits patiently for his present at the Children's Christmas party in 1990.

Above: Dorothy Dean in the Orangery Shop at Chatsworth. She was housekeeper and shop manager from 1968 until 1981.

Left: Antonio Verrio's painting of the 1st Duke of Devonshire's housekeeper, Mrs Hackett, on the ceiling of the Great Chamber. No one knows why they argued, but he got his revenge by painting her in as one of the Furies, *'cutting the thread of life with her abhorr'd shears'*.

Above: the Chatsworth housekeeping team pose for a Christmas photograph in 2013, when the Christmas theme was *The Lion, the Witch and the Wardrobe.*
Front l-r: Barbara Fletcher, Jo Warren, Elaine Taylor, Louise Randall;
Second l-r: Chris Wrath, Catherine Gilbert, Sue Bruno;
Third row, l-r: Liz Tilbury, Jayne Boyd, Jane Birks, Alyson Blackburn;
Back, l-r: Kath Watts, Julie Pelly.

Below: Marjorie Bateman (left) on her retirement as assistant housekeeper in 2010, with another member of the team, Danielle Cullen.

Above: Clive and I enjoy a glorious day at Royal Ascot in 2011, when the 12th Duke provided a coach and tickets for staff to attend.

Below: The Dowager Duchess of Devonshire photographed at the Old Vicarage by Barrie Bateman on her 90th birthday in 2010.

Above: Sue Lumb pays tribute to the Dowager Duchess (seated, left) at the Chatsworth Staff Party on 5th March 2010 to celebrate Her Grace's 90th birthday. I am standing to one side with the 12th Duke.

Below: The Cavendish family at the staff party in 2010.
Front l-r: Lady Emma Tennant, Lady Elizabeth Cavendish, The Duchess of Devonshire, The Dowager Duchess of Devonshire; Back l-r: Lady Celina Carter, Emma Tennant, Eddie Tennant, Alex Carter, Lady Jasmine Dunne, The Duke of Devonshire, Lady Burlington, Lord Burlington.

Above: David Nash's warp and crack sculpture at Lismore Castle.

Below: The circular, one-cut warp and crack sculpture at Chatsworth that Clive made as a gift for the Duke, presented at the Gala dinner in aid of St Peter's Church funds in 2013.

Above: Lord and Lady Burlington with their children on the south steps at Chatsworth, l-r: Lady Nell, Lord Burlington, Lord James, Lady Burlington, Lady Maud, and 'Max', the terrier.

Below: The 12th Duke and Duchess of Devonshire in the Green Drawing room.

The Dowager Duchess of Devonshire (centre) and her sister-in-law, Lady Elizabeth Cavendish (left), enjoy a chat outside the Old Vicarage, Edensor, on the morning of one of Edensor Village Days

Below: Lismore Castle above the Blackwater River in County Waterford.

Above: The statue of Minerva, before and after cleaning during the Master Plan restoration work in 2011. Minerva is the Roman goddess of wisdom, and the 12th Duke was disappointed that she wasn't discovered to be her Greek counterpart, Athena, since she would then have worn a gilded, rather than a plain helmet.

Baby dress and shoes belonging to William Cavendish, who died in 1834. They were discovered in a box of tassels on the Kitchen maids' Landing.

Andrew, 11th Duke of Devonshire, seated in the Lower Library.
His son, then Marquis of Hartington, standing left.
His grandson, Bill Burlington, standing right.

underneath. There were also artists going round the tables to sketch a caricature or cut a silhouette for guests to take away, and there were several magicians working their way round the tables. I have always been fascinated by magicians, and at one point, Clive and I were standing at one of the tables watching one such expert at work. He glanced around the table, chatting as he worked and then walked round the table, passing behind us and back to where he started. Then he took a long balloon from his pocket and proceeded to make a sausage dog from it. As he blew into the balloon, twisting and turning it, he popped something inside the balloon and carried on chatting. I looked hard at what he had put inside the balloon and thought how it looked very like my own wristwatch – but of course, it couldn't be. Then I looked at my wrist and realised that my watch had disappeared, and was now inside the balloon! How had he done it? I have absolutely no idea, but I hadn't felt a thing and knew for certain that I wouldn't want to come across him on a crowded street in London – what an artist!

12

⁓

Talking about Chatsworth

Since my first talk to the Beeley Womens' Institute in 1980, I have spoken on very many occasions, up and down the country, on a number of topics relating to Chatsworth. Amongst the titles are some that prove to be perennially popular: 'Glimpses of Chatsworth', 'Hidden Treasures of Chatsworth', 'Christmas at Chatsworth', 'Chatsworth: A 21st Century Renaissance', 'The History of the Gardens at Chatsworth', and 'Chatsworth: A Personal View'. Sometimes I'll find myself speaking to 300, sometimes to only a dozen, but most are memorable in one way or another, and as a result, I think I could write a handbook on the village halls of England.

One talk in September 1996 was to Sparrowpit WI. Sparrowpit is a one-street hamlet in the wilds of Peak Forest with a handful of houses and one pub called The Wanted Inn. The WI meets in the small village hall once a month, and after the singing of 'Jerusalem' with 20 or so quavering sopranos trying to keep in tune with the tape recording, I gave my talk. WI meetings often have a themed competition as part of the procedure, but on this occasion it wasn't any of the usual subjects, 'A Favourite Photograph of a Stately Home', or 'The Most Unusual Antique', or 'The Best Homemade Cushion' (all of which I have judged, and on more than one occasion). This time it was, 'My Most Useful Kitchen Utensil'. I studied a set of kitchen scales, a food blender, a fancy bottle opener (for those with rheumatic fingers), and even an unusual corkscrew, which nearly got my vote. However, my attention was drawn to a photograph of a chap in an apron and rubber gloves standing at the kitchen sink. It was no contest – I gave it first prize!

One memorable event was a talk to a Ladies Luncheon Club at the Robin Hood Theatre, which is a beautiful little theatre near Newark, built in the grounds of Averham Rectory in 1913 and restored in 1961. We had lunch before the talk in the theatre foyer, where the walls were covered with billboards featuring various well-known names who had performed there. It was astonishing that this tiny little theatre in the middle of nowhere had seen the likes of Cecil Day Lewis, Dulcie Gray, Sir Donald Wolfit, Hinge and Bracket, Anthony Hopkins, Judi Dench and Geraldine McEwan. After lunch I was led onto the stage by a rather dapper woman in tweed trousers and waistcoat. The stage curtains were closed in front of me and there was just a small table in the middle of the stage, as the talk I was to deliver was 'Chatsworth: A Personal View', which didn't need a screen, just a table for a few objects I was going to use during the talk.

My hostess made sure I had a glass of water, and then said, 'I'd just like to point out the emergency exit here at the back of the stage, and then I'll get out of your way. I'll open the curtains for you when everyone's in.' I stood listening to the chatter of 150 women as they filed into the auditorium on the other side of the curtain and took their seats, and for two pins I would have been out of that emergency exit in no time. Like a rabbit caught in the headlights, I stood rooted to the floorboards and blinking in the spotlights as the curtains slowly opened. I think it was one of the most nerve-wracking talks I've ever given…but possibly one of the best!

On 23rd June 1998 I spoke at the Izaac Walton Hotel in Dovedale, near Ashbourne, to the West Sussex Decorative and Fine Arts Society who were on a holiday in the Peak District and planned to visit Chatsworth the following day. It was a perfect summer's evening, the drive to Dovedale was lovely and I was treated to a delicious dinner. The plates were brought in, each covered with a silver lid, and at a nod from the head waiter, all were revealed in one dramatic moment. I told Lord Hartington about it subsequently, and he said that his mother once ruined such a moment. She thought it rather pretentious, and when the covered plate was brought to her place, she took the lid off herself saying, 'Oh, I wonder what we're having!'

Sometimes you know the audience will be large, and on other occasions you have no idea what size it will be – like the time I went the few miles from Edensor to speak to the Monyash WI. Although the audience was small, they had great enthusiasm for the subject, and the lavish refreshments after the talk were magnificent.

In March 1998 I was asked to give a talk to a meeting called 'Group 62', a Jewish group in Sheffield, and subsequently also spoke to a Jewish group in Manchester at their synagogue, where I was given a fascinating guided tour and saw their Torah. I had earlier told the 11th Duke that I was going to speak to a Jewish group, and he told me that his interest in the Jewish cause began as a child when his father invited several Jewish friends to dinner, and he was intrigued with the special way in which meals had to be prepared for their visits. In his memoir, the 11th Duke remembered Chaim Weizmann (who was to become President of the State of Israel in 1948), coming to his parents' house. His Grace subsequently became President of the Conservative Friends of Israel group and visited Israel eight times and even had a forest in Galilee named after him.

In November the same year I was engaged to speak in Chesterfield after the NSPCC Annual General Meeting and although I knew that Lord Hartington was the President of the Chesterfield Branch, it had never occurred to me that he would actually be there for the AGM. How little I knew him! If he is associated with a charity then he is 'in at the deep end' with it and wants to know everything that is going on. It would never have entered his head not to be present at the AGM even though it meant driving up from London and back again on a night of freezing fog. I was anxious that he might stay to hear my talk, but he wanted to get back because of the weather, and although he assured me that I would have had nothing to worry about, I was quite relieved all the same!

Invitations to speak to groups seem to come in batches, as the idea of a talk about Chatsworth spreads from group to group in the same area. As I write, I have a list of invitations from ladies' luncheon clubs in Yorkshire. A few years ago it was Mansfield, and I had no idea there could be so many different clubs and groups in one town. On 11th May 1999 I was invited to speak to the Mansfield Over-50 group in the lovely auditorium at the town library, with about 60 very lively members in the audience. They were interested in my talk and asked many good questions. At the end of the meeting, an elderly gentleman came up to show me a picture, taken of his two children sitting on the log that was then at the entrance to the Farmyard and Adventure Playground. Sitting next to the children was a little figure that was quite definitely a gnome – not a garden gnome, but the sort of gnome you might find in the illustrations of a fairy story. He told me very earnestly that he definitely hadn't noticed the gnome when he had taken the picture, and it only showed up on the photograph once the film had been developed. He said that he had written to Her Grace about it and sent her a copy of the photograph, and he showed me a copy of her reply, handwritten and in a very serious vein, saying how interested she was to hear his story. I followed her lead and told the gentleman how intrigued I was by the picture, but I didn't really know what to make of it. Since then I have always kept a good look out whenever I go up to the Farmyard, although who knows which log the gnome will be perching on now that the old one has finally fallen apart and been removed? When I returned to Chatsworth and told Her Grace about my experience at the talk, she laughed and said that every time she drove His Grace past the Farmyard on their way up to Stand Wood, he always asked, 'By the way, have there been any sightings lately?'

In 2000 the Association of Anglo Swiss Clubs invited Judy Coggins to undertake a 12-day lecture tour of Switzerland in the autumn of 2001, but two weeks before she was due to leave, her father was taken gravely ill. I took her place, desperately sorry for Judy's situation, but delighted to have the opportunity to explore somewhere I had always longed to visit. The Club had offered to pay for the airfare, train pass and accommodation, so all Chatsworth had to agree was for me to take two weeks off work to deliver the lectures. It sounded easy, but as I waited for the minibus at 5am on a wet October morning in a Manchester airport hotel, I wondered what on earth I had committed myself to. The week before had been a frenzy of activity: leaving work schedules for the housekeeping team at Chatsworth, sorting out my family in Edensor, not to mention preparing all the slides to take with me for my talks, and it wasn't until I was on the runway that I had time to think about how I was going to cope when I finally arrived. As the plane climbed through the clouds into the brilliant sunshine and turned eastwards, I knew I would just have to take a deep breath and make it work. It did…I had a ball!

I bought a Swiss travel pass in Geneva and realised how easy the Swiss timetables are to understand and was soon on the train to my first venue in Lausanne. The talk I gave was titled 'A Glimpse of Chatsworth', which gives a snapshot of the House Gardens and Farmyard, behind-the-scenes, and the public areas, when everything is open, when the House is closed, and some of the special parties and events we have enjoyed over the years. On each day I travelled to a new venue, arriving around lunchtime and finding my accommodation. I then had the afternoon to explore the new town before the talk in the evening, which always included a meal with the group.

I loved the steeply winding streets of Lausanne with the beautiful lake below the city and the magnificent cathedral tower rising above it, where the town crier still called the hours between midnight and 4am. At its wonderful outdoor market, all the fruit, vegetable and flower stalls looked so colourful, with beautiful mixed bouquets and tubs of rich roses and bright sunflowers. The vegetable stalls were incredible, selling fresh plum tomatoes, gourds, pumpkins, artichokes and beetroot and over twelve varieties of lettuce on one stall, whilst two champignon stalls were each selling 21 different sorts of fungi. Even a browse around the supermarket was an education, where a huge shallow vat of bouncing white billiard balls were discovered to be glistening globes of Mozzarella cheese, jostling in their tub of salty water.

I was a little disconcerted before that first talk in Lausanne when one lovely lady approached me and in broken English said how much she was looking forward to the talk as she had only been to England once when she had visited Devon, and how many memories it was going to bring back for her to see pictures of the Devon coastline! When that first talk went well, given such a start, I felt confident the other nine were going to be just fine.

Biel/Bienne was the next venue – the only truly bi-lingual town in Switzerland, with street signs in both French and German and with the huge Rolex factory on the skyline. Sylvia and Rudi Jakob, the couple who had organised the trip, met me at Biel station and took me for a delicious lunch at a vineyard restaurant, where we sat outside in the warm autumn sunshine overlooking the lake, watching the workers on the valley slopes below us picking grapes and tossing them into the baskets on their backs.

My third venue was Fribourg, where I stayed with an English couple. They had a plum tree in their garden, and told me that every village has its own distillery where residents can take their fruit to be distilled into schnapps. After the talk that evening, we pushed all the tables together in the back room of the inn where the meeting was held and enjoyed a riotous fondue party. Swiss fondue uses Emmental or Gruyere and Vacherin cheese heated gently together with wine, before Kirsch and cornflour are added to thicken it. My final lecture that first week was in Zofingen, where I awoke to the sound of cowbells outside my bedroom window – now I knew I really was in Switzerland.

I had the weekend to myself and decided to use my rail pass to visit some other places, but was undecided whether to go to Wengen or Grindelwald. Trains left Lucerne on the same platform for both destinations, so I thought I would let fate decide and would just get on the first train to arrive. It took me to Grindelwald, a pretty village and with plenty of hotels to choose from on the main street, but I decided to explore a little before committing to one. I found a wonderful family hotel up a steep side street and with stunning views from my bedroom window, and I was very comfortable there for two nights. It was a perfect opportunity to take a trip on the Jungfraujoch, which is a little train trundling up the Jungfrau, revealing the most fantastic views all the way up. There were breath-taking panoramic views from the top, and spectacular ice caves carved inside the glacier, containing dramatic displays of ice-sculpted tableaux of polar bears, Eskimos and penguins.

On Monday I was back at work, with a lecture in Chur, the farthest east I travelled, and then it was a six hour journey back to Geneva for lecture number six. I had a rather unfortunate experience here, as I wasn't staying in a hotel but in the home of the president of the society, who I discovered too late to find myself a hotel room, was an alcoholic. The next day I was back on the train for a talk in lovely Basel on the River Rhine, before travelling back to La Chauz-de-Fonds for my last lecture.

As my flight the following day was an early one, I needed to leave the hotel well before dawn and change trains in Neuchatel in order to get my connection for the airport train to Geneva. About two minutes before the train was due to arrive in Neuchatel, it stopped at a station and I peered out of the window, but couldn't see a name sign anywhere.

Terrified of being carried on to the wrong station and missing my connection, I got off the train and just as it started to pull away from the platform I realised that I was not at Neuchatel, but somewhere else entirely. I was so relieved that I had taken my luggage off the train with me, but was in despair thinking that I was now going to miss my connection. I had no idea where I was, but taking a firm hold of the impending hysteria, I decided to try to find someone so I could establish where I was, so I walked off the platform towards a small road leading away from the station. It was still dark, and I was drawn towards the lights of a small kiosk, where a man was just setting his stall out ready to sell newspapers and hot drinks. He didn't speak English, but fortunately was able to understand my broken French and smiled at me, gave me a thumbs-up and a free cup of wonderful coffee whilst he made a telephone call. Within ten minutes a taxi arrived and whisked me away to Neuchatel, where I was able to catch the next train to Geneva and made my flight on time. What a relief!

Not long after my trip to Switzerland I took a booking for a WI Group meeting, which is an occasion where a group of around six WIs get together for a social evening, sharing news, having a speaker and entertainment. On this occasion the venue was Sudbury Prison near Derby. It was a dreadful October evening with high winds and torrential rain and I was so glad when I finally arrived. I was pleased that some of the women were already arriving so that I could see where I had to go. The searchlights and barbed wire were rather off-putting, and we then had to pass through an area where mobile phones had to be handed in. Eventually I arrived at the very well-equipped prison theatre to give my talk and after the refreshments, the host WI put on a very entertaining one-act play about a stately home, which was highly amusing.

Talks like this are usually planned well in advance but sometimes I find myself stepping into the breach when there is a problem. A few years ago, I was just leaving work at 5.30pm when my pager sounded. I went back into the switchboard and was told that Mrs Tennant was on the phone and would like to speak to me. She is the wife of Eddie Tennant who is the nephew of the 12th Duke (and grandson of the 11th Duke), and lives with her family in a farmhouse on the Chatsworth Estate. She is very much involved with the local charity, Helen's Trust, which had sold tickets for a talk by the Sheffield MP, David Blunkett, who lives on the Estate and was due to deliver his talk that evening in Bakewell. However, he had telephoned Emma that afternoon to say that he had to stay in Westminster for a whipped vote in Parliament and would be at least an hour late for the talk in Bakewell. Desperate to know what to do with the audience whilst they waited for him, Emma asked if I would give them a talk for an hour before he arrived. Of course I agreed, the talk was well received and I really enjoyed listening to David's talk once he finally arrived.

In 2008 Jackie White took a call at the switchboard and rang my extension, saying, 'Hi Christine, I've got a gentleman named Joop on the line, from Holland, wanting to book a talk – I'll just put him through now.'

'Hello, Christine Robinson here, I understand you are interested in a talk?'

'Yes, that's right. Several talks actually. I'm organising a series of lectures in the Netherlands for the Nederland-England Society – is this something you would be interested in doing?' Would I be interested! I went straight down to the switchboard after Joop came off the phone to thank Jackie for putting him through, and the following April, Clive and I flew off to Holland. Chatsworth had agreed that I could be away for nearly two weeks without losing any of my leave allowance, and they paid my usual salary, whilst the Nederland-England Society paid my travelling expenses. It was great that Clive was able to take some annual leave to accompany me, and it made the visit so much easier as we could use a car, rather than going by public transport.

As with my previous trip to Switzerland, it was arranged that we would arrive at my speaking venue mid-afternoon, where Clive and I would enjoy a cup of tea with our hosts before going out for a meal. After I had given the talk we then went back to our hosts' house where they had a small party for us. The following morning they proudly showed us round their locality, and then it was off to the next venue; an exhausting two weeks with eight lectures to deliver the length and breadth of Holland. We travelled on the weekend before the tour began so that we had a chance to explore the wonderful Koekenhoff Gardens, a long-held ambition, and to visit the fascinating city of Leiden and the Delft factories in Delft.

The first talk on 20th April 2009 was in Breda, where we stayed with a delightful couple who made us very welcome. On the morning after the talk they showed us round the town and then said, 'You need to eat before you leave for Hengelo, how about lunch in Belgium?' So off we went to Belgium for lunch before heading off for the next venue in Hengelo, where the talk took place in the modern library in the middle of the town, which had suffered extensive damage during the war, so most of the buildings were quite modern.

The talk that evening went well, apart from a disturbing incident during the question and answer session at the end, when the chairman of the society asked, 'I understand that the Duke of Devonshire is one of the greatest landowners in England. Please could you tell us a bit more about that?' This question would have posed no problem at all had I not misheard 'landowners' as 'philanderers'! I thought very quickly and then rather haltingly started talking about the 8th Duke of Devonshire and his relationship with the Duchess of Manchester. I was just getting into a description of the 6th Duke and his lady friends, when it became obvious that something was amiss, and the questioner interrupted, 'No, no, I said landowner!' Phew!

Our hostess in Hengelo was a delightful lady with a passion for toys and had actually persuaded her family to move to a house with a large enough space above the garage for her to house her enormous collection. It was also their guest room, so we were surrounded with every kind of toy and game imaginable. She had a special interest in an ancient European board game called the *Game of the Goose*, which we had never heard of before, but we certainly knew plenty about it by the time we came to leave!

She was also a guide at nearby Twickel Castle and we were delighted when she said that she had arranged for the curator to give us a private tour of the castle the following morning. It was a glorious day as we drove up the very grand approach to meet Jan-Wilhelm, who took us below stairs for coffee in the old kitchens, which looked as though they hadn't been altered in over a hundred years. We were shown the principal rooms and then taken up to the old nursery, where there was an amazing array of old toys and games – including yet another *Game of the Goose*. It was a fascinating castle and we felt privileged to have been shown the interior, as it is only the gardens that are generally open to the public. These had been recently landscaped and were truly magnificent, especially since all the tulips were in bloom.

Once we bade farewell to our hostess we set off for Deventer, an interesting town with its historic centre built almost on an island in the River Isjle, which flows along one side of the town, carrying vast tankers and other shipping to the northern coastal ports, and south down the river to Germany. The talk to the Deventer group went well, with the most interest being shown in the *trompe l'oeil* image of the Chatsworth violin hanging in the State Music Room, as the audience could not believe it was only a painting.

We stayed that night with a lovely lady called Els, and ate at her home before the talk. It was an opportunity to chat on a more personal level and learn a little more about what it had been like for the Netherlands to be occupied during the Second World War. Els said that her mother had been a ten- or eleven-year-old girl when the Germans occupied Holland, and they were forced to have a young German soldier billeted with them. Apparently he had a daughter the same age as Els's mother, and had wept every night because he feared that he would be sent to the Front and might never see his little daughter again and Els's grandmother would try to comfort him.

The following morning we had a long drive to Groningen in the north, through the region of Friesland, with its own language and a very different landscape, with field upon field of Friesian cattle. There were no hedges or fences here, just dikes, or polders, separating the fields, and windmills to pump water into them from the land and drain it away to the sea. The group I spoke to in Groningen were also very friendly. We stayed with Joka and her husband, Jakob, whom we didn't meet until after the talk as he was late back from a rather special luncheon appointment where he had been seated at a table of only eight people, including the Queen of Holland and the King and Queen of Sweden!

The last talk of the week was in Utrecht, another long journey all the way down to the south of the country and we were looking forward to staying with Joop and Carol, who had been my main contacts in the planning for the tour. The talk went well, for by this time I knew that I had to be careful to enunciate carefully and to speak neither too quickly nor too slowly so that they could follow what I said.

160

The following day Carol and Joop took us to Het Loo, the palace built for William III, Prince of the House of Orange and his English wife Mary. The palace and gardens were recently restored and immaculate, with many connections with Chatsworth, including copies of the Cibber figures in the *Seahorse Fountain* at Chatsworth and porcelain pieces copying our silver-gilt pilgrim flasks. It was a reminder of the international importance of the Chatsworth collection when we saw that the descriptive label with the ceramic flasks noted that they were 'a copy of the silver-gilt flasks at Chatsworth House in England'. We left Carol and Joop on Saturday and drove to The Hague, ready for the talk there on Monday, so we had the Sunday to explore the galleries and sights.

The talk in The Hague on 27th April was perhaps the most interesting location, in an old bank now used as a conference centre. The talk took place below ground in an old vault lined with drawers, although sadly all of them were empty!

Our journey the next day was long and wet, from The Hague to Maastricht, in the long thin finger of Holland tucked in between Belgium, France and Germany, called Little Switzerland by the Dutch because of its hills – a surprising feature in Holland. We were fortunate again with our hosts in Maastricht, staying with a wonderful couple called Tilly and Hubert, with whom we have become firm friends.

Their house is where Tilly grew up, built by her parents in the 1920s, and she and Hubert had lived in it all their married lives. Tilly told us that during the Second World War they had to hide their bicycles, lest they were stolen by the Germans who, towards the end of the war would desert back to Germany, over the border not far from Maastricht. Tilly remembered her mother hiding their bicycles in the rows of runner beans in the back garden.

The Germans surrendered to the Allied Forces in Maastricht on 14th September 1944, eight months before the rest of Holland was liberated, and Tilly recalled the German surrender being announced and the celebrations that morning. Later that day she was in the upstairs bedroom that Clive and I were sleeping in, which offered a clear view down the road out of a corner window. She had gone to the window because she heard a tank coming down the street and she could see an American soldier waving from the open tank hatch. As she watched, a shot rang out and he fell dead across the top of the tank, shot by a sniper.

The eight-year-old Tilly was badly affected by this, and even after so many years she could still remember the incident vividly.

She told her story a few years ago at a meeting of NAILS, a Dutch-American group. There were some US servicemen present and one commented that there was only one American killed on Liberation Day in Maastricht, so it should be possible to find out who he was. Tillie did some research on the Internet and discovered the soldier's name, and that he came from Michigan. She posted more questions on relevant US websites and was delighted when a young boy recognised the family name as his own and replied and Tillie then wrote back to him.

At this point the boy's mother intervened as she was suspicious about someone emailing her son, but when Tilly explained, she was told that the young boy was the dead soldier's grandson. His body had been returned to the USA and was buried in Michigan. The dead soldier's brother refused to believe Tilly's story, but his son did, and Tillie invited them to come to Holland to see for themselves where his father had died. When Tilly and Hubert subsequently went to Michigan to see his grave, they met the sceptical brother, who finally believed her story; it was a very poignant meeting.

When, a couple of years later, we were asked to do another lecture tour in Holland, it was an opportunity to meet new people as we stayed with our hosts in different towns. We had a rather awkward experience at one location where we arrived as usual in mid-afternoon. It was a traditional farmhouse, with one side of the building designed to house animals, and the other side for the farmer and his family, but the couple living there were no longer farming and just kept a few horses.

After the talk later that night, we discussed what time we needed to leave the next morning as we had a long drive to Maastricht for the next talk, and we agreed that we should get away by 9.30am. I set our alarm clock and we were up early the next morning, but there was not a murmur from our hosts, so we went into the kitchen and hunted round for something to eat for breakfast, and finally left at 9.30am without seeing anything of them. I said to Clive that I was worried that they might have been murdered in their beds and we would be the prime suspects, fleeing the scene of the crime, but no one came after us!

Over the years I have been to many places to talk to many lovely people and I find it strange to remember what a shrinking violet I was at school.

13

❧

The Tercentenary

In 1994 we celebrated the tercentenary of the Devonshire Dukedom. In 1988 it had been 300 years since the 4th Earl of Devonshire helped William of Orange to take the English throne in the Glorious Revolution of 1688, and in 1694 his title was elevated from Earl to Duke, so what better way to celebrate than to have a grand party at Chatsworth! We had enjoyed a magnificent firework party on 5th November 1988 to celebrate the Revolution, and so were greatly excited to hear that there was now to be another one to celebrate the Dukedom.

Planning for the Tercentenary celebrations began in 1992, although it was not until 12th May 1994 that the event actually took place. An evening garden party with a themed buffet was held in marquees by the river, together with a masque, specially commissioned by the Duke and written by the son of our local doctor, actor Richard Evans, which briefly depicted the history of each Duke. The first evening was to be for the 3,500 Estate staff and their families, pensioners and tenants, and the second night on the 13th was to raise funds for the Children's Society, with tickets for this evening priced at £45. The invitation said:

The Celebration setting will be a purpose-built tented village and auditorium on the banks of the river opposite the west front of the house.

The setting will be designed and appointed to capture an atmosphere of the 17th century, and the evening will comprise a Supper Party with period entertainment, a Masque Performance and Grand Firework Display.

The supper party between 7.30 and 9.30pm will be held in marquees and the open air within the tented village. 17th century entertainments will be staged during supper and the food will reflect the times with some dishes produced from recipe books such as 'The Complete Cook' 1681 and 'Mosley's Derbyshire Recipes' 1699 - 1712.

The Masque performance in drama, music and dance will follow at 9.45pm. The auditorium will be built on the river bank facing the House with the stage on the opposite side linked by a bridge. The Masque, specially commissioned by the Duke and written by local actor Richard Evans, will tell the story of the Cavendish family and Chatsworth from Bess of Hardwick to the present day. The performance will involve a cast of over 150 professional and amateur actors as well as children from the estate and local schools.

The grand finale at approximately 10.30pm will be a magnificent firework display set to music.

Set-building for the stage and auditorium began on 28th April, with work having been in progress for several weeks prior to that building the tented village on the west side of the river. The stage builders included divers to correctly position the underwater props, as it was intended that the stage would overhang the river.

A special Tercentenary logo was produced and as a surprise for the Duke, this was worked into a huge flag to be hoisted on the Hunting Tower on the morning of the Tercentenary. The flag was 25 feet by 16 feet and required 70 metres of fabric. It was produced in the Sewing Room by Christine Thompson and her textile team. The only place large enough to lay it out was the floor of the Painted Hall, where one piece was laid out flat and the other half was 'walked' over the top of it so the two pieces could be tacked together to make a flag that weighed 28 pounds. This activity was carefully timed so as not to clash with His Grace making his way along the Catwalk for breakfast, but it also had to be over and done with before the visitors arrived. Once finished, it looked magnificent, fluttering away on the top of the hill. However, the flagpole on the Hunting Tower is incorporated into the four poster in the room below, and the constant flapping nearly drove the Duke's grandson, Eddie Tennant mad, so it was taken down after a week or so. The Hunting Tower is now a holiday cottage, but Eddie lived there for quite a number of years until his wife was expecting their first child, when they decided the spiral staircase was not suited to a young family.

It must have made a great bachelor pad; he even managed to fit a snooker table in the basement.

The dress rehearsal for the Masque on 11th May was a chilly evening and so the Duke arranged for mulled wine to be available. He wanted parents and relatives of the cast not eligible to come along to the main performance to have the opportunity to see the dress rehearsal, and he also arranged for one maroon to be let off, so the audience could see at least one giant firework. The cold of the evening also caused him to be concerned for the comfort of the guests on the subsequent evenings, so Helen Marchant was tasked with ordering enough plastic rain capes (all with the Tercentenary logo on them) and 6,000 rugs from the Army and Navy store to be available for anyone who needed them. The blankets are still in constant use as packing for works of art as they are transported round the House and in and out of storage.

There were 418 costumes used in the Masque, most of them borrowed from theatres all over the country and brought together by Annie Brown of the Royal Exchange Theatre in Manchester. Christine Thompson was her assistant and helped with all the fittings, alterations and running repairs. One of the alterations was due to the fact that the actress playing the part of Bess of Hardwick was six months pregnant, so it was a good job that her costume was so all-enveloping.

The day of the event was a busy one in the House, and there was a lot to do before we were able to enjoy the party. Christine Thompson and the textile team were fully committed with last minute alterations to costumes, and in the House it was business as usual for us, with the visiting staff from Lismore Castle to take round the House, and a dinner in the Painted Hall for 40 of His Grace's private guests, before the party outside in the tented village began.

It was a much warmer evening than it had been the night before, and it was delightful to stroll across the Crobs (the hill between Edensor and Chatsworth) to the party with Clive and the boys and all the other villagers bound for the event.

The food, drink and entertainment were themed from the 17th and 18th centuries, with costumed jesters, jugglers, fire-eaters and stilt-walkers. The serving staff were in costume, and I shall never forget the magnificent stuffed 'peacock', surrounded by wonderful things to eat, that was borne shoulder-high into the scene. The food was served from a carvery, and our six-year-old son Michael's face was a sight to behold as he tried to bite a strawberry that looked as large as an apple in his hand.

The children of Pilsley School, all in costume, put on a colourful display of maypole dancing, and as the time for the main performance drew near, the signal was given for the guests to move to the auditorium for the start of the Masque. This involved a number of actors from Buxton's Drama League, dressed in long black curly wigs, dress coats and jabots, knee breeches and white stockings running through the crowd, and presenting a very convincing Court of James II. At the same time, others from their company appeared as a magnificent troop of revolutionaries who stormed across the bridge, calling for the people to sign their petition and join them in the plot to bring William of Orange from Holland to take the English throne. Philip and Michael signed their names, along with the larger-than-life Vicar of St Anne's Baslow, the Reverend Martin Leigh, scratching away with a quill pen to do so.

Local amateur acting companies and local schools provided many of the actors for the Masque. Pilsley School appeared as North American Indians in the scene depicting the 9th Duke of Devonshire's time as Governor General of Canada. The story of the Dukedom was narrated by Donald Sinden, whose resonating tones took on the persona of the 'Spirit of the Derwent'. He linked the characters of the Masque together, at one point summoning Bess of Hardwick to warn her descendants of the pitfalls that would lie ahead. The Buxton Sea Scouts enacted the arrival of William of Orange in 1688, when they rowed the King and the 4th Earl of Devonshire down the river and 'landed' them directly onto the stage.

In order to depict the tradition of the Dukes of Devonshire for the purchasing of works of art, the House painter and decorator, Lawrence Udall, copied two of the paintings in the Devonshire collection onto massive canvases. During the performances these were then carried onto the stage and could be clearly seen from the back of the auditorium. One of these canvases is still tucked away in the joiners' wood store, whilst the other, a portrait of Henry VIII, is on the wall in the men's mess room.

The children from St Anne's School Baslow were charming as the children of the 3rd Duke, and my deputy housekeeper, Judy Coggins, was proud to see her husband, Dick, play Lord Frederick Cavendish, who was shot within 24 hours of his arriving in Dublin, in the Phoenix Park massacre of 1882. I think one of my favourite parts of the Masque was the minuet danced by the man who would become 4th Duke, and his wife, Charlotte Boyle, staged against a backdrop of dozens of tiny candles reflected in the river. The visit of Queen Victoria at the time of the 6th Duke was spectacular as she was driven onto the stage in a horse drawn carriage, and when Paxton's Great Conservatory (made for the 6th Duke and much admired by Queen Victoria), was destroyed in the 1920s, the sound of breaking glass was deafening!

Schoolgirls from Lady Manners School in Bakewell played the Penrhos College years beautifully, and the aerial attack on the House was captured brilliantly as the House air raid siren sounded, and firecrackers in Stand Wood exploded all along the ridge.

The finale included a very moving tribute by His Grace, speaking from his place amongst the audience, and he then pressed the switch to start the magnificent firework display, which was set to music and was truly amazing. On the first night's show, one of the fireworks set fire to a bush in the garden, causing many of the staff's pagers to start bleeping wildly.

An artist was commissioned to paint the Masque whilst it was happening, and the resulting painting was turned into a greetings card, and the painting now hangs in the Cavendish Club.

The housekeeping team enjoyed the event as guests on the first evening, and on the second, were involved as stewards, so were lucky to see the whole thing all over again, and we were also invited to attend the 'wrap' party at the end of the evening, which was great fun. I can remember seeing Sir Joseph Paxton and Capability Brown deep in conversation, which seemed so appropriate, although I doubt whether the two actors were discussing gardening.

14

❧

Filming Chatsworth

Chatsworth has been a focus of interest for film makers for more than 50 years, either for those wanting to make a programme about how Chatsworth is run today, or about a character connected with Chatsworth, or perhaps a feature film, or just to provide the scenic setting for an unrelated subject entirely. Mostly, if the subject matter does not compromise the character and ethos of Chatsworth, the request is accepted, since not only do such films sometimes offer a generous facility fee, but they always generate advertising for the House.

'Fly-on-the-wall' documentaries are always favourites with the general public, but often create misgivings for those who have taken part in them, but there is no doubt that they increase our visitor numbers and no matter how mundane we think the subject matter is, it is invariably of interest to viewers.

My first experience of taking part in a 'docusoap' was in 1993-4 when Judy Leybourn and Sean Gilmartin of the Clear Picture Company spent a year following us about with a camera, including the filming of the fantastic Tercentenary parties. It is surprising how quickly they became friends, but as we felt less wary of them we were more in danger of letting slip something that ought not to be revealed! It is also interesting to note how many viewers of these programmes are prompted to write to Chatsworth, often about the oddest things. I was amazed to get a letter from a male viewer complaining about my language. He picked me up on the fact that when I had been describing the pattern of work, I had talked about the men going into a room first to erect the scaffolding, and then the ladies going in afterwards to polish furniture and so on. He said I was being disrespectful to men and should either have called the ladies 'women' or the men 'gentlemen'!

The next Chatsworth documentary was in 1999-2000 when the television company Bazal filmed *Great Estates*. On this occasion it was the fabulous party in July 2000 that featured in one of the episodes. One of the programmes also included a piece about our shade ring pliers, which we had thought were unique to Chatsworth. The pliers are an ingenious tool for removing the glass shades from the lamps in the Painted Hall. They have a wing nut that tightens the two jaws of a clamp around the brass ring that holds the shade in place once the light bulb has been removed. There is no space to get one's fingers round the ring to remove it, but the pliers allow a tight purchase on the ring so that it can be taken off easily and the shade removed for cleaning. I had been talking about these at one of my housekeeping demonstrations, when a man in the audience, called Alan Eades, asked if he could make a reproduction of them for sale in the Orangery Shop. This coincided with the filming and we thought it would be of interest to viewers, but were amazed that when it was broadcast, over 40 people telephoned to say they had got a set, or wanted one. Strangely enough, most of the people who already owned these pliers were living in Dundee.

Another item to feature in the programme was a story about the tin plates Her Grace had commissioned for sale in the Chatsworth shops. Her story generated so much custom for the plates when the piece was shown on television that they sold out immediately in the Orangery Shop and more had to be ordered. The plates are copies of some in the Collection at Chatsworth and are so realistic that apparently on a family picnic one day, Her Grace threw one to her son, shouting, 'Catch, Sto!' and he was terrified of dropping it as he thought it was the real thing!

The last television documentary about Chatsworth was aired in 2012 and covered the whole year's activities on the Estate in 2011. It was very well received and had a significant impact on our visitor numbers in what might otherwise have been a quiet year for us due to the poor weather. We were encouraged to suggest items of interest for filming if they came up unexpectedly, and we dutifully did so. However, this was something we later came to regret, since the one thing that many visitors now talk about when they are in the Great Dining Room is the struggle we had to get the creases out of the tablecloth.

The BBC Antiques Roadshow has visited Chatsworth twice, in 1996 and 2010, and has been extremely well-attended on both occasions, with the marquees erected on the private West and South Lawns and the queue of people stretching all along the West Drive and down the footpath as far as the bridge. The night before the event in 1996, there was a champagne reception for the Roadshow team in the Painted Hall, to which some Chatsworth staff were invited: Clive and I, Christine and John Thompson, Peter and Wilma Day and John and Margaret Oliver. It was great to meet Lars Tharp, Henry Sandon and the rest of the Antiques Roadshow team at the reception, and gratifying to realise that they were just as interested to meet Chatsworth staff and hear what made Chatsworth tick, as we were to hear their stories. We did have to 'sing for our supper': Peter talked to the group in the Library, and Christine and I gave a talk in the Great Dining Room. Clive still talks about how the furniture expert, John Bly, couldn't help peering underneath pieces of furniture and lifting things up, eyes darting everywhere whilst we were speaking. After their tour of the House we walked up to the Carriage House restaurant for a delicious dinner, where Clive and I were lucky enough to be seated on Her Grace's table next to Hugh Scully, Eric Knowles and Hilary Kay. Hugh Scully gave Their Graces an excellent vote of thanks, though I was surprised how nervous he seemed beforehand!

When the programme was broadcast, they showed an item from the art collection that they thought viewers would find interesting, a model aeroplane about 8 inches by 16 inches by 15 inches, made of tinplate and celluloid and with a clockwork motor. Made by the Märklin factory and listed in their 1909 catalogue, it was probably bought for Edward Cavendish, future 10th Duke of Devonshire (1895-1950). The item aroused great excitement when it was broadcast and His Grace thought it would be good to put it on display for visitors to appreciate, but our insurers were less enthusiastic as it had been valued at £120,000. However, the Chatsworth plumber, David Moran, is a keen model maker and he was able to make a replica that was displayed for the visitors. Dave is quite a character; not only is he an expert plumber and model maker, but is also on the first aid team and the fire team, he can pick a lock in no time and mend a broken key, and he can also juggle nine balls and swallow fire!

In October 2003 we took part in a different sort of programme when the 'BBC Breakfast' production team was commissioned by BBC One to make a week long series called *The Day Team From Chatsworth* presented by Nicki Chapman, and presenter of the BBC's Countryfile programme, John Craven. It took a behind-the-scenes look at Chatsworth House for an hour-long live broadcast every day for a week. It was a magazine programme that included live interviews with people such as interior designers, gardeners, cooks and farmers, and there were also daily recipes from the cooks at Chatsworth, both in the private kitchen and also in the kitchens at the Carriage House Restaurant, and they also requested housekeeping tips from us. When they first spoke to us about the filming, they said they would like to have two housekeeping tips for each programme, so we had to come up with ten for them to film in advance. Jayne Boyd and I had a lot of fun with it. We had to be certain that none of the tips we demonstrated would harm the objects we were cleaning, but amongst the tips we demonstrated were using salt and vinegar to clean old brass; gently rubbing a piece of stale white bread on the walls to remove grubby marks; how to refresh tired-looking imitation pearls; and fluffing up feather pillows by popping them in the tumble dryer with a tennis ball. The film crew wanted to make it entertaining, so we had to place the pillow in the tumble dryer, and then throw the tennis ball in from a distance away. It took time to get that right – Jayne and I will never make it into the Chatsworth cricket team! One cleaning tip that was especially enjoyable was cleaning the chandeliers with gin. I had been given the tip some time before but had not been able to try it out, but the droplets of the chandelier really did sparkle when we had finished. We thought it was probably a good job that we tried it on a small chandelier, as the fumes were quite overpowering.

At the beginning of every new visitor season and also at the start of Christmas opening, we often have a visit from local television to promote the attractions, and I remember just before the Christmas opening a few years ago, the local television company came along to cover several items which were filmed around our Christmas displays. They had invited a number of outside experts to talk about different topics relating to the festive season. It was a live broadcast and after I had done my piece to camera in the Library, I looked after some of the other contributors as they waited to be filmed. One of them was an absolute bag of nerves, and we tried all sorts of ways to help him relax, but could not put him at his ease. When it was finally time for him to go on air we were very surprised when he was announced, not as someone who would talk about festive cookery or table decorations, but as the expert who was going to talk viewers through the ways in which they could cope with the stress of the Christmas season!

Chatsworth has been used for many films over the years, particularly the wider Estate. D H Lawrence's *The Virgin and the Gypsy* was filmed in Beeley village and on Beeley Moor. Another novel by Lawrence, *The Rainbow*, was filmed in 1988 using an unoccupied cottage in Edensor and on the River Derwent alongside Beeley Meadow, where they filmed a nude bathing scene. Charlotte Bronte's *Jane Eyre* has been filmed in the Park on several occasions, and whilst this is a popular novel, nothing could match the excitement when we learned that Jane Austen's *Pride and Prejudice* was to be filmed at Chatsworth in the autumn of 2004. The attention to detail was so particular, and it was such an interesting thing with which to be involved.

The film company asked to use the Sculpture Gallery as the room where Lizzie Bennet comes upon the portrait of Mr Darcy, but in this production it was decided to use a marble bust as the likeness, instead of a painting. Mr Darcy was to be acted by Matthew MacFadyen, and so a marble resin bust of him was cast for use in the scene. It arrived several months before the filming was to begin and we stored it in a cupboard near the old switchboard. Ever a devotee of Mr Darcy, I enjoyed taking a secret peek inside the cupboard now and then to make sure he was all right.

At that time the Sculpture Gallery was hung with tapestries over red and green velvet covering the walls, and the production company asked that they be taken down for the filming. It was a huge task and I thought that the amount of effort involved would be disproportionate to the fees that the House would receive for allowing the filming. None of us anticipated the actual outcome, which was that we were so thrilled with the appearance of the Sculpture Gallery once the tapestries and velvet had come down that it was decided not to put them back again afterwards. Once the 12th Duke and Duchess came to Chatsworth, the project to restore the room to how it would have been in the 6th Duke's time commenced, and all the pieces of sculpture originally in that room were returned there and are now shown to best advantage.

Before the filming of *Pride and Prejudice* began, there was the usual reconnaissance visit by the film crew, and although there were lots of them, I have never seen a group so well organised. The coach deposited the team at the north front door and they all immediately sprang into action to determine lighting, angles, approaches on horseback, permissions to use various rooms, and how they were going to co-ordinate their filming with visitors in the House. The actual filming went like clockwork, and although we had to ask visitors to wait whilst shots were taken in the Sculpture Gallery, the guides did it so well, entertaining the visitors with stories whilst they waited, that we had no complaints, and they seemed to enjoy the experience.

Lighting was something members of the film crew were concerned about in the Sculpture Gallery since they wanted to use a number of '360 degree shots' and any lighting rig would be in the way. The solution was to use helium balloons to contain the lighting strips, requiring long hoses from gas tankers outside in the Gardens to keep the balloons filled. They looked like vast killer whales as they bobbed about, black and white, within the skylight at the north end of the room. A new 'wall' was built to obscure any view into the Orangery Shop, and special plug sockets were made and painted in case they were spotted by an eagle-eyed viewer.

This incredible attention to detail spilled over into the Gardens, and in the weeks before filming began, the gardeners were instructed to mow the lawns without a roller so that they would not look out of place for an early 19th century landscape. One woman was busy working at a trestle table in the office passage for the whole five days of filming, doing nothing but make pretty paper lanterns that were taken into the garden to go along the edge of the Canal Pond for the end shot. We felt so sorry for her because they looked incredible once they were lit, but the director decided that it wasn't the look he wanted and consequently they were not used in the film.

We were lucky that Chatsworth was the last location for the filming and was therefore the location used for the 'wrap'. Helen Marchant's organisational skills were tested in arranging the most amazing party in just two weeks, and those of us who had been closely involved with the filming were invited to attend. A marquee was erected near the House Bridge opposite Mary's Bower and although the weather was atrocious on the evening of the party, with a howling gale and driving rain, the moment we entered the marquee we were transported to another world. Beautiful chandeliers hung from the roof, cosy sofas and armchairs were scattered over plush carpets and the food and drink were wonderful. Champagne was served in frosted glasses with lemon iced onto the rim, and all the food was in miniature – tiny bamboo baskets of mouth-sized fish and chips, bangers and mash and hot dogs, followed by tiny ice-creams and chocolate éclairs. A ceilidh band provided some of the music and a disc jockey had been brought from London for the dancing, led by Keira Knightley, who had played Elizabeth Bennet.

The film was released the following year, in September 2005, and in the same week as the London premiere, Chatsworth was chosen to host a special advanced showing of the film for regional press and tourism representatives and the Duke and Duchess allowed this to take place in the newly refurbished Chatsworth Theatre. Universal Pictures rented us the digital projection equipment for a second day so that we could have an extra two screenings for Chatsworth staff. It was a truly magical evening, when everyone dressed up and the Carriage House staff served drinks as we arrived and supplied ice-creams in the interval.

For many visitors, Colin Firth is still the definitive Mr Darcy, and I remember being approached by a lady outside the Lodge who asked, 'Could you tell me please where the lake is that Mr Darcy came out of?'

'It's at Lyme Park, Madam,' I replied, 'about half an hour's drive from here on the Stockport road.'

'Oh no, I think you'll find it's at Chatsworth!' she retorted. 'I'm surprised you didn't know that. I'm meeting my friend beside it in half an hour!' As she strode towards the entrance to the Chatsworth Gardens, I wondered how long her friend would be waiting for her beside the lake at Lyme Park.

In early 2008 Chatsworth was transformed into a dilapidated ancestral home for a remake of a 1940s classic, *The Wolfman*. It starred Anthony Hopkins, Benicio Del Torro and Emily Blunt and was to cost Universal Studios a staggering $85 million to produce; even Sir Anthony Hopkins said that he had never witnessed a production on this scale.

Parts of the Garden needed to be converted into a neglected and overgrown wilderness and a 'greens team' was employed to help with the transformation. Several members of seasonal staff helped with this and our younger son, Michael, and a couple of his friends also joined the team, so our house was overtaken with weary young men all needing to be fed and housed. The daily rate of pay was excellent, but as the work started in February and ended in March, the length of hours they were expected to work extended as the daylight hours increased and the young lads were aggrieved that their rate of pay was for the day and not for the number of hours worked!

For three nights the south front of the House could be seen ablaze, an illusion created with lighting rigs in every window and smoke machines positioned on the roof and along the riverbank, where they had placed huge tubes with holes at intervals along them. A smoke machine pumped smoke through the tube and gave the illusion of fire, and similar tubes were also placed on the House roof. It was so realistic that the emergency services had to be alerted as people driving through the Park were dialling 999 to call the fire brigade. Clive and I walked across from Edensor one evening to watch the filming from the bridge, and found it really rather disturbing to see the House 'on fire'. I was touched at the end of the filming to be given a bouquet of flowers by the director, who apologised for the disturbance they had caused inside the House. That was the only time that happened with a film crew, apart from when Sean and Judy spent the year filming with us in 1994.

When *The Wolfman* was released in 2009, Clive and I saw it at our local cinema in Chesterfield. Our gasps of horror were not those of the rest of the audience, as we were gasping not at all the gory slaughter, but at the terrifying and all too realistic burning down of Chatsworth!

15

⳥

Community

Chatsworth is far more than a just stately home; it is a family home, and has been a family home for the last 500 years not just to the Cavendish family, but also to all the families who live and work within it and on the Estate surrounding it. In these days of intense competition, the House and Gardens need to continually strive to find new ways to present what is on offer to visitors and encourage them to make return visits to Chatsworth. I am sure that this must be the goal for many other visitor attractions, but the thing that sets Chatsworth apart and makes it special is that its setting is within a living community of which the Cavendish family is still very much an active part.

There are four villages surrounding Chatsworth Park, and one village actually within it. Edensor is within the Park boundary, Beeley is to the south, and Baslow and Pilsley are to the north. There are now only a handful of houses in Beeley still owned by the Chatsworth Estate but the village is still proud of its Estate connections. It has a school built by Joseph Paxton in 1841 which since its closure has provided accommodation in the form of two flats.

Towards the rear of the old school is a building called the Duke's Barn which was built in 1791 to provide accommodation for the Duke's carriage horses when they were not required at the House. They were stabled in the barn and grazed on Beeley Meadow and an old field name, the 'Horse Pastures', between the village and the river, harks back to where the horses were buried. In 1983 when the Very Reverend Ron Beddoes (previously Provost at Derby Cathedral), came to take over as Priest-in-charge on the Chatsworth Estate, he admired the Duke's Barn and, as he was a governor of the Derby Royal School for the Deaf, he thought that the Barn would make a splendid place for the school's outdoor pursuits centre. The 11th Duke agreed, and the Barn was converted to become the Deaf Centre in 1986. It now provides an outdoor pursuits centre for youth groups generally, employment for some of the residents of the village, and, in addition to the village hall, a venue for village activities.

When Beeley School closed in the 1960s, the children were transported by a bus provided by the Chatsworth Estate to the school at Pilsley. This is still the case today, with an Estate bus doing the rounds of all the communities, and delivering the children to school at Pilsley.

Pilsley, also the location of the Chatsworth Farm Shop, is about two miles north-west of Chatsworth on the Bakewell Road. Pilsley is entirely owned by the Chatsworth Estate, providing accommodation for Estate workers and pensioners, and is also the home of the Estate School, which was built by Joseph Paxton in 1849. When Edensor School was demolished in 1950 the stone was taken to Pilsley to build a pair of memorial cottages on the main road as a memorial to Billy Hartington, the 11th Duke of Devonshire's elder brother, and a second pair of cottages was built alongside in 1970. By 1967, with only 14 pupils on the roll, there were serious concerns for the school's future, but numbers picked up and the school has since been extended several times, in 1969, 1998 and 2002. A key date in the Pilsley diary is the well-dressing week every July, celebrations for which include the Village Fair and the crowning of the Queen.

There are still several Estate cottages in Baslow, and most people on the Estate use the Doctor's surgery there. I don't think I have ever been to the doctors' without seeing someone from the Estate in the waiting room, although I don't think we are a particularly unhealthy lot! I think the residents of Baslow are pleased with their connection with the Estate, and certainly enjoy the walks through the kissing gate into the Park. This kissing gate was specially commissioned by the 11th Duke following a request from a Mrs Cannon, who wrote to him because she was unable to access the Park through the gate in her wheelchair. The Duke had a special gate designed to allow wheelchairs through into the Park, but not bicycles, and the gate was called 'The Cannon Gate' in her honour.

There is a longstanding tradition within the Cavendish family of kindness to others, stretching as far back as the Eyam Plague of 1665-6 when the villagers, led by their Rector, quarantined themselves away from the surrounding area in order to prevent the spread of the disease. The 3rd Earl of Devonshire ensured that food was placed for them at the Boundary Stone so the survivors would not starve. Over the 14 months that the plague raged, 260 lives were lost from Eyam's population of 800.

More recently, Baslow had two resident tramps, one of whom, Harry, lived in a cave on the Chesterfield Road. He always looked extremely dirty because he kept warm by sleeping in an old bath over a fire in his cave and so was continually being smoked like a kipper. He wore overcoats that were given to him by the villagers, and these were always singed by the fire. The other Baslow tramp was Davy Crocket, who Her Grace allowed to live in some redundant outbuildings at the Old Peacock Hotel. When the Peacock was about to be renovated to become the Cavendish Hotel, the outbuildings were needed so she bought him a railway carriage to live in, which was placed near to the main car park. John Thorp, who used to be the local milkman, remembers delivering milk to him, and how proud he was of his new home and wanted to show him round. Davy Crocket was a keen animal lover and kept a menagerie of cats, dogs and chickens, but after a few years the residents of Baslow complained about the noise of his cockerels waking them in the morning, so Her Grace paid for his railway carriage and contents to be moved into Chatsworth Park, where Davy continued to live the rest of his years. He was always clean, and had a wash every day in the river.

One of the Chatsworth characters who retired to Baslow was Maud Barnes, Her Grace's lady's maid. She was born in 1918 at Lismore Castle in Ireland where her father was clerk of works to the Estate, and the Barnes family and their six children moved to Hardwick in the 1920s when her father took on the same job there. Maud stayed on at home to care for her ailing parents, and after her mother died in 1944 she continued to look after her father and also managed to snatch a few hours out of the house to become a guide at Hardwick. When her father died in 1959 she moved to Chatsworth to become lady's maid to Her Grace. Maud retired in 1980 and moved out of Chatsworth House to a lovely little cottage in Baslow until her death in August 2000. Her Grace gave a wonderful eulogy at her funeral, as she had done at Ron Beddoes's funeral. Both tributes were poignant and entertaining, perfectly summing up the characters of the two very different individuals. Maud was a great friend to me when I first came to work at Chatsworth, fiercely loyal, very outspoken, incredibly nosey, but great fun to be with, and she loved tagging on with the young ones when we went out and about in the evenings after work. She was a staunch member of the WI and gave a word perfect rendition of 'The Green Eye of the Little Yellow God', a monologue written for the music hall in 1911 by J. Milton Hayes, which, with costume and actions was guaranteed to have the audience rolling in the aisles when Maud took to the stage at WI Group Meetings.

Edensor has been an Estate wholly-owned by Chatsworth for so long now that it's easy to forget that two centuries ago parts of the village belonged to other people, and what is now part of the Park was then sub-divided into small cultivated fields in order for the 400 or so inhabitants of the 80 village cottages to support themselves. It is still possible to see the ridge and furrow traces of their strips of land in the Park when the sun is low in the sky or if there is a thin covering of snow on the ground. Edensor today is confined within a wall, wholly to the west of the road through the Park, but until the 1760s the village straddled the road, extending across the flat land to the south of the hill known as The Crobs as far as the river below the House. When the 4th Duke decided to build a new bridge in 1763, the old bridge, the old mill and some cottages in the vicinity were taken away. The removal of the remainder of the village was completed by Paxton and the 6th Duke some 70 years later, when the 'new village' was built, including the house where Clive and I live today, which dates from 1840.

The stables in Edensor were designed by Decimus Burton in 1836 at the same time as he was assisting Joseph Paxton with the designs for the Great Conservatory. The stables subsequently became the Estate Office until 1958, when the office was moved to its present location next to the main road. The old stables then provided accommodation as eleven flats, primarily for Estate pensioners.

The two lodges on either side of the gate at the north entrance to the Park near the Estate office were built by Sir Jeffrey Wyatville, ten years after he had completed the North Wing of the House. At that point the 6th Duke and Paxton started the work on the new Edensor village. There is a lovely story that when the 6th Duke asked Paxton to design a style of cottage for the village, Paxton drew up several suggestions for the Duke to choose from. The 6th Duke couldn't make up his mind and said, 'Do me one of each!' However, it was actually John Robertson who created the designs using the pattern books of John Loudon and P.F. Robinson to create the wild mixture of styles to be found in the village, from an Italianate villa to a Norman villa and with everything you can think of in between.

The new buildings included a school for boys on the village green built in 1839 to a design by Paxton, which was closed and demolished in 1950. Mr Wragg (father of the librarian Tom Wragg), was headmaster in the early part of the 20th century, when the boys were beaten for being late or for having dirty boots. He was furious when they were taken away from their studies to caddy for guests at Chatsworth who wanted to play golf!

At the north end of Chatsworth Park there is a large stone which used to be known as Elephant Rock due to its unusual shape. With the approach of Queen Victoria's Golden Jubilee in 1887, the local physician, Dr Wrench, proposed that the rock be inscribed to commemorate her jubilee and be renamed the Jubilee Rock. Ten years later, to mark the Queen's Diamond Jubilee, the dial of the clock on Baslow Church was redesigned by Dr Wrench and officially started by Duchess Louisa.

With this Jubilee Rock in mind, John Oliver, the comptroller at Chatsworth, suggested doing something to commemorate the Millennium, and favoured having a Millennium Rock placed in a prominent position on the Estate. Henry Sheldon, Brian Gilbert and David Spencer spent time hunting for a suitable stone and eventually found a four tonne rock near to the Duke's Seat in Stand Wood. It then had to be approved by both Her Grace and Carl Wragg, who was going to carve it, before being moved with webbing slings into position at the top of The Crobs. The stone was aligned between the west front door of the House and the top of the Paddocks Avenue, west of Edensor. Just before it was finally fixed into place, two walkers who had wandered from the path to see what was happening were invited to put something beneath the stone. They both dropped a coin into the hole, having nothing else in their pockets at the time, but this led to the decision to place a set of coins, minted in 2000, in a jar, along with the current Chatsworth leaflet and photographs of the group who had been involved with the project.

Every village has its share of characters and Edensor has been no exception. Every village has a busybody who likes to know what's happening, but without whom nothing would get done. Jayne Boyd and I remember, as young mothers in the village, chatting about the two busybodies of our day and wondering who would take their place when they had 'moved on' into the churchyard. Jayne suddenly looked at me in consternation. 'You don't think it will be us two, do you?' she asked. Needless to say, Jayne and I still live in the village, but neither of us thinks we fit the bill – not yet, anyway!

The Estate villages are special because the inhabitants all know each other and are all linked by a common bond – Chatsworth. Everyone living in Pilsley and Edensor works or has worked at Chatsworth, and the people living in the couple of houses that are tenanted join in with village life with great gusto and are very much a part of the community. Young families live side by side with spinsters, young singletons and pensioners, and we all join together to share the joys and sorrows of everyday life in a way that most communities lost over 50 years ago. The Cavendish family are part of this community too, always taking part in village events, be it school assemblies or the Village Fair at Pilsley, or Edensor Village Day and Church services, and they know the people who live in the villages and how the fabric of the whole slots together.

Charles, a pensioner living in Edensor, emigrated to New Zealand at the age of 80 to be with his family just outside Christchurch. It was a huge decision for him as he had been born on the Estate, lived there all his life and started work in the Estate Office when it was in the old stables. We had been neighbours for many years and used to have his dog to stay with us when he went to New Zealand to visit his family, and I kept in touch with him after he left. He was always wistful when we spoke on the telephone, and each time I felt he was making the best of it and would really have preferred to be living back on the Estate, though he was so grateful for the welcome he had received from his son-in-law and his new wife.

The Duke and Duchess went on holiday to New Zealand in 2010 and the Duke asked me for Charles's address as they wanted to visit him whilst they were there. They had only been back in England a couple of days when the earthquake struck Christchurch in September 2010. I couldn't get in touch with Charles for several days, but eventually I received an email from his son-in-law to say that they were all well, but the house had suffered and everything was in a bad way. It was a great relief to finally speak to Charles, but he was very unhappy and the aftershocks of the earthquake were very frightening. He contacted the Estate and it was arranged for him to return to Edensor, and he now lives in one of the Cavendish flats. I went to collect him from Manchester airport on 29th April 2011 and it was a touching reunion, with both of us in tears. I drove him home on the scenic route, the weather was glorious and the spring flowers were out and he was so glad to be coming home.

Sadly Charles wasn't back in time for the series of lunch parties that Her Grace held for Edensor villagers in February 2011. She hosted the parties at her home in the Old Vicarage, held over several days and with a dozen of us at a time. It was fun to get together, as although we see each other most days, everyone is always so busy and there isn't the opportunity to chat, especially in the winter months when we aren't in our gardens as much and just wave from one car to another. Her Grace gave us a real treat and it was so very typical of her to think of doing it.

The village is dominated by the presence of St Peter's Church, situated on the top of a hill and with a great spire that soars above it. The church was completed in 1867 by the 7th Duke of Devonshire to plans by the architect Sir Gilbert Scott and it replaced a 14th century church on the same site. The 7th Duke was a deeply religious man, devoted to the memory of his wife Blanche who had died when she was only 28, and to whom he taught algebra on their honeymoon. The church is very much a part of the Estate life, with an annual Sheep Service each spring, a tradition that was started by Ron Beddoes and is still ongoing. We give thanks for the sheep on the Estate that are an intrinsic part of the landscape, one they help to create, since the Park would look very different without the short-cropped grass that feeds them. The children from Pilsley School come to the Sheep Service and to the services for Mothering Sunday, Harvest Festival and the Christmas Carol Service. We also have services linked to special events over at the House, such as the Tercentenary Thanksgiving service held on 15th May 1994, which was followed by lunch on the Vicarage lawn attended by Their Graces.

The church used to hold a St Peter's Day Garden Party, but now joins with the whole village in our annual Edensor Village Day and Open Gardens, which raises money for charity and for the church. It is a vast church, far too large for the community it serves, and it costs a fortune to run, so the Parochial Church Council is constantly organising fund raising activities to meet running costs and pay for the upkeep of the building. Over the years church fund-raising events have included garden parties, azalea walks in the Chatsworth Gardens, flower festivals, concerts and gala dinners. Eric Knowles was the guest speaker at one such dinner in 2000, and in 2013 we invited Alan Titchmarsh, who very generously gave his time for nothing and the Duke and Duchess very kindly accommodated him in the House.

Alan has been visiting Chatsworth for many years and has been associated with the Country Fair for several years. He has stayed with the Dowager Duchess at Edensor, or in the main House on many occasions. In 2013 he came with his wife Alison, and was charming to everyone he met. It was a most memorable, idyllic summer evening, and following a reception in the Painted Hall, the guests strolled through the North Wing of the House and then up to the Carriage House restaurant for dinner. The gardeners had done a wonderful job with the table decorations, incorporating peonies, alliums and hosta leaves in metre-high cocktail glasses, with spikes of foxgloves flying out of the top. After a delicious meal, Alan entertained us with a talk about the garden he and his team had designed in South Africa for Nelson Mandela. He also told of an occasion when he had welcomed Her Majesty to Chelsea Flower Show, and later gave a talk to the ladies of the Sandringham WI. 30 ladies had assembled in the village hall for their WI meeting, when The Queen arrived to take part in the proceedings as a WI member. After the photographs had been taken, Alan stood up to give his talk, with the Queen seated on the front row and with a table between them.

'You're awfully close, Ma'am!' said Alan feeling rather hemmed in. 'Shall I just move this table?'

'Yes, you pull, and I'll push!' replied Her Majesty.

Later, in 2000, when Alan received his MBE from the Queen, she surprised him by remarking, 'You've given a lot of ladies a lot of pleasure!' He obviously understood this to be a reference to his WI talk, but it must have intrigued other people within earshot!

We wanted to present Alan with a present as a 'thank you' for his generosity in coming to speak to us, and also give the Duke a gift for accommodating Alan and his wife at Chatsworth. After much thought, we decided that Clive would make them both something out of wood, as he is a keen pole-lathe turner and worker in green wood. He turned a garden dibber for Alan, and made something for the Duke in the style of some of David Nash's work that we had seen at Lismore Castle – a block of wood 12 inches square by about 16 inches high, that David Nash had sliced horizontally with a chainsaw not long after the tree had been felled so that the wood warped and cracked as it dried out, creating a wonderful effect.

Clive decided to cut a circular piece of alder for the Duke only a couple of days before the dinner so that the cuts were all straight when we gave it to him, and the Duke would then have the pleasure of watching it twist and split as it dried out. The Duke appeared delighted with the gift and we were thrilled that he decided to put it on one of the tables in his private apartments. We were subsequently relieved that it behaved properly and warped and cracked into a lovely work of art.

16

❧

Fifty Years of Loving and Giving

On 20th September 1997, the 11th Duke of Devonshire had held the title for longer than any of his predecessors and in the year 2000 it became his 50th year in that position. Not only that, but 2000 was also the year of Their Graces 80th birthdays, so they had three reasons to celebrate and parties were duly organised for the 14th and 15th July. Planning for the parties began many months prior to the event, but the physical preparations began two weeks before, when a huge marquee was erected, occupying two-thirds of the South Lawn. Extra 'arms' of the marquee extended towards the House, with a small pagoda for the jazz band who were to play during the reception. At the south end, near the Canal Pond, there was a huge awning for viewing the fireworks, should the weather be inclement.

I had to give a talk in Mansfield at the Mansfield Leisure Club on the afternoon of the 14th July, but was back home with just enough time to prepare for what was going to be the party to end all parties!

The invitation had specified fancy dress or lounge suit and initially it had been His Grace's intention that everyone should dress from one of the five decades since he became Duke in 1950. In the end it was decided that any fancy dress would be acceptable that could be said to vaguely connect with the historical theme so that guests would then not feel too restricted, but at the outset it seemed as though no one wanted to dress up. As the day approached, however, a kind of party frenzy swept through the House and spread across the Estate, so that on the night about a third of the guests did dress up, and I'm sure that the other two-thirds certainly wished they had! Most of the Cavendish family dressed up too, which all added to the fun and sense of atmosphere.

Days of dreary, cold windy weather did not bode well, and the day itself didn't dawn very fine. We had no idea what was inside the marquee. Once it was erected, we could peep inside from the State Apartment windows to see the wooden flooring going in, with raised terraces down each side and white fencing round the Seahorse Fountain, but once that was in place, the marquee flaps were firmly closed and no one was allowed to see inside, except the building yard team who delivered their contribution and left again. I went to see Helen Marchant for something a day or two before the party, knocked on her office door, and His Grace called,

'Come in!' so of course I had no option but to enter. 'Helen's in the tent, Christine,' he said when he saw me.

'Oh, right, thank you. Sorry to have bothered you, Your Grace. I'll come back to see her later.'

'No, no, come in and see me. How are you?' His Grace wanted to talk about the party and was really pleased to hear that so many people were going to be dressing up. 'Splendid, splendid!' he cried.

'What about you, Your Grace?' I asked. 'Will you be dressing up?'

'Oh, I'm just going to wear my navy blazer and a perfectly vulgar pair of black and white shoes and a straw boater. William's dressing up... he mentioned something about a pair of tights, but I'm not sure what he's going as!'

Throughout the House, there was a great air of anticipation and excitement, with stifled giggles and sudden silences as secrets were kept. Entering the sewing room and finding a great heap of straw-coloured silk and blue letters gathered in a heap on the table, I said, 'What's all this about? Is it the children's banner?'

'Never you mind, you'll have to wait and see!'

The fancy dress hire shop in Matlock did a roaring trade, coping with the Chatsworth party in addition to Cromford Carnival, and anyone who went in reported seeing at least two other people from Chatsworth wanting to try on costumes of one sort or another. 'How many people are going to this party?' cried June, the proprietor. 'What, twelve hundred? I'm sure I must have had at least half of them through here!

It's like being Cinderella and working my socks off but with no chance of ever getting to the ball!'

I had collected our costumes at the very last minute on my way back from the talk in Mansfield, and we had just an hour to prepare ourselves for the party. I had decided to dress up as Charlotte Boyle, the daughter and heiress of the Earl of Burlington. She had married the son of the 3rd Duke of Devonshire in 1748, and it was through this marriage that the wealth of the Burlington family became part of the Devonshire inheritance. I wore a gold and black hooped skirt and overdress, and a veiled tricorn hat, and Clive was in costume as my consort, William, Lord Hartington. He was dressed in a pair of knee breeches, white stockings, my best black shoes, a red and gold waistcoat, a white ruffled shirt and jabot, and a fabulous chestnut brown embroidered velvet frockcoat. To crown the whole thing off, he wore a black wig and pigtail. He looked wonderful, and the moment he put the costume on, his whole demeanour seemed to change and I felt obliged to drop him a curtsey!

Coaches had been laid on from Baslow, Beeley, Pilsley and Edensor, but I was afraid I might have difficulty getting onto the coach with my hooped skirt, and as we also knew we wouldn't have long to get ready, we decided to go in the car. My mother had come over from Chesterfield to look after Philip and Michael, and we were very excited as they waved us off. However, as we waited to pull out onto the main road at the bottom of the village, every car that went past seemed to be filled with sober-suited occupants, with not a single sign of fancy dress in any of them. What had we done? Full of misgivings we joined the queue of traffic turning off at Sandy's Turn to make our way across to the House.

It was with enormous relief that we spotted a highwayman in the distance, and then parked next to David Oakley and James, the vet from Bakewell, who were both in fancy dress, James as another highwayman, and David as an Elizabethan page. We walked in together, thinking 'safety in numbers', and it didn't seem to matter that we couldn't see anyone else in fancy dress; we were all four determined to enjoy ourselves. As we strolled down the Broad Walk we saw Victoria Edwards dressed as a ringmaster in a frockcoat, fishnet tights, a lurex waistcoat and a silk-banded top hat, whilst her husband Mike was Biggles, in jodhpurs, a leather bomber jacket, wellingtons, a flying helmet and elaborate moustaches. The party had begun! As if on cue, the sun came out, and it turned into a balmy summer's evening as we swept down the Lion Steps and made our way through the reception tent, to be presented to the Duke and Duchess by the Master of Ceremonies. As everyone turned to gaze at those in fancy dress, any doubts we may have had about dressing up swiftly disappeared. The champagne flowed and we had a ball!

It was lovely to see so many people enjoying themselves, entertained by the jazz band playing beneath a little pagoda in the middle of the lawn. Her Grace looked breath-taking in the costume that Louisa, wife of the 8th Duke, had worn to her own Devonshire House Ball held in honour of Queen Victoria's Diamond Jubilee on 2nd July 1897, when she appeared as Xenobia, the Empress of Palmyra. His Grace had told me that the party was being held in almost the same week as the Duchess of Devonshire's Ball, and I wondered if that was what had inspired Her Grace. The dress Her Grace wore had been made for Duchess Louisa by the House of Worth in Paris, which was founded by Charles Frederick Worth (1825-1895), the great Parisian couturier, and was made from cloth of silver and gold, and silk gauze, with a full train in emerald green velvet stitched with sequinned peacock feathers. The costume had been carefully preserved at Chatsworth over the years, and was even displayed in the American exhibition of 1979. To complete the outfit, Her Grace wore a green velvet cap held in place with Louisa's tiara and decked with extra multi-coloured dyed ostrich feathers, which also featured in her dramatic plumed fan. She looked as though she was having a great time, and in fact when I spoke to her about the party on the following Monday she said, 'I thought at my age I had been everywhere and done everything that was worth doing, but I have never enjoyed myself so much in all my life. It was wonderful!'

His Grace wore his navy blazer and his black and white shoes, together with his straw boater, and he looked as though he was really enjoying himself. Lord Hartington went as a university don, in cap and gown, and Lady Hartington looked very demure in a costume that might have been worn by Bess of Hardwick or Mary Queen of Scots – a black velvet gown with a white cap, and she looked lovely. William (Lord Burlington) went as the 6th Duke, in knee breeches and a black velvet frock coat.

Other costumes were imaginative and varied. Nicky Dunne (the young man who would marry Lady Jasmine in 2003), was dressed in a toga, laurel wreath and carried a watering-can – the Emperor Fountain, of course! The Chatsworth housemen invited His Grace's grandson, Eddie Tennant, to join them in their dressing-up, appearing as His Grace's racehorses, two men per horse. Christine Thompson had made the saddlecloths in the Duke's colours, and each cloth had the horse's name appliqued onto it in blue lettering: Duck Row, Teapot Row and Emperor Fountain, and the housemen's wives were the owners. Rob Law, gamekeeper, dressed as an Arab owner, Tony Hubbuck (House electrician) was the trainer and John Riley (car park attendant) was the bookie, in a white coat, bowler hat and a blackboard with all the odds on it, and his name at the top, 'Honest John'. Someone somewhere carried a bucket which offered 'Top quality horse muck, 50p per bucket', and the jockey, of course, was Eddie Tennant. He was dressed in his grandfather's straw-coloured silks, riding hat and all the gear, and he kept the whole lot on all evening, including the riding hat and the bow-legged stance. His fiancée had poured herself into a leather catsuit with a magnificent cat mask and she looked fantastic. As the evening wore on, the wine flowed and the dancing began, and I can remember seeing Eddie leaning against a tent pole and sliding gracefully to the floor.

The land agent, Roger Wardle, went as Elvis, wearing a blue Teddy Boy suit with blue suede shoes and a black Elvis wig, and his wife Sue was one of his groupies in a little pink number with a blonde wig. There was another Elvis there as well, Peter Day, who wore the real thing, a gold suit that Elvis actually wore on the cover of one of his albums. Peter hired it in London, paying a large deposit for such a historic garment. His wife Wilma painted his shoes gold, and he dyed and back-combed his hair. Wilma had back-combed her hair too and wore a purple and black sparkly dress. Charles Noble and Kitty were from the Twenties, with Kitty wearing an original dress that had belonged to her grandmother, whilst Charles wore a striped blazer and a straw boater. Another person from the Twenties in a black dress and feathered headband was Jo Wood, wife of the deputy land agent, Nick, who, because it was also Bastille Day, was dressed as a French revolutionary with a red scarf round his head.

Judy Coggins was dressed as Antonio Verrio's interpretation of the 1st Duke's housekeeper, Mrs Hackett, depicted on the ceiling of the Great Chamber. She was draped in grey tulle, with a laurel leaf head band and a pair of shears, reflecting Verrio's painting of Mrs Hackett as 'The Fury of Atropos cutting the thread of life with her abhorred shears'. Judy's husband, Dick, was dressed as the artist Verrio, with false Italian moustaches, a white smock, velvet artist's beret and carrying a paint palette. Judy told me that he had been desperate to dress up as something as he could no longer fit into his lounge suit!

Clive's brother, Frank, had been invited because he was a tenant farmer, and he dressed up as his great-great-great-grandfather, the first miller in the Park. David Spencer, the Domain supervisor, was eye-catching in the costume of a North American Indian, with braids in his long hair and red face paint, showing a black hand across his face. Mrs Symonds appeared as the Veiled Vestal, copying the renowned Monti statue placed initially in the Sculpture Gallery when it arrived from Compton Place in December 1999, and she looked almost funereal, veiled and draped in white. Sean and Lorraine were the 6th Duke and his escort, looking pure Mr Darcy and Elizabeth Bennet.

There were many guests that I did not know. One lady, dressed as a bunch of grapes, had clearly put much thought and effort into her costume. It struck me that it was easy to do as all Clive and I had done was to hire a costume, but this woman must have spent hours making her amazing outfit. She was quite small, in purple tights and a purple leotard, with her torso covered in purple balloons. On her head she wore a pointed green cap as the stalk of the bunch of grapes. We were amused to see that the balloons got in the way when she was given a glass of champagne – she simply produced a pin from her hair and popped a couple of balloons to solve the problem.

Mr and Mrs Penrose went as a pair of leprechauns, both looking rather strange. He wore a weird Uriah Heap sort of costume with a green face, and Mrs Penrose wore a peasant's outfit, a wig of ginger ringlets and a headscarf, and had outlandish eyelashes painted onto her cheeks. Bob and Joy Damerell went as two Cavaliers in long black wigs, feathered hats and thigh boots, and Diane and David Naylor made gilded picture frames to carry like sandwich boards with holes for their faces, masked as Georgiana and Henry VIII.

The hour-long reception on the south lawn was over in no time, and the master of ceremonies invited us to take our places for dinner. Now was the moment to see what had been hidden inside the marquee, and we approached the doorway in great excitement. Jaws dropped as we entered and stood for a moment, spellbound by the wonder of the scene. A myriad of fairy lights studded the black silk roof like stars glittering in the night sky. Floodlights illuminated the Seahorse Fountain and the stage at the south end of the tent. The dance floor in front of the stage was made of marble flagstones, and the floor and stage were enclosed by girders forming the shape of the 11th Duke's 1970 display greenhouse. The revolving stage had a rainbow hoop of colour above it, and as we entered, the band was playing Big Band music, which they played superbly throughout the meal. Waiters and waitresses in white-gloves held the table numbers on poles so that it was easy to find our places, and when we were seated, Michael Gowdey, Vicar of Edensor and Beeley, read a special Grace that he had composed:

For fifty years of loving and caring,
For fifty years of trusting and daring
For fifty years of tending and striving
For fifty years of growing and thriving
For fifty years of laughing and weeping
For fifty years of waking and sleeping
For fifty years of welcome and giving
For fifty years of grateful living
We thank thee, Lord of all Creation
And pray Thee, bless our celebration
Amen

Dinner began with ballotine of Scotch salmon, followed by rosette of English spring lamb, and finished with strawberry shortcake, Hartington Stilton and Wensleydale cheeses. The service was brilliant, with over 200 staff waiting on, and 20 chefs in the carefully hidden kitchens running the length of the tent, unseen by the guests. Lord Hartington, Roger Wardle, and the Duke spoke at the end of the meal, and then the dancing began. The dance bands were superb, with a seamless transition from one to the next as the stage revolved. As a special surprise for Her Grace, Helen Marchant had organised an Elvis impersonator to be part of the entertainment. Her Grace seemed enthralled by the performance and I wished that I had taken a photograph of her, representing such an absurd juxtaposition of characters and times – the Empress of Palmyra, hands clasped, transfixed in front of the stage as the King himself (or so it seemed, he was so good), held us in his thrall. At the end he offered his thanks for being invited to perform and said how much he had been made to feel at home, concluding, 'What with His Grace, and Her Grace… It sure feels like Graceland!'

I was an extraordinary evening, with people of all ages throwing themselves with utter abandonment into having a thoroughly good time. We danced until four in the morning and I wore a hole in my shoes! I have a photograph of His Grace, at one point sitting alone at a table, just so evidently enjoying watching everyone else having such a good time, that it really did seem to sum up the man and his incomparable generosity.

The Lavatories! These certainly deserve a special mention, for we had never seen such sumptuous Portaloos before, nor have we since. Beautifully carpeted and decorated, gold taps and with framed pictures on the walls – what a palace! I even took a photograph of them.

There were four bars, one in each corner of the marquee and each serving free drinks throughout the night. They were each decorated to depict a different aspect of the Estate in photographs and objects: The House, The Farmyard, the Gardens and the Farm Shop. The walls of the tent were hidden by arched rustic 'stone' which were actually wooden blocks made by the building yard, and reminded us of the stonework in the Stableyard and the wonderful arches at each end of the maze. All along the 'walls' between the bars were photographs of the 11th Duke and Duchess during their 50 years at Chatsworth.

The firework display was announced at midnight, and the guests gathered on the south lawn. A full moon hung perfectly above the Canal Pond and John Oliver told me later that someone had calculated that it would be 500 years before the moon would again be in the same place at the same time on the same day of the year. The positioning was critical and Helen Marchant had checked ten minutes before the displays began. She was horrified to see the moon was in exactly the wrong place for the Aquatique display, and feared it would ruin the whole effect.

However, by the time midnight arrived, the moon had moved on and was in exactly the right place for the most ethereal and magical display.

We had been wondering what the large 'swimming pool' between the marquee and the Canal Pond had been intended for, and now we were to find out. The pool had been filled with water and the pipes running within this were pierced with tiny holes from which a fine mist of spray was thrown upwards to about 30 feet, and onto this faintly moving spray were projected images of Their Graces from the time they first met right through to the present day. It was the most dreamlike, ghostly display imaginable as the images wavered and shimmered before our eyes, and the music, bursts of coloured laser beams and amazingly timed, magnificent fireworks burst above us. We knew that we would never see the like again. Her Grace said that it was utterly fairylike, just like the drawings of an Inigo Jones masque.

Fortunately, some of us were lucky enough to see it all again, as there was a second party the following evening for people from the county who had given something to the county, or to Chatsworth, or to the Duke and Duchess personally. The guests included people from the Red Cross, our local councillors, doctors and the local vet, Her Grace's hairdresser and the man who sold His Grace his newspaper at Chester-field station when he was catching the train to London.

Clive and I qualified for an invitation to the second evening because Clive had been chair of the local Chatsworth parish meeting for over 30 years. For the second evening, the dress code was black tie. The reception took place as it had the night before, with the Master of Ceremonies announcing the 1,200 guests, and when it was our turn he announced, 'Mr and Mrs Clive Robinson, in their normal clothes this evening!' as he evidently remembered we had come in fancy dress the night before!

After the champagne reception, with music by Moment's Notice, we went through to the marquee as we had done the previous evening, and on this occasion we were seated next to Ian Lawson and his wife. Ian was the auctioneer who sold the Duke's sheep at Chatsworth's annual sheep sale, selling upwards of 6,000 sheep in a single day. He had never missed an auction, even though the event often fell on his wedding anniversary. Grace was said by the Bishop of Derby, and music was provided during dinner by the young people of the county in the form of Derbyshire City and County Wind Band, The Peak District String Orchestra, The South Derbyshire Youth Orchestra and The Amber Bells, a group of hand bell ringers from schools in the Amber valley. Once again, a lovely booklet was produced as a guide to the evening, which was a great memento to take away. The Toast was made by HM Lord Lieutenant for Derbyshire, Mr John Bather, and at midnight, there was once again fireworks and the Aquatique show, before everyone went home… exhausted!

17

⚜

Treats!

Although the north entrance of the House is no longer the entrance used by the family, it is still the way in for the thousands of daily visitors to the House, and also many who come to charitable events, special evening events, and even on occasion, the way in or out, for royalty. On 4th July 1986, Her Royal Highness Diana, Princess of Wales, was due to attend a Barnardo's charity tea for 7,000 helpers on the South Lawn at Chatsworth, so there were a lot of preparations to spruce things up a bit before she arrived. There wasn't going to be enough time to paint everything that should be painted and as the Stables windows were especially in need of redecoration, it was decided that only the outside window frames that might be noticed should be painted. We were living at the Stables at the time, and our windows were scheduled for painting. Pendletons, the local painters and decorators, came to do the job, and I can remember young Kevin Pendleton at the top of his ladder with his paint pot on the windowsill. I passed a mug of tea out for him, but he was so intent on his nattering whilst he worked, that he dipped his brush into the tea instead of the paint pot and nearly fell off his ladder when he realised what he was doing!

It had been arranged that at the end of the tea party, the Princess would be driven down the North Drive. However, once she realised that the children of members of staff and their families had been invited to line the drive, she decided to walk, so that she could meet them, and there was great excitement amongst the well-wishers as the Princess came into view. She was dazzling in a navy blue skirt and polka dot jacket, topped with a blue straw hat set at a jaunty angle, and she seemed to have a special word for everyone. Our elder son Philip, then aged nearly two, had been primed to offer the Princess a posy of pansies, and as she came along the line of eager children she paused and smiled at him and held out her hand. I think Philip had been expecting a storybook princess, complete with gown and crown, and was reluctant to hand the flowers over to anyone else. Grandma stepped in to help. 'Give the flowers to the lady, Philip,' she said. The Princess smiled as she bent down to take them from him.

'Are these for me, Philip?' she said. 'Pansies! My favourites. Thank you!' It was a lovely moment, but sadly not one that Phil would remember.

In December 1994 I was lucky to be invited to be presented at the Court of King James's Palace. The Prince of Wales was always very grateful for the times he came to stay at Chatsworth over the years, usually in the winter time when we were all extremely busy with the House deep clean. We got on with our work without any fuss and he could just relax and enjoy himself. For a couple of years he invited a handful of people from Chatsworth to go to St James's Palace, and Clive and I were thrilled to be invited, along with Jane Brindley and Sue Shafie, who at that time did all the buying and window dressing for the House shops. Their Graces used to own a wonderful house on Chesterfield Street in Mayfair, and they made it available for us on the occasion of the St James's Palace visit. I made a point of keeping a detailed account of the wonderful time we had.

We travelled by train to London, arriving at Their Graces' house in good time to change for the visit to the Palace. At 5pm there was a ring on the doorbell to say that our taxi had arrived, and with great excitement we told the driver, 'St James's Palace!' The taxi dropped us at the courtyard to the Marlborough Road entrance, where several people were already gathering.

Once inside, we passed two enormous malachite *tazze* – great dishes of green Siberian marble, set on pedestals on the red carpeted stairs – and into the first reception room, where the walls were lined with royal portraits: Henry VII, Charles II, Prince Rupert and others, and on either side of the fireplace were two beautiful pedestal flower arrangements with Christmas greenery, fresh pineapples, roses, gypsophila, spirea, and with six white candles lit in each arrangement.

As we entered the reception room, we were offered drinks and we chatted there until about 6.30pm, when we were directed to a queue for the presentation to His Royal Highness. The queue passed through a room of armoury, overlooking the courtyard by which we had entered the Palace. As we progressed slowly forward, we admired the stunning display of swords, scimitars and guns on the walls and a huge bowl of amaryllis and roses on the table. At the doorway to the next room we were presented to the Prince of Wales, and exchanged a few words about our journey and where we were staying. We then moved through a room hung with tapestries into two State apartments, again both with red carpeting and red damask curtains. There were two huge pier tables in each room, one with an enormous ormolu and tortoiseshell clock upon it. There was also a vast Christmas tree, which must have been over 25 feet high, hung with tiny golden lights.

As we entered the room, we were offered drinks and footmen came round with canapés, served on salvers decorated with leaves and orchids. Once Prince Charles had greeted everyone, he came into the room and circulated among the groups of people. He greeted us with, 'Ah, and how's the Chatsworth contingent getting on?' He chatted to us for quite a while about the Orangery Shop and said how much he liked the Farm Shop.

The Prince told us that he had been walking with his dog in the Old Park at Chatsworth the previous weekend, when a shepherd in a Land Rover came chasing after him, and then recognised him. 'Oh, it's you!' he exclaimed, 'I was just going to give you a rocket for trespassing.'

He also told us about meeting Edward Kennedy that weekend, during a tree planting ceremony at the Golden Gates. They each planted a lime tree in the avenue of golden limes, newly placed to commemorate the 11th Duke and Duchess's golden wedding anniversary in 1991. The Prince said that Edward Kennedy especially enjoyed the lunch that was served after the planting ceremony and that, when he then visited the Edensor churchyard to see his sister Kathleen Kennedy's grave, he was side-tracked into the tea room for a cream tea!

The event ended at about 8pm and we strolled back to Chesterfield Street through the festively decorated streets of London. It had been a fantastic experience, so special that I wrote it all down before I went to bed.

Our visit to St James's Palace was a wonderful, unique experience in our lives and quite unforgettable. But there are other less dramatic occasions that stick in the mind. One such event was on 6th March 1995 when Judy Coggins and I travelled by coach from Chatsworth to Hardwick Hall where Lord Burlington was to plant a tree at Stainsby Mill. We were given a tour of the Hall, including the roof, the attics and store rooms which, like those at Chatsworth, seemed to hold a vast collection of old and interesting items. After lunch in the old kitchens, His Grace made a very moving speech in which he said that it was the first time he had been back to Hardwick since it had been handed over to the Treasury in exchange for death duties and given to the National Trust in 1959.

It was, perhaps, a small event in the diary but one that once again illustrates the strong sense of family that has long been fostered by the Dukes of Devonshire, involving their staff in the many events and celebrations that feature in their busy lives.

The 11th Duke of Devonshire was Patron of Chesterfield Football Club, and in 1997 the team reached the semi-final of the FA Cup for the first time. The game would be played against Middlesbrough at Old Trafford, and knowing that his staff would appreciate going to the match, the Duke organised two coaches and tickets for staff and families. Philip, Michael and I were in the party and we had the most fantastic day. On other occasions we were treated to seats at Wimbledon, for His Grace was connected with the event and had tickets that he chose to use for his staff. I was lucky enough to go several times to see play on Number One Court, watching the all-time greats of John McEnroe and Bjorn Borg. Another treat was a trip for every member of staff to go to the Sheffield Arena to see *Les Miserables*, paid for out of His Grace's own pocket – he was such a generous man.

I think the most bizarre treat I have ever enjoyed was when I was invited to attend the Barmote Court at Chatsworth on 2nd November 2010. The courts were established in 1288 and are still held in the lead mining districts of Derbyshire. Their original function was to settle disputes arising between the individual miners and landowners and also to record the miners' claims so that they could pay the necessary royalties and tithes to the Church, the Crown and the landowner.

Although packed with tradition, the Barmote Court is still a legal entity, with a legal job to do. Lisa Bloor, one of the Estate Office accountants, Steve Porter, head gardener and I had been invited to attend the court in session at the Cavendish Rooms and Lisa and I were the only women in attendance.

The court and observers assembled at the bar of the Covered Ride at the Cavendish Rooms, where Eddie Tennant, as Barmaster, bought everyone a drink as they arrived. To hold with tradition, the drink was half a pint of beer and as I would not have dreamed of asking for anything else, I enjoyed my half pint of Chatsworth Gold along with the men, together with the traditional slab of bread and a hunk of strong cheese. We stood chatting until the bailiff called, 'Oyee, Oyee, Oyee!' and then announced the Court was in session. He called a roll of the jurymen, 24 in total since it was a joint session of two separate courts. Each juryman answered, 'Here Sir', and then the twelve jurymen from the first calling were taken through to their seats against the window in the coffee room that served as the courtroom. The second batch of jurymen were then called through and sat in the seats in front of them. The visitors were called next and we were directed to seats at the back of the courtroom. Finally the bailiff came in, calling, 'All rise', and we stood up as the Barmaster, the Duke's representative (Nick Wood), Henry Stephenson, and the legal barrister came in.

On the table in front of them stood the engraved brass measuring dish presented to the Barmote Court in 1509 by Henry VIII. Normally empty, it represents the authority of the Court, but on this rare occasion it was filled with galena, lead ore – the first time that any of the Court had seen it used. The ore was the last takings from the Mill Dam mine at Glebe Mine, which was due to close at the end of the year. It was a truly historic moment, the continuation of 500 years of tradition, and it felt a great privilege to witness it.

There was a very elaborate swearing in on the Bible of the first twelve jurymen, who then elected a foreman. The Barmaster then announced how much lead had been mined in the individual mines during the previous year. The second hearing was then heard, which meant that the jurymen from the first hearing had to change places with the twelve jurymen from the second hearing, and the whole process was repeated.

When the Court had been heard, we went into the Burlington Room for lunch. An ancient Grace was said, which heralded a delicious meal of soup, roast beef and Yorkshire pudding and then an almond tart with fruit and aniseed ice-cream followed by coffee and truffles. Finally a huge silver punchbowl and silver ladle was carried in and steaming green punch was ladled into large tumblers, which were well over half full of the concoction of lemons, rum, brandy, Curacao and Guinness. The punch was passed round and then the speeches began, all of which were most interesting. At the end of each speech there was a toast, so we ended up drinking the whole tumblerful of punch. In earlier times the procedure would have included the smoking of clay pipes, each pipe being inscribed with the owner's name. The pipes were still present, duly engraved, but naturally we were not allowed to smoke them because of the smoking ban – but what a lovely treasure to take home!

18

◈

Christmas

C hatsworth must have been a wonderful setting for family
Christmases over the years, and it's such a pity that tantalisingly
little is known about what happened. I remember hearing my
grandmother talk about Christmas parties at the House for the Estate
children, and the excitement of travelling there with the children from
Beeley School and from other schools in the area.

We catch glimpses of the excitement here and there in documents in
the Chatsworth archive, such as one found in the 9th Duke's papers,
possibly written by his agent, Mr Cockerell, in 1917 whilst the Duke
and Duchess were in Canada, where the Duke was Governor-General.
On that occasion, the Estate children's Christmas party was held in the
Cavendish Hall (then called the Chatsworth Institute), on the afternoon
of Saturday 22nd December, when 250 schoolchildren of all ages
gathered in the Recreation Hall.

At that time during World War I the building was used as a
convalescent home for soldiers and sailors. They had been busy for days
with their preparations for the party, hanging bunting, evergreens and
tinsel, and with a tall mysterious something draped in white to the side
of the stage. The children were entertained on the stage by a conjuror
and ventriloquist, and then the 'cinema machine' was turned on and
the children were captivated, watching films of Charlie Chaplin. Tea
was then served in adjacent rooms, with the sailors waiting at table,
before everyone went back into the hall for the distribution of the
presents. Mr Cockerell's letter reports:

Suddenly, at the signal of a shrill whistle, the gaslights went out.
Simultaneously the white covering was removed from the tall mystery,
revealing a beautiful Christmas tree glittering with 50 sparkling electric
lights, the cinema lantern was directed onto the stage, the curtain arose,
and there, standing amidst a shower of falling snowflakes, was a real
live Father Christmas. Slowly he descended the steps with his capacious
sack, from which he produced a multitude of crackers and sweets. Not
only were there presents in the big bag, but tables set around the room
were loaded with them, all arranged according to the ages of the
children. The boys, as becomes this war-like time, were well supplied
with ships, swords, rifles, knives, drums and trumpets; the girls
received model domestic utensils, tea sets, work boxes and baskets,
candy stores, pianos, books, skipping ropes and other games. Everyone
received a present. Nor were the staff of the Hospital forgotten, the
nurses and voluntary workers each received an appropriate gift at the
hands of Mrs Cockerell, who also presented a pocket-knife to each
patient at the Hospital.

In the early years of the 20th century, a charabanc from Hulley's (a
bus company still operating in Baslow), used to collect the schoolchildren and choirs from Beeley, Edensor, Pilsley and Baslow and bring
them to the annual Estate Christmas party. The charabanc had a canvas
roof and seats right across the width of the bus and a door for each row.
Reg Taylor of Baslow remembered that it was driven by Ben Hulley,
who was about 16 at the time. On its arrival at Chatsworth, the children
were taken up to the Theatre for a conjuring, or magic lantern show
followed by tea in the Orangery. They were then led to the Painted Hall
where Her Grace presented each child with a gift. On one occasion, Reg
received a No 2 Meccano set.

Another person with memories of the children's parties was Jack
Sheldon. Writing in his book about Baslow, he remembers his time as
a pupil, and later as headmaster at Baslow School.

Those happy and exciting Christmas parties at Chatsworth House, the
feelings of awe and wonder with which we gazed on the magnificent
Christmas tree in the Sculpture Gallery, and the journey back home
through the park in the old game vans, clutching our presents, happy
faces showing dimly in the light of the lantern swinging from the roof,

and the steady clip-clop of the horses' hooves sounding loudly in the frosty air.

Lady Anne Hunloke (born in 1909), was the youngest daughter of the 9th Duke of Devonshire. In documents in the Chatsworth archive are her reminiscences about children from Baslow, Beeley and Pilsley Schools visiting the House after Christmas. They arrived in the middle of the afternoon and went straight up to the Theatre for an entertainment, usually a conjuror, and then coming back down to the Orangery where they had tea and crackers at long tables. After tea, they went through into the Sculpture Gallery where the Christmas tree had been brought from the Painted Hall, to receive their presents from the Duke and Duchess. When all the presents had been given out, the children stood round the tree, the Edensor Vicar called for three cheers for the Duke and Duchess, and as the children left they were each given an apple, an orange and a bag of sweets.

Lady Anne's elder sister, Lady Maud Baillie (born in 1896), remembered one family Christmas where she and her brothers and sisters were given roller states, which, she says, 'Led to the most exciting games of hockey among the statues in the Orangery and Statue Gallery and wild races down the long passages'.

Countless Estate children over the years must have remembered these Christmas parties all their lives and it is wonderful that this is still the case, with parents who once enjoyed the parties themselves, now bringing their own children along to be equally spellbound. When Michael and Philip were small, the parties were held in the Painted Hall, where we set out long trestle tables laden with a magnificent tea and attended by the family and any guests staying at the time. After tea, the children were led up to the private dining room for an entertainer, usually a conjuror, or perhaps Punch and Judy, whilst the tea things were cleared away from the Painted Hall. When that was over, the children would be led back down into the Painted Hall to await the arrival of Father Christmas, who brought a present for every child, and never the same gift twice!

Once the Chatsworth open season extended until 23rd December, we tried having the children's party on 24th December, but over 100 children late in the afternoon on Christmas Eve proved to be not a very good idea, as they were all as high as kites, so we have reverted to having the party around the 20th December, held up in the Theatre. The children and guests, including the Duke and Duchess and their grandchildren, enjoy a fabulous tea followed by a conjuror and entertainer.

The proceedings are always started by Sean Doxey, now head of special projects, but for several years the House comptroller. Sean tells the children that he has been in touch with Father Christmas on his radio, and the sleigh is about an hour away, so they have plenty of time to enjoy their party. After the entertainer has finished, Sean returns to the stage and says that Father Christmas has been on the radio again, and that he has some good news, and some bad news. The good news is that Father Christmas has arrived, but the bad news is that he has landed on the wrong roof!

By now it is 6 o'clock, and all the visitors have left, so we are able to lead the children back down through the House to the Painted Hall. A couple of years ago I was standing at the Theatre door as the children jostled their way out onto the staircase and overheard one little girl saying to her friend, 'Honestly, you'd think he would have remembered which roof to land on wouldn't you?' Once in the Painted Hall, the children go out into the Inner Court. Here, they have to be very, very quiet until they hear the tinkle of sleigh bells, and spot Father Christmas and Rudolf on the roof. But there are so many chimneys on the rooftop at Chatsworth that Father Christmas doesn't know which one to come down, so the children have to rush back inside and shout up the chimney in the Painted Hall. Once they have shouted loudly enough for him to hear, he rattles down the chimney, preceded by a couple of sooty bricks which tumble out into the hearth, and he brings with him a sack containing a gift for every child. What could be more magical than that?

We had a crisis in 1986 when the new turbines were being installed and someone dropped a spanner in the machinery, plunging the House into darkness. The emergency generator failed to start, so 100 children had to wait patiently (and some impatiently), in the private dining room whilst poor Gerard Coleman ran all the way up from the turbine house to the House to start the generator manually, since the House electrician, Tony Hubbuck, was otherwise occupied with Father Christmas, who happened to be up the chimney at the time.

Foot and mouth disease broke out in Britain in February 2001, and Chatsworth was haunted by the fear of the disease spreading to animals on the Estate. Many people remembered the previous epidemic of 1967-68 which had a great impact on the tenanted farms of the Estate and on Chatsworth itself, as the whole Park was closed to traffic. In 2001 the decision was taken to delay the opening of the House and Gardens from mid-March to 7th April in order to try to minimise the risk, and events like the staff party (usually held at the beginning of March), and the Duke and Duchess's Diamond Wedding party, were postponed. Since deer are cloven-hoofed and are susceptible to the disease as well as sheep and cattle, an 800 yard wire fence was put up to act as a sterile corridor, and the aim was to drive the deer into the area west of the river so that they were removed from human contact. The deer are not used to being handled, and in effect run wild in the 1,000 acres of Parkland, so it was not easy to move the animals into the safe area. A huge human chain was constructed of anyone and everyone on the Estate, master-minded by the head keeper, so that one team drove the deer over the river at the shallows by the cricket ground, whilst another team closed in on them near the golf course so that they were safely secured, and disinfectant mats were then installed at the entrances to the Park.

Public footpaths were closed throughout the country, and although the House and Gardens re-opened on 7th April, the footpaths remained closed for a long time afterwards. As a result, visitors were reluctant to visit the Estate and our season looked set to be a very poor one, with a similar prospect for local businesses as well. After much debate it was decided to extend the season until Christmas, just for one year, and introduce Christmas displays to encourage visitors to come. This decision was taken in the August, so we had a tremendous amount of work to do to get everything ready, since the whole of the House was to be decorated, including all the rooms on the second floor.

It had been suggested to us that a company in Huddersfield, KD Decoratives, might be able to help and so Tony Hubbuck and I went to visit them in the old mill where they were based. We dubbed it 'Fairyland', and have known it as that ever since. We had a wonderful day, especially on the longest grotto train ride in Europe, which featured every kind of Santa's Grotto imaginable, full of fantastic animatronic figures, dancing, singing, flying, and story-telling. The one that captured our hearts was in the reception area, where a mother polar bear snoozed on a large iceberg with her two cubs, which stretched from time to time, and then slumbered on.

The company's packing rooms were already busy, dressing boughs with fairy lights and baubles, before packing them into huge boxes ready to be shipped off to decorate P & O cruise liners, or to city shopping centres and large international airports. The team from KD later visited Chatsworth and came up with some wonderful ideas for decorations throughout the House, but we eventually decided that as we didn't want to end up with the 'Cruise Ship Chatsworth' in dry dock, we would do the bulk of the decorating 'in house', just using one or two of KD's larger displays.

Several meetings between House and Gardens then followed, resulting in the Chatsworth gardeners undertaking the decorating of the fireplaces, and the housekeeping staff tackling Christmas trees and candles. In September, Tony and I made several trips to a warehouse in Nottingham, where we bought nearly a thousand Christmas tree baubles and innumerable sets of tree lights, followed by a further two trips to Leeds to buy the eleven artificial Christmas trees required for the House, along with all the garlands and trimmings that the gardeners were going to need for the fireplaces. Work began straightaway, with the gardeners piecing together the garlands so that they would be ready for installation in the House, and the housekeeping team wiring all the baubles and sorting them into colour groupings, which would speed things up when we came to dress the trees.

Once decorated, the House looked spectacular, with wonderful garlands up the staircases, a fantastic kissing bough suspended from the stag chandelier on the Oak Stairs, tinsel on the marble busts (at Her Grace's request), and a sumptuous display on the Great Chamber table, including silver gilt from the vaults. The State Drawing Room displayed two period beds complete with hot water bottles and bulging Christmas stockings (which were actually Her Grace's shooting stockings) hanging alongside the wartime painting of the Penrhos College girls using the room as a dormitory. Candles were carefully lit throughout the House. We just had the odd snag, which was only to be expected when bringing trees indoors, and when there was a dog living in the house.

The Stables looked equally magnificent, and we even managed to persuade Father Christmas to come along and take up residence in the Stable yard, in the area now occupied by the Garden Shop, with several ice maidens helping him to look after all the children. I called in to see him to check that he was all right and had to laugh when he told me that one child had arrived clutching a scrap of paper with the Argos catalogue number of the gift he wanted!

That first year, 2001, we had a staggering 88,000 visitors through the door, all eager to know what we were going to do the following year. Our policy of only opening for one year had to be re-thought. The extra revenue made such a difference to what we were able to achieve with regard to restoration, so it didn't take long before we agreed to repeat the Christmas opening the following year.

The House had been decorated to a traditional theme that first year, and we wondered if people would want to come and see us again if they thought it would be along the same lines. It was decided, therefore, to have a different theme for 2002, 'Christmas from other Lands', depicting Christmases in Holland, Germany and Russia, and this seemed to go down very well with our visitors. The Oak Room was the setting for the display depicting Christmas in Holland, where tradition has it that Sinterklaas arrives from Spain with his Moorish helper, Svarte Piet, on his feast day, 5th December. On this day, Dutch children fill their shoes with hay and a carrot and wake up to find them filled with sweets and nuts. However, when we did this in the Oak Room, we found that a mouse came in through the French windows during the night to steal the sweets, leaving us with just the wrapping paper.

We try to use items from the historic collection where possible and this has worked well, especially if we can incorporate the Chatsworth sleigh into the decorative theme, and it has been used in several locations over the years. Mark and the joiners make a low bottomless box to pen the sleigh inside, and we roll white curtain wadding underneath the sleigh and then sprinkle 'snow' on top. We take the opportunity to incorporate artificial snow into some of the displays whenever we can, as it lends real atmosphere, to the delight of the visitors. I had a struggle finding where to buy the snow, until I discovered a company called Snow Business, which deals in snow all year round. They turned out to be one of the world leaders in the supply of snow to the film industry; their snow having appeared in *101 Dalmatians, Gladiator, Bridget Jones's Diary* and *Harry Potter*, to name but a few. They also have a White Wedding department dedicated to providing falling snow at the church, whatever the time of year! They offer a staggering 168 different types of snow, all of which are fully flame retardant!

This second year of Christmas opening was launched with a visit by Father Christmas in a candlelit parade on 8th November. Nine schools from Derbyshire and Sheffield were invited to be part of the parade, plus all the tenants and employees of the Estate. The Redhouse Carriage Museum at Darley Dale provided a coach for Father Christmas and the parade of children carrying candles was due to follow him via the Stables and up to the Farmyard. The parade was to be accompanied by a stilt walker and a drummer, and the evening was due to end with a firework display at 8pm at the top of the Crobs. We had planned everything down to the last detail. The car park would open in plenty of time to allow the children time to collect their candles and candle holders in readiness, and Father Christmas was timed to set off from Darley Dale in his horse drawn 'sleigh' ready to arrive at the Bastion wall below the House at 6.30pm, ready to lead the procession.

However, in the event, it was chaos. More people turned up than we anticipated and the crowd arrived too early. It was a terribly stormy, wet night. People were slipping on the mud as there was no floor covering, and the tent in which we were distributing candles was too dark and too small. Some people had travelled a long way and were complaining because they had expected to be able to buy food when they arrived. The invitations had not specified an age limit for the issue of candles so some older children were expecting candles too and so there were not enough to go round. Father Christmas was very anxious about the crowd of people and made his own decision to set off earlier from the Bastion Wall than the planned time, so no one was ready for him in the Farmyard. It was an absolute disaster, but that is how lessons are learned.

Planning for the 2002 Christmas display had begun at the start of the year, which allowed us to take advantage of buying at source. We visited the Spring Fair at the NEC, and have done so every year ever since then. It's a great way to see what the trends are, to buy decorations in bulk directly from the suppliers, and to tie in what we buy with what the Chatsworth shops are going to be selling, so that our visitors are able to take a little bit of Chatsworth home with them. The displays have always been devised, bought and installed by the housekeeping team, with assistance from the gardeners and textiles team, and they all enjoy working together on the project. With the arrival of the 12th Duke and Duchess at Chatsworth, the Duchess has become very much a part of the Christmas planning team, and she and I, together with Janet Bitton, Matthew Hirst, head of art and historic collections, and Susie Stokoe, textiles supervisor, form the team who put forward the plans for what we are going to do, and then Janet and I do the bulk of the planning and buying.

In 2003 our displays depicted 'A Victorian Christmas', and the joiners made us a wonderful Yorkshire Range to form the Cratchit family's kitchen hearth in one of the displays. Since that year the joiners have played a large part in helping us to depict our theme. Once we have decided what we are going to do, we get together with Mark Rhodes, the House carpenter, our painter, Richard Elliott, the House engineer, Paul Neale, and the House electrician, to tell them the effect we would like them to achieve in a particular display, and they have never let us down.

The Farmyard has also become a favourite Christmas destination for many visitors. There is free entertainment and the opportunity for children to make their own Christmas crafts in a lovely warm marquee. With all the usual animals and outdoor activities to enjoy, there is no wonder that it has become so popular. The Farmyard team also organises Christmas Nativities for children to take part in, with beautiful costumes made by the textiles team at the House. The animals also take part in the Nativities, and seem to enjoy doing so – they even know their cues, and the donkey sets off up the aisle towing Mary along behind her as soon as her musical cue of 'Little Donkey' begins!

In 2004 our theme was 'Christmas through the Ages', which we began with an Elizabethan Christmas staged in the Great Chamber. This was the year when I first met the food historian, Ivan Day, who made us the Elizabethan banquet that still gets brought out for different displays most years. We progressed through the ages from the Elizabethan Christmas right through to the 1950s, and had a great time in researching and sourcing material for all the displays.

In 2005 our theme was 'Aspects of Christmas', where we devised tableaux depicting different aspects of the Christmas season, including Christmas carols and a favourite pantomime, Cinderella, as a finale in the Sculpture Gallery, and this was the first year in which we used real trees throughout the House, rather than just in the Painted Hall. Real trees add a wonderful atmosphere, with the scent of pine throughout the building and as I now buy mostly Nordman pine or Noble fir for inside the House, we have very little problem with needle drop and they last from early November until well into the following January.

In 2006 there was important restoration work that needed to take place in the State Apartments, which meant that those rooms had to close at the beginning of November, with the work not being completed until the following March. I had also been uneasy for a couple of years that extending the visitor season until Christmas had required some trimming of the deep clean programme for the House. We had less time to complete it thoroughly, and it was an additional cause for concern that having so many people through those sensitive and important rooms at a wet time of year increased the humidity, potentially damaging the fabric of the building. It was therefore decided to close the State Apartments, Sketch Galleries and Scots Apartments, and to confine our Christmas displays to the ground floor of the House and the North Wing. The bonus was that visitors were now able to see the whole of the ground floor, including some areas which are normally 'private'. It also meant that visitors with mobility problems were now able to see the same as everyone else, as previously, wheelchair access to the second floor had been extremely limited.

The theme in 2006 was 'The Twelve Days of Christmas', and it was judged by our visitors as one of the best we had done. It was the first year that the Duchess was fully involved with the displays, much to our benefit. I had originally planned to use decorative birds for the two turtle doves, but the Duchess announced, 'Oh no, I think we should have real birds!'

Mark made a fabulous dovecote and aviary to place on the West Sub-corridor, and two white fantail doves were loaned by a friend of the Duchess. The doves were beautiful, and aroused a lot of interest from the visitors, especially when the billing and cooing progressed to such an extent that they laid eggs and we ended up with several birds! It produced a marvellous effect on visitor numbers, since visitors came to see the birds, came back when they had heard that they had laid eggs, and then paid a third visit to see the chicks!

The Christmas theme in 2007 was 'A Christmas Kaleidoscope', featuring all the colours associated with Christmas and culminating with a larger-than-life kaleidoscope made for us by the House maintenance team.

In 2008 we worked with the children's illustrator, Jan Pienkowski, using designs from his pop-up book, The First Noel, A Christmas Carousel. Jan's designs were turned into tableaux, nine feet high, telling the Christmas story, from the Annunciation by the Angel Gabriel right through to the visit of the wise men. It made a beautiful back drop for our Christmas displays.

The following year, in 2009, we took the fairy stories of Hans Christian Andersen as our inspiration, and in 2010 we enjoyed filling the Christmas route with snow as we brought the feeling of a 'A Russian Christmas' into our displays. This was one of the years when we had a proper winter, and had to actually close the House, Gardens and Farmyard for three days as there was so much snow!

We had thought for some time that Christmas carols would be a good theme to choose, as visitors would be able to identify our displays immediately, and so in 2011 we took 'Deck the Halls' as our theme. We decided to depict the carol While Shepherds Watched their Flocks by Night on the West Sub-corridor, and the Duchess thought that it would add a touch of humour if we had a small washing line across the passageway, with a line of children's socks hanging from it, to fit with the schoolboys' corruption of the carol to 'While shepherds washed their socks by night'. We were rather taken aback subsequently by one of the notes in our comments box which said, 'Excellent day – one small problem – our visitor from Thailand is a Buddhist, and they are not allowed to walk beneath clothing!'

In 2012 we tried get more interaction between our guides and visitors, which was an easy thing to achieve when the theme was 'Pantomime'. Our male guides needed no prompting to get into makeup and high heels as Widow Twankey, and the women loved playing the Wicked Witch.

The interaction between guides and visitors was once again a feature of the Christmas theme in 2013, 'The Lion the Witch and the Wardrobe', which was another popular event. By this time we had been collaborating in our Christmas installations for several years with a company in Derby called SetOne, who specialise in making sets for the stage. They have made a number of realistic figures for us over the years, from Puss in Boots, to Peter Pan, a crocodile, and a realistic pack of wolves. In 2013 they supplied a beaver in a bath, together with a 'breathing' Aslan, the lion. Just as in the story, Aslan was depicted tied down to a stone table, with animatronic mice nibbling him free. This proved to be a real show-stopper, but also a bottle-neck, as all the visitors wanted to stop and photograph him.

The 2014 theme, 'Alice's Wonderland', was well into the planning stages before we closed at the end of 2013. Christmas trees were ordered, and a number of props and decorations were bought at the NEC Spring Fair in February – it's amazing how well ahead we are these days!

I have often been asked if all the advance Christmas planning has spoiled my own personal Christmas at home, but I still love the festival of Christmas and feel very lucky that I can enjoy it all year round!

19

❧

The End of an Era

Over the years, the housekeeping role at Chatsworth has carried on pretty much the same since I took over from Mrs Dean in 1981, with the additional responsibility of Christmas opening since 2001, and the pinch this gave to our opportunities for the deep clean. Other events have developed and grown too, and I have also become heavily involved with the Flower Festivals organised with NAFAS (National Association of Flower Arranging Societies). Change is an inevitable part of everyday life and we accept it as the years pass, but the greatest change of all was to come in the early summer of 2004.

The 11th Duke was a wonderful man, much loved by his family and staff, and we were all devastated when he died at 11.30pm on 3rd May 2004. John Oliver telephoned to tell me the sad news at 7.40 the following morning, and all the House staff met in the Painted Hall at 8am for the land agent, Roger Wardle, to speak to us. We walked into the Painted Hall and stood in a subdued silence until Roger entered and told us what had happened. He broke down at the end as he said, 'It is the end of an era…a golden era'. The two portraits of His Grace in the House were draped in black and a notice was placed on the gates and around the Park announcing the death of the Duke, but that the House would remain open in accordance with his wishes.

Plans then began for the funeral to be held at St Peter's Church, Edensor, on Monday 10th May at 2.30pm. It was decided to close the House, Farmyard, shops and restaurant for the day as a mark of respect, and also so that staff would be able to pay their respects if they wanted to, but the Gardens and car park were to be open without charge so that any visitors arriving at Chatsworth and not knowing that the House was closed, would still be able to see something.

The District Council closed the road through Chatsworth Park and the funeral procession left the House led by John Oliver. The family walked behind the coffin, except Her Grace and the older members of the family who followed by car. Staff lined the road all the way to Sandy's Turn, joining the procession as it passed. Because there was no traffic in the Park, the deer had come down from the hillside and stood alongside, as if they had also come to say farewell to this lovely man.

The Park was bursting with birdsong, and with the lush fresh green of springtime, and the sun came out as the procession wound its way across from the House. The church was packed, with the service relayed to an enormous crowd outside and in accordance with His Grace's instructions, there was no eulogy, just a really beautiful service. As the procession made its way up the churchyard to the family burial ground, a flight of micro-light aircraft flew overhead in homage to the Duke, who had been patron of their society.

After the service, everyone was invited back to Chatsworth and family, staff and guests gathered on the South Lawn. There was a lovely afternoon tea and a brass band – just the kind of afternoon His Grace would have enjoyed himself.

In the days following the Duke's death, Her Grace received over 2,300 letters, cards and messages of condolence – a marvellous tribute to a very special man, who never missed an opportunity to tell the world how fortunate he felt himself to be.

Although the 11th Duke died in May 2004, the Dowager Duchess did not move into Edensor until December 2005, and the 12th Duke and Duchess then moved from Yorkshire in January 2006. They had spent a lot of time at Chatsworth in the intervening period, and in May 2005 decided to organise a 'Tour of Attractions' for nine members of staff from Bolton Abbey and Chatsworth, which would provide a good way of getting to know some of their staff, and also learn what other visitor attractions were up to. I was in the Chatsworth group, with Margaret Norris (Farmyard and Adventure Playground manager), Charles Noble (keeper of the collections), Simon Seligman (marketing manager), Sara Sweetland (head of trading), and Sean Doxey (assistant comptroller). We caught the train from Chesterfield station and were met by taxi at

St Austell, which took us to a lovely hotel in Fowey, where we met the team from Bolton Abbey and the Duke and Duchess.

It was a fascinating few days, though extremely hard work as we were expected to have an opinion on everything we saw, and to discuss whether some of the things we saw could, or could not, be transferred to our own situation at Chatsworth or Bolton Abbey. A lively debate continued over meals, in the bar and in the train or coach to the next destination. It was a good way to get to know each other better, and also for the Duke and Duchess to get to know us.

In Cornwall we enjoyed the Eden Project and the Lost Gardens of Heligan, where our guide was an elderly gentleman, a real character with a pronounced West Country accent, and he really brought the gardens to life. We tried to go incognito, as we thought we would have a truer experience than if it were known that we were from Chatsworth. It produced an amusing exchange at Heligan, when our guide asked a question and the Duke answered correctly, the guide announced, 'Well, the old codger's got it roight!' We had to stifle a smile, but when the same thing happened again, and the old man said, 'And the old codger's got it roight again!' it was just too much! We then caught the train to London to discover the Science Museum and Hampton Court Palace, and finally, it was up to Yorkshire by coach to visit Harewood House and Castle Howard.

There have been many visits since then to see what other attractions are doing, some with the Duke and Duchess, and some without them, including Muncaster Castle, Edinburgh Castle, Stirling Castle, Blenheim Palace, Warwick Castle, Leeds Castle, Waddesdon Manor, Shugborough Hall, and the Manchester Science Museum. One especially exciting visit took place one New Year when four of us flew to Paris with the Duke and Duchess to visit the Christmas displays at Vaux le Vicomte and Fontainebleau. We had so much fun we had to remind ourselves that it was meant to be work!

The 12th Duke is a Director of Sotheby's and at his invitation in September 2005 Chatsworth was visited by about 30 of the company's most senior international staff for the company's 'annual retreat', a chance to review the past year's performance and to discuss future policy. Many of them had not visited Chatsworth before, but by the end of the weekend they realised that Chatsworth would make the perfect setting for an annual selling exhibition of modern and contemporary sculpture, similar to one that they already held every year in Florida. This led to the first selling exhibition in 2006, and since then 'Beyond Limits' has been a popular part of the Chatsworth calendar, bringing significant pieces of contemporary monumental sculpture out into the provinces, and also a whole new audience to Chatsworth, eager to view these works.

There has been much to learn during the process, for both Sotheby's and the Chatsworth team, and the event has become one which the Duke and Duchess look forward to hosting every year. That first exhibition of 2006 included my favourite piece of all the Sotheby's exhibitions we have enjoyed: Dale Chihuly's *Sunset Boat*. This comprised a wooden boat filled with pieces of yellow and red glass blown into all manner of interesting shapes, creating glorious reflections in the water of the Canal Pond where it was situated. The Sotheby's exhibition curator needed the help of the Chatsworth gardeners to place the boat in the pond, and then took up the offer of the gardeners' foreman, Alan Froggatt, to place the pieces of glass inside it, thinking they would rearrange it afterwards. However, they were so pleased with the effect Alan had created that nothing needed to be changed and the piece was a great success with the crowds who flocked to view the exhibition. Since then, the Chatsworth team has been responsible for the installation of all the pieces, a few of which are sometimes placed inside the House. Again in 2006, one such piece was Duane Hanson's *Sunbather*, a polychromed bronze life-sized figure of a woman on a sunbed, which was so life-like it made the visitors jump. I found it quite unsettling to be dusting it at the weekend as I expected a slap from the woman at any moment!

When the Duke and Duchess moved to Chatsworth, they left behind the most beautiful home at Beamsley Hall on the Bolton Abbey Estate in Yorkshire. They brought with them their own private housekeeper, chauffeur-cum-valet to the Duke, and Chrissie, their cook, who has now retired. I miss seeing her and her little dog, Rags, who used to belong to Lady Jasmine, the Duke and Duchess's younger daughter. Rags was always angling for a fight with the Duchess's own small terrier, Snug. Chrissie told me that one day at Beamsley the two of them somehow managed to get together, and whilst the Duchess was trying to separate them, Chrissie filled a bucket of cold water as she had heard that is one of the best ways of separating fighting dogs. Unfortunately, she threw the bucket of water with rather too much force and not enough precision, and managed to drench the Duchess in the process. Snug has been such a lovely little dog, but does love to roll in anything smelly she can find, and I am sure most people would not believe that the Duchess always bathes Snug herself when she's been 'rolling'.

The Duke and Duchess both love having their grandchildren to stay. I believe that when the children were first told that their grandparents would be moving to Chatsworth, they were rather dismayed. They had visited Chatsworth to see their great-grandmother, the Dowager Duchess, but whenever they came they found it difficult to remember where to find things because there are so many rooms. The Duchess devised a clever solution to the problem. She cut out large dinosaur footprints and laid them on the floor so that the children had a path to follow, and put photographs and arrows outside various doors to guide them towards the Duke in his study, Chrissie in the kitchen, or the secretaries in their office.

The long service corridor at Chatsworth is a great place to play games and ride up and down on a skateboard, roller skates or even a bicycle, especially if it's too wet to play outside. My office is one of the open doorways off this corridor and we often hear them playing, and if the dogs run along the corridor ahead of the Duchess, they often whizz in to say 'Hello'. One day as I sat at my desk, I heard the sound of skipping feet and someone chanting, 'Clip clop, clip clop, clip clop'. The sound got gradually nearer, and then came galloping into my office, with a loud, 'Naaaaaay!' It was the Duchess with her grandson, Barney, on her back. She said nothing, just galloped up to the window, and turned and neighed at me.

'Hello Barney,' I said. 'I do hope your horse is behaving itself!'

'Naaaaay!' said the horse, and made as if to throw him over its head before galloping off again.

I suppose every Duke of Devonshire over the years has had time to consider what he would like to do at Chatsworth, both to make his mark, and also to improve and enhance what he has inherited. After years of painstaking planning, work began on the Master Plan in 2006 to begin alterations with the intention of developing the House route and displays for visitors, improving the facilities in the family part of the House, and ensuring that the 12th Duke and Duchess will hand on a House in good repair to the 13th Duke of Devonshire when the time eventually comes. The Master Plan required detailed research, expert advice, and a full planning process which culminated in permission being granted by the Peak District National Park Authority and English Heritage. The work has involved changes to both the interior and exterior of Chatsworth, and there are also plans to extend this work into the surrounding parkland and buildings such as the Stables and Game Larder.

In an attempt to make more sense of the 1st Duke's State Apartments, built for the visit of William and Mary (who never actually made it to Chatsworth), the Duke and Duchess began extensive research to redesign the displays within these rooms. The carpets and furniture disappeared from the State Dining Room, now renamed the Great Chamber, to recreate the space where courtiers hopeful of being received into the presence of the King would have gathered, and whilst they waited, they would have been left in no doubt as to the wealth and importance of the Duke, by the fabulous display of wealth in the form of items from his vaults.

Many of these items are now on display, such as the silver-gilt plate from the time of the 1st Duke, on a new 'buffet' arranged on the table that was already in the Great Chamber, with several tiers resting on it to provide the shelving. Ivan Day, the food historian, recreated food from the period, whilst florist Charlotte Hepworth meticulously recreated garlands of flowers in wax and paper, to reflect the seasons, and these were arranged by the renowned florist, George Smith. In the State Drawing Room, furniture was moved to the sides of the room, as if to allow the courtiers to gather in that space, and in the next room, the State Music Room, another display of wealth became obvious in the elaborate Boulle furniture of brass and tortoiseshell inlay.

Finally, in the State Bedchamber and Closet are displayed the fabulous toilet service with the arms and monogram of William and Mary, a gift from the King to the 1st Duke. The textile historian, Annabel Westman, advised on the new curtains for the State Bedchamber and Closet, and a special damask, woven to match the State Bed, was used to furnish the curtains and pelmets and to cover the dressing table. The same project involved the House joiners raising the bed by twelve inches to its original height so that the valance was visible once again.

The 6th Duke created the Sculpture Gallery in 1833 to display his collection of masterpieces by Canova and other neoclassical artists, a fashionable, contemporary space in which to view what was then modern sculpture. In the winter of 2008-9, following detailed research into the room's history, the gallery was returned as far as possible to its original state, returning to the gallery several sculptures, coloured columns, inlaid marble tops, specimen marble tables and minerals, and the relocation of pieces which have been added since the 6th Duke's time. The intention was to present the room as it would have been arranged in 1857, the year before the 6th Duke's death, and it now looks absolutely spectacular.

In the winter of 2009-10, work began on the walls of the north side of the House to clean and consolidate the stonework. This involved extensive scaffolding on the north front of the building that had to be free-standing so that the stonework was not damaged. The scaffolding was secured in place by 115 blocks of concrete weighing a total of 403 tons, and on average there were around 70 contractors on site each day. A structural survey of the roof later revealed extensive weathering; some of the stonework was badly worn and must have been in danger of falling to the ground for some time. This resulted in a whole new programme of work to restore, consolidate and clean all the stonework and re-gild the finials. In order to achieve this work, Chatsworth was under scaffolding for nearly a year, and was the only time that I have been able to spot Chatsworth out of an aeroplane window coming in to land at Manchester airport, seeing a vast white sugar cube in the middle of the landscape. It was a special moment when the scaffolding was finally removed.

The next phase of work involved the creation of an improved visitor route for the start of the 2010 season, by reopening the doorway at the end of the West Sketch Gallery, creating a new North Sketch Gallery, and providing fresh access to the Scots Apartments. At the same time, the 9th Duke's glass skylight above the Oak Stairs was taken down, to reveal the wonderful moulded plasterwork in the space above, thereby restoring the Oak Stairs to their original 19th century splendour, and now hung with family portraits.

During the work, previously blank windows into the courtyard were opened from the second floor, revealing superb new views from the North, West and South Sketch Galleries. Visitors can now see the three-hundred-year-old carved stone martial trophies, which are in the form of suits of armour and weaponry, which have been restored and cleaned, along with all other stonework in the Inner Court. A number of pieces in the Inner Court were beyond restoration and have been re-carved, and in keeping with tradition, the stonemasons also carved a couple of new contemporary pieces, a tank and a Remembrance poppy, which are both tucked underneath the carved skirts of the martial trophies. All this extensive and expert work has been done by Chatsworth's in-house craftsmen, assisted where necessary by specialists from across the country. The programme has been managed by the comptroller, Sean Doxey, now head of special projects.

Scaffolding on the outside of the building provided secure access into the House for workmen, and as the walls on the South Sketch Gallery were stripped of their fabric, an opportunity was thereby provided, in September 2009, for every member of Chatsworth staff and all the Friends of Chatsworth to sign their name on the walls before the new fabric was applied – an immense graffiti exercise that future generations will discover when the restoration is repeated. There has always been an unofficial tradition of staff writing their names on the walls in the hidden spaces of attics and roofs, or sometimes etched onto window panes high up out of sight. There are some of these in the Scots Dressing Room, high up on the windows: 'Robert Bowman from Bakewell 20th Day of April 1782'. Also, 'Strangways July 1691' and 'Cornelius Bellney plumber and glazer [sic] Bakewell April 3 1811'. There is another signature and etching of the Cavendish coat of arms on a high window in the Orangery, and one rather rude one signed by a member of the Burdekin family, dated 1697, on a window in the Painted Hall.

Along the South Sketch Gallery, one of the wooden doors and shutters that had been re-used to block the windows in the 19th century contained a fragment of handmade wallpaper and a large chalk signature dated April 1836. Elsewhere, the windows of the West Sketch Gallery were blocked with custom-made panels, each constructed from smaller rescued boards found to contain pencil and ink architectural drawings and a date of 1838.

Once the building work had been completed, it was time for the furnishing to begin, a busy time for the textiles department. The new fabric they needed to make curtains and pelmets, and to cover the walls of the three new sketch galleries, required 650 metres of green silk to be woven.

The South and West Sketch Galleries have been displayed to a traditional design, but the North Sketch Gallery has given the Duke and Duchess the opportunity to arrange changing displays of works of art, sometimes traditional, sometimes more abstract. Two years ago, a teacher with her school group was overheard to ask the children which pictures they thought were the oldest – those in the West Sketch Gallery they had just passed through (where there are traditional paintings depicting the history of the 3rd Earl of Burlington), or those where they were standing, in the North Sketch Gallery, with an exhibition of contemporary art. The children thought for a moment, and then one boy said, 'The ones in here, Miss!'

'Oh, and why do you think that?' the teacher replied.

'Because they haven't learned to paint properly yet!' answered the child.

Whatever the display, visitors have always found the contents of these galleries interesting to explore, on the walls and in the two fitted cabinets, both perfect for metalwork or ceramics. In November 2013 Jacob van der Beugel began the installation of an ambitious commission for the Duke and Duchess, to create a permanent ceramic installation in the space. The work involved the attachment of over 600 tiny ceramic tiles set out in the pattern of the DNA of the Duke, Duchess, Lord and Lady Burlington, and 'Everyman' on the south wall, together with blocks of mirror on the north wall, which catch the sunshine beautifully as they reflect the designs on the opposite wall.

One of the early decisions of the 12th Duke and Duchess was to install a lift for visitors, so that all may share the same experience of the House. Prior to this lift being installed, an elderly American couple toiling up the Oak Stairs arrived at the top just as a nearby clock struck the quarter past the hour. The lady turned to her husband and said, 'Hear that honey? There must be an elevator around here somewhere!'

Further Master Plan work has involved decorating and rewiring the private apartments, and essential upgrading of heating, security and fire-safety systems throughout the building. The Duke calls this 'dentistry' – all the important and necessary upgrades that have to be done, but which are usually out of sight. Some of this essential work took place in the particularly cold October of 2010, and there was no heating at all in the House. I came into work one day to find an enormous box of chocolates on my desk and a note from the Duchess, 'This box of chocolates is for the guides who are being so wonderfully cheerful while there is no heating in the House! Roll on the day when the boilers are back in action.'

It had long been a cause for regret that the Old Master drawings in the Collection could not be put on public display, because there was nowhere with the necessary low light levels for them to be shown safely. One of the next phases of the Master Plan included the creation of the Old Master Drawings Cabinet, which allows some of these fragile items to be displayed in a carefully controlled environment. This was not possible for 200 years, but the drawings are now greatly enjoyed by visitors and staff alike.

There is also a New Gallery, created in 2011 from old bedrooms on the Bachelor Corridor, where exhibitions of changing subject matter are staged. These have included paintings by the Duke's sister, Lady Emma, items from other collectors, including Frank and Cheryl Cohen, or topics such as Chatsworth in wartime. The first display in there was in 2011 to celebrate the 6th Duke on the 200th anniversary of his attaining the Dukedom in 1811, and some would say that it is largely thanks to him that Chatsworth is such a special place today.

A team of archaeologists has been employed for the Master Plan, led by Oliver Jessop, to ensure that nothing of importance was lost or overlooked. The team members were specialists in the survey and interpretation of historic buildings, and their role has been to monitor the Master Plan building works as they progressed. The work involved taking photographs, making drawings and detailed notes to document and interpret evidence relating to the earlier development of the House. An extensive photographic survey to record the condition of rooms and corridors was made before any work began, and the team was then on hand to look under floorboards, behind plasterwork and in the roof during the course of the refurbishment works. There was great excitement in 2008 when they found evidence within the South Front first floor apartments for the original room layout dating to 1687-89, preserved in the form of mortise holes for partitions within the floor beams, and also the base of an earlier chimney and doorway. What stories the House could tell if only it could speak!

Possessions of the Cavendish family over the last 500 years have arrived at Chatsworth from Burlington House in Piccadilly, Bolton Abbey and Londesborough in Yorkshire, Lismore Castle in County Waterford, Holker Hall in Cumbria, Chiswick in Middlesex, Hardwick Hall in Derbyshire and Devonshire House in London, and over the last century, these items have been stored in any available space. With the reduction in the number of servants required in the House, the space available for storing things has expanded into servants' attic bedrooms, lofts, outbuildings, the Theatre gallery, the Stables, and even the 6th Duke's plunge bath. In order to make space in the House for the Master Plan developments, a careful inventory was made of everything, and following expert advice, certain items were put to one side with a view to keeping them in an off-site storage area, whilst other items were considered for sale.

One such occasion was the Attic Sale in October 2010, which offered for sale architectural items like the marble fireplaces once at Devonshire House, and pieces that had once been on display at Chatsworth but were no longer considered important enough to remain in the collection. I found it quite hard to see items that I had lovingly cherished for many years (and coveted, if truth be told), go under the hammer, always achieving prices that Clive and I found impossible to match. Clive took the week off work so that he could attend the sale in the hope that we might be able to purchase something, but alas, absolutely everything was beyond our reach. Even old suitcases and EPNS silver, went for large prices. A cast iron armorial fireback dated 1657 fetched £18,750, a bunch of 40 carved oak flower heads made £12,500, and the ruby glass *epergne* (an ornamental centre-piece for a table), that I had cleaned for 33 years and had admired so much, made an unaffordable £950.

20

⤝

The Challenge of Change

In January 2006, the 12th Duke and Duchess arrived from Yorkshire, in a wonderfully organised removal orchestrated by Denna Garrett, who was at the time, private secretary to the Duchess. It was the starting point for many new developments at Chatsworth.

In time, the Master Plan was conceived and executed, but the changes we first experienced were in the management structure at Chatsworth, and I think this has been the most difficult thing for the staff to absorb.

In 2001 Roger Wardle, land agent, had announced his intention to retire when he reached the age of 60, which was in April 2006, and John Oliver, comptroller, also decided to retire when he reached 60 in August of the same year. With both of them retiring at more or less the same time, the Duke decided to rearrange the structure of the Chatsworth management team, appointing a newcomer, Richard Reynolds, to a new position of chief executive, and he took up that role in May 2006. Richard and the Duke then reviewed the existing management structure in the light of the evolving business of Chatsworth and its offering to visitors and devised a new structure that it was hoped would more effectively manage the visitor experience. Sean Doxey was promoted from deputy comptroller to comptroller, with responsibility for the maintenance of the House, whilst the visitor side of things, previously managed by John Oliver as comptroller, was to be the responsibility of a new general manager.

I decided to apply for this new position as I was excited by the challenge of taking on the role and knew that I had many ideas for bringing more visitors to Chatsworth and thought that my knowledge of Chatsworth would be well-suited to the job. Sadly I was unsuccessful, but there was strong competition! The post was taken by Sarah Montgomery, who was general manager at Warwick Castle, but she was unable to start this new role at Chatsworth until the summer of 2007. In the meantime, the guides needed someone to manage them and in October 2006 I was offered the position of visitor welcome manager, in addition to my role as head housekeeper. I had always enjoyed working with the guides and I loved working with the visitors. It is always a privilege and gives a huge sense of enrichment to feel that you can make a difference to their day, or to show them something they might not otherwise have noticed.

Some visitors have questions about their visit that one would never dream of, but we follow through on them all. I remember hearing about one visitor to the coffee shop in the Farm Shop who was concerned that the bleaches and ink used in the manufacture of the napkins might contaminate the food. The supplier of the napkin was contacted and he in turn spoke to the manufacturers in England and Germany who made the paper and ink. The analysis concluded that a customer would have to actually consume more than 12,000 napkins in order to suffer any ill effects from the ink. The total cost to complete the investigation and eight-page report was £200!

On another occasion, a family of Australians arrived at the House wanting to hand over some cash. It transpired that their ancestors had been deported to Australia for stealing a pheasant from the Duke of Devonshire, and his descendants wanted to clear the family name!

Joe Clark and his wife Lynne are the organists at St Peter's Church, Edensor, and he is also the musical director of the Derbyshire Singers, who provide choral music for special events at church and also at Chatsworth, such as family christenings in the Chapel in the House. Joe is also one of the guides at Chatsworth, and whenever he sees someone he knows, he begins the conversation with, 'Darling! And how are you?' or, 'Now then, my dear!' He was once taking a guided tour round the House of a large group that had been subdivided into several smaller groups. As inevitably happens in such cases, the first groups were rather slow to move on, which resulted in a log jam in the Ante-Library. As Joe's group waited to go through into the Great Dining Room, Joe announced, 'Never fear, my dears. I will entertain you while you wait!' and he promptly took his seat at the grand piano and played to his group until the Great Dining Room was clear. They enjoyed it so much that they didn't want him to stop!

On another occasion, Joe came to see me at the end of the day. 'Brace yourself for a complaint, my dear!' he announced as he came through the office door.

'Why, whatever's happened, Joe?'

'Well, this morning a school group came through the House and I couldn't make out what language they were speaking so I asked them which country they came from.'

'So what did they say?' I asked.

'Well, the teacher in charge was very cross with me and said they were from Liverpool!' replied Joe. No complaint was forthcoming, so we both heaved a sigh of relief!

When Sarah Montgomery took up her new appointment, she asked me to take over the ticket team as well, and in March 2008 we appointed Paul Hayes as supervisor and named the team the visitor welcome team. Paul and I were now also responsible for the car parking team, which previously had been the remit of the comptroller. I have endless admiration for the car parking team, outside in all weathers, and being endlessly polite to all our visitors, some of whom don't realise how exasperating they are. For example:

Customer: 'Can I leave a space next to my car so that when you see my mother you can direct her to park next to me.'

Car parker: 'But I'm afraid I don't know your mother…'

I thoroughly enjoyed all the new roles that had grown around me, but it was undoubtedly hard work to combine the roles of head housekeeper and visitor services manager. A further reorganisation of the management structure in October 2011 redefined the scope and responsibilities of the 'front of house' teams and resulted in the replacement of the general manager and head of trading positions with a new appointment to combine the two, as chief operating officer. The effect on my role was that my position was split again. I was sad to lose the close contact with the visitors that I had so enjoyed, but it meant that I was able to revert to my first love, the housekeeping team.

The immense success of Chatsworth has brought big changes. There are now more staff than ever working at Chatsworth, meaning a growing human resources department, a larger health and safety team, and a new sustainability office, as Chatsworth takes its responsibilities very seriously with regard to 'green initiatives'.

The family is still heavily involved with the Estate, and the future of the Chatsworth landscape is being wholeheartedly embraced by Lord and Lady Burlington, who, together with their children, are the future of Chatsworth. Very many workers still have family connections with the Estate, and will continue to be vital to the success of Chatsworth into the 21st century.

Before the Duke and Duchess moved to Chatsworth in 2006, work began to prepare an office space for the Duke, which involved drilling through walls over three feet thick, and lifting floorboards for computer cabling to pass through. The office is just off the visitor route, and one of my routine tasks prior to the visitors arriving is to lock the door. While the work was underway, I couldn't resist the temptation to open the door each day and peep inside the room to see how the work was progressing. One morning when I looked inside, one of the joiners was working in there on his own. He looked up and said, 'Come and have a look at this!'

I went into the room, and we peered down into the hole beneath the floorboards, where we could see three nails lying half-buried under layers of dust. I bent down to lift the nails out of the hole, and held them in my hand, wondering for how many years they had been lying there in the dark. They were square, and about six inches long and made of wrought iron, and I could even see the layering in the metalwork where they had been folded and beaten to give them strength. I kept them, not wanting them to be hidden away for another three centuries, and thinking they would be an interesting thing to show people on Behind-the-Scenes days.

A few days later, the housekeeping team was cleaning in the old laundry, where the shelves are filled with box upon box of old vouchers, receipts and bills, all waiting to be catalogued, and I idly opened one to see what was inside. Tied up in bundles of pink tape was a random assortment of bills, several of which were from an apothecary who had visited Chatsworth to prescribe various blood lettings, purges and ointments for the staff. However, tucked in amongst them was a bill for nails from William Shaw dated 22nd March 1735. They were priced at ten shillings for a thousand twelve inch nails, eight shillings and four pence for a thousand ten inch nails, and so on, down the list of nails supplied to the House. To my mind, in their own way the nails are just as important to Chatsworth's history as the Rembrandt hanging on the wall. They might be a very small part of the story of the House, but it could not have been built without them.

The history of the Cavendish family is well documented, as is the building of Chatsworth and the acquisition of its contents, yet so little is known about the people behind-the-scenes who worked here. At best, they appear just as a name on a wages ledger, or in a bill for nails. Where did they live? Who were their families? What did they think about the changes to the House when the 3rd Earl started to make alterations to Bess of Hardwick's Elizabethan house, or when the 1st Duke built the State Apartments and rebuilt the east, west and north fronts, or when the 4th Duke made further alterations to the House, followed by the 6th Duke adding the North Wing? Not to mention all the work outside in the Park and Gardens over the last 300 years!

We can only guess what they thought, but one thing I am sure is certain – they were all committed to Chatsworth and to the Cavendish family and justly proud of the part they played. In her book Round about Chatsworth, Her Grace sums up the sentiment perfectly:

'Change itself is a tradition at Chatsworth. There has always been something new to see, something going on. It has never stood still, never been frozen into inaction at any particular time. I think it would be a tragedy if it were made to do so.'